Consumer
and
Commercial
Collection
Deskbook

Jon R. Lunn

Institute for Business Planning

A Prentice-Hall Company

ENGLEWOOD CLIFFS, N.J. 07632

Library of Congress Cataloging in Publication Data

Lunn, Jon R.
    Consumer and commercial collection deskbook.

    Includes index.
    1. Collecting of accounts—Handbooks, manuals, etc.
I. Title.
HG3752.5.L86   1985   658.8′8   85-2470
ISBN 0-87624-097-X

What This Deskbook Will Do For You

Today, virtually every credit sale is a gamble—no matter how well established the customer or how reliable the credit information. But that doesn't mean you can't sharply reduce your credit risks and pare bad debts right to the bone.

In my new CONSUMER AND COMMERCIAL COLLECTION DESKBOOK, I've finally gathered, refined and updated the most effective strategies and action-getting letters I've come across in working first with Dun and Bradstreet, and now with Stanley Tulchin Associates, one of the top collection agencies in the nation.

For example, with the tell-tale signs I spell out for you, it's not only possible but surprisingly easy to spot the accounts most likely to wind up in the bad-debt column. By zeroing in on these high-risk accounts before they show large balances, you can prevent horrendous losses from surfacing somewhere down the road.

And to help you immediately solve any cash-flow problems and give profits a sizable boost, I've provided a complete arsenal of innovative and hard-hitting techniques to collect what's owed you, fast and in full—even from seemingly ''hopeless'' slow-payers.

These are tough, no-nonsense tactics straight from the firing line. I know they work.

Take the two big chapters devoted to turning the telephone into a potent weapon in the fight against credit abuse. Here I detail how to prepare for that critical first call so a customer can't get ''off the hook.'' I show you precisely the right time to initiate action, plus the special tricks of the trade to keep full control of the phone conversation. There are even proven ways to handle evasive customers and others trying to stall.

What's more, I show you how to tackle out-of-the-ordinary or tricky collection situations with remarkable ease. For instance, how to collect from the military and from minors . . . how to deal with freight claims . . . how to get money from corporate debtors . . . the best way to take care of international collections . . .

the best way to skip-trace . . . how to recognize certain costly scams—the "overbuy," the "bust out," the "sting"—and what to do about them.

There's also a whole chapter on how to collect from insolvent or bankrupt debtors. I cover everything from the advantages of a voluntary settlement to how to take someone to bankruptcy court. Each step of the way I point out how to protect your interests, and where possible, to get your money or merchandise returned with the least effort and expense.

Of course, for slow-paying customers whose business you'd like to keep, you'll need an entirely different kind of approach. Here I reveal how to apply the art of motivating people to speed up payments—giving you the actual words, phrases and appeals I've found most effective in persuading customers to live up to their financial obligations. This is "psychological dynamite" that can quickly break through a slow-pay barrier, without any loss of good will.

And in my new CONSUMER AND COMMERCIAL COLLECTION DESKBOOK, you'll find over 100 of the best action-producing and cost-effective letters ever gathered in one place. They range from some 50 ready-to-use models of the remind and request type . . . all the way to 29 bombshell sample letters that can work even when everything else has failed. Yet all of these more than 100 letters have one thing in common: the tested ability to get more cash into your hands rapidly, whether you're owed $10 or $10,000.

It's a fact of life, though, that despite your best efforts some debts may require more time and work to collect than you care to spend. In that case, your wisest move could be to place the account with a professional collection agency. Based on my years of first-hand experience in this field, I can take you behind the scene and show you exactly what to do to get the top payoff from such an arrangement.

For starters, I highlight how to select the right collection agency for your particular needs. I give you specific guidelines for when to place an account. I brief you on how to keep an agency on its toes and get it to do the best possible job for you. I explain the legal ramifications of using an agency, plus much more.

The credit policies, collection tactics and model letters in my new Deskbook put at your fingertips the most innovative and powerful tools now being used to minimize the threat of heavy losses and maximize the inflow of cash. They can have a dramatic impact on a company's bottom line.

Every credit manager, collection manager, accounts receivable manager—indeed, any wide-awake businessperson—will want to keep this invaluable new aid close at hand. It cannot only help you solve the "money problems" you face all the time, but turn those problems into daily opportunities to hike profits and enhance your personal reputation.

—Jon R. Lunn

Summary Table of Contents

Chapter 1—Using Action Letters To Bring In Big Dollars

How To Get The Most From Your Collection Efforts . . . Should You Use A Statement Or Letter As A First Attempt? . . . Essentials Of A Good Collection Letter . . . Ways To Add Spark To Your First Letters . . . What Opening Statements Should Include . . . The Payment Request . . . Examples Of Effective Collection Letters . . . How To Get The Most From A "Payment Appeal" Letter . . . The Final Demand . . . Ten Useful Tips For Creating Effective Collection Letters . . . Special Requirements For Retail Collection Letters . . . Collecting From Professional Accounts . . . When To Use Telegrams, Mailgrams, Or Overnight Letters . . . How To Handle NSF Checks—and much more.

See detailed Table of Contents on page 101.

Chapter 2—Model Collection Letters: Reminders, Requests And Appeals

REMINDERS—Action Approaches: Let's Be Brief; Did You Forget?; Customers Tell Us They Like To Be Reminded; Little Things Are Often Overlooked; Has Your Payment Gone Astray?; Statement And Invoices Enclosed . . . PAYMENT REQUESTS—Action Approaches: Won't You Agree, Pay, Or Advise?; We Are Surprised Not To Hear From You; We Are Concerned About Your Past-Due Balance; Protect Your Credit; Future Credit Approved, But Past-Due Balance Must Be Paid Now; Advise If There Is Any Problem; Clear Balance Before Year-End . . . PAYMENT APPEALS—Action Approaches: If We Are Wrong, Please Explain; How May We Help? Advise Or Pay; Straight-Forward Appeal To Call Us; For Part Payment: Restore Trust, Faith, And Confidence; We Serviced You Promptly; Please Pay Us; Final Appeal: Write Or Call Right Away; Seasonal Payment Appeal—and much more.

See detailed Table of Contents on page 201.

Chapter 3—How To Get The Jump On Marginal And "Problem" Accounts

How Best To Handle Marginal Accounts . . . Which Accounts Are Likely To Be Marginal? . . . Evaluating Marginal Accounts . . . Signs Of Trouble—And What To Do About Them . . . How To Handle A Check Marked "Paid In Full" On a Disputed Account . . . The Compromise Settlement . . . Advantages of Settling Out Of Court . . . A Model Settlement Work-Up . . . How To Use Personal Guarantees Successfully . . . What To Do About Customer Reluctance . . . Late-Payment Interest And Service Charges . . . Providing For Your Right To Impose A Service Charge . . . How To Deal With Improper Customer Deductions . . . Protecting Yourself By Becoming A Secured Creditor—and much more.

See detailed Table of Contents on page 301.

Chapter 4—Model Collection Letters: Demands That Get Attention And Action

PAYMENT DEMANDS—Action Approaches: Make Your Payment In Five Days; Last Chance To Respond Amicably; To Preserve Business Relationship: Pay In Seven Days; Phone Us At Once To Arrange For Payment; Distributor Agreement May Be Cancelled; Send Certified Check; Call And Tell Us Your Problems . . . FINAL DEMANDS—Action Approaches: After Several Calls And Letters; You're Leaving Us No Alternative; Sight Draft Will Be Drawn; Pay Now Or We'll Proceed Further; Part-Payment Received; Mail Balance; Pay In Five Days Or Face Attorney Action—and much more.

See detailed Table of Contents on page 301.

Chapter 5—Tested Telephone Collection Techniques That Control The Conversation—And Get Results

Making Effective Use Of Pre-Call Reminders . . . Essential Fact-Finding Questions For Pre-Call Planning . . . Key Elements Of A Successful Collection Call . . . The Opening, Body And Close Of The Call . . . How To Take Control Of The Conversation . . . Two Keys To Improved Telephone Effectiveness . . . Action Words That Get Results . . . Dealing With Evasive Customers . . . Uses Of Collect Calls And Toll Calls . . . The Impact Of The Initial Reminder . . . The

Double-Teaming Approach . . . How To Make Installment Arrangements . . . Answers To 16 Commonly Raised Objections About Post-Dated Checks . . . What A Letter Of Commitment Does—and much more.

See detailed Table of Contents on page 501.

Chapter 6—The Fine Points Of Telephone And Follow-Up Collections

Telephone Collection Situations—And How To Handle Them . . . Case Examples: The Broken Promise; The Hard-Pressed Customer; The Last Try; The Convincing Staller . . . How To Improve Your Telephone Technique . . . Laws And Regulations To Keep In Mind . . . Guidelines For Debt Collection Calls . . . Bolstering Your Efforts With A Follow-Up System . . . Collecting Face To Face . . . What About Sales People As Collectors? . . . The Value Of Bringing Up The "Big Guns"—and much more.

See detailed Table of Contents on page 601.

Chapter 7—Special Collection Situations, And How To Handle Them

Collecting From Stockholders For Corporate Debts . . . How To Protect Yourself . . . Collecting As A Secured Creditor Under The Uniform Commercial Code . . . How To Validate The Security Agreement . . . Collecting Freight Claims . . . Collecting From The Military . . . Collecting From Minors . . . International Collections . . . A Good Way To Prevent Collection Problems: Letters Of Credit . . . Skip Tracing: A Good Way To Locate A Customer . . . How To Recognize Scams, And What To Do About Them—and much more.

See detailed Table of Contents on page 701.

Chapter 8—Model Collection Letters For Use In Special Situations

BACKING UP CLAIMS—Action Approaches: Enclosing Invoice Copies At Customer's Request; Documentation Requested By Customer; Request For Reimbursement For Unpaid Freight Bill . . . REQUESTING CLARIFICATION—Action Approaches: Questioning Difference Between Your Statement And Customer's Payment; No Record Of Payment . . . CONFIRMING SPECIAL

ARRANGEMENTS—Action Approaches: Debtor Promises Payment In Full Within 30 Days; Confirming Telephone Call With Promise Of Payment; Acknowledging Part Payment . . . Suggesting A Repayment Plan . . . Requesting Evidence Of Payment . . . Seeking Information On A Debtor . . . MAKING SHIPMENTS TO DELINQUENT CUSTOMERS—Action Approaches: New Order Shipped On Past-Due Account; Pay Now, And We'll Fill New Order; Factoring Company Notification Of Past-Due Balance . . . Customer's Check Returned—and much more.

See detailed Table of Contents on page 801.

Chapter 9—How To Get Money From Insolvent Or Bankrupt Debtors

Voluntary Vs. Involuntary Settlements . . . The Benefits Of Extension Agreements . . . How Are Creditors Protected? . . . What A Creditors' Committee Does . . . An Anatomy Of An Out-Of-Court Settlement . . . An Assignment For The Benefit Of Creditors . . . What To Do About Insolvent Customers . . . What You Must Know About Bankruptcy Law . . . Chapters In The Bankruptcy Law—And How They Affect You . . . Adjustment Of Debts For An Individual With Regular Income: Chapter 13 . . . A Chapter 11 Bankruptcy Petition—and much more.

See detailed Table of Contents on page 901.

Chapter 10—How To Get The Best Recovery From Accounts Placed With A Collection Agency

What To Do Before You Place An Account For Collection . . . Benefits Of Using Collection Agencies . . . When To Place An Account For Collection . . . What To Look For In Choosing A Collection Agency . . . How Best To Work With Your Collection Agency . . . Legal Phases Of Collection . . . What Happens In A Collection Lawsuit . . . Ways That Collection Actions Can Be Resolved . . . Compulsory Arbitration . . . Collecting Through Small-Claims Court—and much more.

See detailed Table of Contents on page 1001.

Chapter 11—How To Gear Your Collection Efforts To Today's Business Conditions

The Impact Of Slow Collections . . . "Consumer" Vs. "Commercial" Indebtedness . . . Matching Collection Techniques To Your Special Needs . . . Setting A Policy That Promotes Sales . . . Your Long-Term Investment In Trade Receivables . . . Holding Collection Problems To A Minimum . . . Setting The Best Collection Policy For Today . . . Collection Policy: Written Or Unwritten? . . . Putting Your Collection Policy Into Action . . . The Importance Of Timing . . . Payment Demand Schedule: Intervals For Follow-Up . . . Keeping Collection Policy And Procedure Sharp And Effective—and much more.

See detailed Table of Contents on page 1101.

About The Author

Jon R. Lunn is President and General Collection Manager of Stanley Tulchin Associates, one of the largest commercial collection agencies in the nation. He is an authority on commercial credit and corporate debt collections, and a frequent guest lecturer for the American Management Association and other credit management groups.

Mr. Lunn is a graduate of the College of the City of New York, and has completed studies at the graduate school of Credit and Financial Management, sponsored by the Credit Research Foundation at the Amos Tuck School, Dartmouth. He is a recipient of the school's "Executive Award." Mr. Lunn is a member of the faculty of the New York Institute of Credit, and a member of the Commercial Law League of America.

Dedicated to

Elena, Eric and Gena, my family

1

Using Action Letters To Bring In Big Dollars

Table of Contents

1

Using Action Letters
To Bring In Big Dollars

Business people are often called upon to write many kinds of letters in the course of their day. Perhaps the most difficult one for them to write is the collection letter. Yet it is among the most commonly used method for asking for payment today. While it is obvious that circumstances surrounding each indebtedness will directly affect the type of letter that is written—how friendly or how firm it is—there are few things that people resent more than getting a request for money that they owe.

How To Get The Most From Your Collection Efforts

Obviously, no one letter or series of letters can be devised to fit all situations. However, form letters may be prepared that will satisfy a majority of collection requirements—as long as they can be modified as special exceptions arise. A collection letter must always firmly convey the message to pay the bill—without injury to the customer's feelings, or the loss of good will and business. Customers whose accounts are past due must of course expect to receive collection letters. But good letters can keep them as customers.

Letters, to be effective, must command attention. They should be prepared so that they get the reader's attention and response. However, most Collection Managers do not expect that every letter in every instance will get a response from the delinquent customer. Some letters may even be hastily read and thrown aside or routed to different departments—ignored in anticipation of receiving more urgent appeals, or totally discarded.

On some occasions, customers receiving letters from their suppliers may correctly infer that the communication is a collection letter—and totally ignore it, leaving it on the desk unopened. The customer, knowing that he is being dunned, however, really didn't ignore it; and in fact the letter may have accomplished its purpose by prodding the customer closer towards payment.

A collection letter is written, obviously, to get paid. You must sell the customer on the idea of paying you now, rather than later. The best experts agree that the longer a bill remains unpaid, the greater the probability that it will never be paid.

SHOULD YOU USE A STATEMENT OR LETTER AS A FIRST ATTEMPT?

The Statement

Correspondence as a collection procedure actually begins when the account becomes due. A statement of account, listing the open invoices outstanding, is the most widely used and simplest collection effort. For the most part, such a statement is sent without a covering letter, but may have a pre-stamped message on it about when payment is expected. The statement generally contains sufficient information to permit a customer to check the items billed against his own records, for accuracy.

The statement generally results in a substantial number of accounts being paid on time, thereby considerably reducing the number of accounts requiring any follow-up. Many organizations, however, have eliminated the use of the statement, and instead use a collection letter, enclosing duplicate invoices, in its place. Copies of customer invoices frequently are used to bring accounts to the attention of those in charge of making payment.

The Collection Letter

Collection letters, in order to be successful, must convey to the customer the advantage of paying—and do it in a natural friendly and cheerful way. Letters often referred to as "written demands" must motivate, in other words. Most customers recognize that they should pay what they owe; therefore appeals should be made to good will, pride, self-interest, fairness and the advantage of a good credit reputation.

The first collection letter sent to a delinquent account is the most important one. It should be as brief as possible, identify the charges that have become due, and serve as a reminder for payment. Such a written request for payment lends itself more easily than any other type of communication to the use of a form letter. For the most part, the initial letter actually contains little more than the same information that would appear on a statement of account. Nonetheless, the collector should never assume that the customer knows everything about the account. A smart collector quickly learns that customers actually rely on collectors to remind them of their obligations.

The specific amount and original date due, and the date payment is expected, are therefore essential items in all collection correspondence. Because of the briefness generally associated with the initial reminder, there is usually only a limited variety of correspondence that can be prepared. However, where a statement is used, most experts agree that in order for it to be used as an effective collection tool, it should not include current items. Only those items that are *past due* and that require the attentive follow-up of your customer should be indicated on the past-due reminder.

ESSENTIALS OF A GOOD COLLECTION LETTER

In order for a collection letter to generate the greatest amount of attention and have the greatest impact, and therefore the greatest success ratio, it should be clear, courteous, sincere and to the point. It should be composed of short sentences with language that will motivate your customer to act. It should also include words and phrases used in regular everyday conversation—not unnatural, stilted, strained, or exaggerated language.

The collector must remember that he is representing his company, and that the image inspired by the correspondence will greatly affect collection results—as well as the potential future business relationship. It is therefore necessary that strict attention be paid not only to the style you're using in writing the letter, but also to the mechanics of writing in terms of spelling, slang, and grammar.

While some people resort to "high-balling" (asking for more than the amount that is actually due) to get attention, it is always best to ask for the correct amount that is actually owed. Nothing irritates a customer more or quicker than being asked to pay an amount that is not due. In addition to creating serious doubt as to the validity of future notices, such practices are likely to give the customer a bad impression of your company. They may not even be legal, in some areas.

The lead sentence must command the customer's attention. It should indicate the purpose of the letter and relay the message that you wish to be paid, clearly and understandably, so there's no doubt in the mind of the customer as to the purpose of your communication. Here's how:

Ways To Add Spark To Your First Letters

There are numerous ways to add spark to your first collection attempts. For example, you may isolate the reminder sentence of the letter from the remaining body, by skipping two spaces before continuing. Or you can use bold type, different color inks, or different style types for special effect. In addition, you may underline the first sentence, or it can be shaded with highlighted colors.

Regardless of the variation you choose, *don't overdo it* or strain for effect. Remember to maintain your company's image and play it straight. Sure, people will react to a threatening letter, but usually in a hostile way. Sometimes you may be able to use humor in your letters, but it must be done in a simple and straight-forward way. And always resist the temptation to be sarcastic.

What Opening Statements Should Include

The first reminder is meant to call attention to the fact that an account has fallen due. It should contain a mild statement of fact, and command the appropriate attention and motivation—so that the customer who hasn't been properly informed is likely to react. It must tell the customer what is expected.

Naturally, the timing of the notice may result in its being sent to customers whose payments may have crossed in the mail. Thus, it should contain a face-saving mechanism for those who have already sent their payment. By incorporating "If payment has already been mailed, please accept our thanks," you provide the necessary "out" for customers who have already paid.

Sample opening statements include:

1. Our records indicate the following invoice(s) remains open on your account.

2. We have not received your check.

3. Credit is a privilege; good credit is an asset.

4. Payment in the amount of _____ would be very much appreciated.

5. We ask that you kindly forward your check.

6. Your attention is requested to the following invoice(s) that are now due.

7. The payment we are sure you intended to send in the amount of _____ has not been received.

8. Has your check gone astray?

9. We are always glad to extend every consideration to a customer; your check will be appreciated as was your business.

10. Did you forget that our payment was due?

11. This is to remind you that we have not received payment of your account now past due.

12. Our records indicate the following balance is due. What do your records show?

13. Did you know that your account is still unpaid?

14. Is this an oversight?

15. Have you forgotten to mail your payment?

16. We extended you credit; please extend to us payment. We gave you a chance; please give us your check.

Regardless of the type of reminder sent, the success of any collection effort is partially based on forming a good foundation with persistent consistency. Whether you fix a pressure-sensitive label reminding your customer that the account is past due, or whether you have used a stock-pile form letter or individually typed personal demand, the initial reminder is your first line of defense.

What About Preprinted Forms?

When you engage in a discussion of "to form or not to form" with credit executives, be prepared for a battle. Those who insist that the use of form letters produces substantial savings of time and expense are contradicted by an equally impressive number of experienced executives who suggest that only specially written communications will produce the desired results. They argue that, since form letters are detectable, using them would be ineffective. I'm sure you'll find that both positions are substantially correct. However, as a general rule, form letters seem to be most effective in the preliminary stages of collection, and less and less effective as the delinquency becomes more serious.

A form letter, generally speaking, is a collection letter preprinted in bulk quantities with certain variable information left blank. Because of the wide variety of customers it must appeal to, the content is usually relatively simple and general. However, it is this universal use that makes the form letter a very important collection tool, which should therefore be well written. Where large volume follow-up is required, the sheer number of accounts to pursue would render corresponding to customers on an individual basis cost-prohibitive.

With the advent of automatic typewriters, memory typewriters and computers, form letters too have progressed, and are now at a point where you may find it difficult to recognize them. They're now, on occasion, being individually typed.

The fact that you are communicating by way of a preprinted form should not give your customer the idea that the account is less serious or getting less attention than would otherwise be received. It must still seem individual.

Cost-Saving Ideas When Using Preprinted Forms

The content and quality of all communications between you and your customer may prove critical. There are many ways that you can phrase your collection correspondence to get the desired results. Form letters should be written in simple, direct style with visual impact. They should be brief and flexible with empathy and sincerity. But they must be constantly revised so they don't become recognizable by repeat slow payers.

Among the most effective ways to balance both individuality with the cost advantages of form correspondence is to create a library of ten variations of each letter within your demand sequence. Then each and every time your customer receives notice, either your computer or your collection staff should mark the file indicating that the customer received letter #1, copy #1. In that way, the next time the account reaches the same delinquency stage, letter #1, copy #2 will automatically be sent. If ten seems too much, then shorten it to four. By employing this technique, you'll be giving the necessary individuality and attention to each account, and maximizing the effective use of your correspondence.

What Approach Is Best?

Most credit and collection personnel at one time or another believe they have stumbled upon or created the literary masterpiece that will produce the greatest collection result. Undoubtedly there are thousands of letters in a variety of volumes, suggesting that certain approaches are more effective than others. What is common to all, however, is that none would likely go down into the annals of history as a great literary work. Thus, you need not slave over your hot dictaphone in an attempt to create a literary masterpiece; your object is *collection*.

Having made your opening statement based on examples previously suggested, you must now determine what posture you wish to convey to your customer. For example, do you wish to remain "neutral"? This means repeating the facts as you know them, and simply requesting payment by a specific date. The "neutral" approach is most frequently used as a general payment demand, after first appeals for payment have been made. However, neutrality is not easy to maintain; and many people find themselves attempting to encourage customer compliance by showing an optimistic attitude. This optimistic approach tends to praise the customer, and encourage him or her to perform in accordance with the original terms of sale. The optimistic approach is found most frequently in the initial-payment reminder.

Then, of course, there's a "negative" communication, reminding the customer of the punishment for not paying the account on time. By informing the customer of the consequences of default, you are hoping he or she will see the light and respond. For the most part, it is not necessary to indicate exactly what you intend to do. Leaving your intended reaction a question mark in the mind of your customer is often more effective than stating specifically what procedures you will pursue to recover. An example of such an ambiguous communication would be, "Unless we have your check within ten days, we will proceed to take further action." Well, proceed may be very subjective and mean different things to different people. But suppose you say, "How do you expect us to fulfill your future orders while your account remains unpaid?" This more specific message suddenly implies that future credit is impaired until payment is made.

The examples of the negative approach can be limited only by the imagination. Such negatives are usually reserved for the tougher accounts in the later stages of your collection effort.

Whatever your approach, invariably each and every communication is going to have a beginning, a middle and an ending—where the beginning is designed to attract immediate attention; the middle is likely to inform your customer of the indebtedness, and the ending will attempt to motivate payment.

How To Personalize Your Demands, For Extra Pulling Power

One of the best ways to improve customer response to a letter is to be sure that it is individually signed. Nothing is worse than a reproduced signature. The customer is sure to see the letter as nothing more than the work of a robot. Similar caution is urged in the use of form letters when your type-face insert, as part of a variable, is different from the body of the letter. It stands out like a sore thumb.

Another excellent way to strengthen your communication is by personalizing it with a message written especially to the customer. This certainly gives the impression that you're taking a personal interest in the customer's account, early in your collection effort. This personalized approach gives a certain amount of empathy and sensitivity which comes alive as the customer reads it. An example might be "Call me if you need any assistance," "I would really appreciate your check," or even "Please adhere to our credit terms." Any appeal can be used, since the main purpose is to show personal attention and get personal attention in return, in the form of a prompt response and payment.

The Importance Of Knowing Your Customer

A good collector must recognize the *psychology of collection*. That means trying for the best way to strike that responsive chord that will motivate customers to pay. By appealing to instincts, emotions, and attitudes, a collector uses these ideas as tools for payment.

Effective collection efforts and appeals must take account of customer attitudes. An appeal to shame or fear—when the appropriate motivator is one of fairness—will fail. Throughout the collection effort, it is quite common to receive customer responses concerning promises of payment or giving excuses for non-payment, or sending part payments of their account with or without explanations for the balance. Understanding the debtor's financial attitude, his past relations or experience with your company as a customer, and how outside business conditions might influence him, will help you to assess these—and to determine the right appeal at the right time. After all, good credit and reputation are only meaningful to those who value it. For the most part, action and reaction call for the use of common sense and good business judgment. The most effective correspondence will lose its potency if the choice of appeal does not fit the occasion or circumstance.

How Persistent Consistency Pays Off

Be more determined than your customer. It is a given fact that, from time to time, your correspondence will prove ineffective. Regardless of the approach you take, it may appear that your efforts are in vain. However, while this may be a surface observation, the account may be far from entirely lost! Though your customer may not have reacted to the point where payment is forthcoming, each step of the way your payment demands may be influencing the account a little bit more towards recovery. With each reminder and the subsequent payment appeals and demands, it is very probable that you are prodding your customer closer towards recognizing the obligation and keeping to the agreement by making payment.

The power of suggestion is an active ingredient in the collection effort. The collector, ever confident that the bill will eventually be paid, must bring the debtor to the same conviction. The collector's natural objective—to bring the account current in as short a period of time as possible, while still maintaining the customer's good will—is a strong motivator. With the aid of the variety of appeals at the collector's disposal, the persistent repetition with increasing intensity, requesting payment will eventually lay the groundwork for the desired result.

Timing Is Everything

Even the most effective notices will lose their pulling power if not properly scheduled. Timing in your collection effort may involve such factors as the debtor's attitude, mood, and financial conditions. There is no way for you to know just what mood your customer is in when the correspondence reaches him, nor can you determine just how preoccupied your customer may be with other aspects of running the business—besides bill paying.

Obviously, the best time to make your appeal for collection is when the customer has the money. Of course, you could wish that your collection letter was so good that your customer would adapt and use it to collect his own accounts—after having paid you.

While a collection effort is generally not a seasonal one, collectors should try to make their own luck; and the greatest effort should be put forth when success seems most certain (in the event your customer's operation is of a seasonal nature). To the extent that there may be a *best time* to *demand payment* or a best appeal for a given situation, there may also be a *worst* time. A final demand when your customer is experiencing health problems, even though there is no way that you could know that, may provoke a resentful reply.

Once the reminder has been sent, you must determine precisely what sequence will be used for the subsequent demands. Most collection managers seem to believe that sending more than four notices will not produce any significant results; but further recognize that a good deal of time and energy can be saved by properly timing and sending out the notices on schedule. Of course, where consumer installment credit is involved, the customer often has a payment book—therefore, no preliminary statement or reminder is necessary.

Because it is more difficult to collect accounts as they age, the strength of each notice must increase as time passes. You must consider everything from mailing time to payment terms, customer attitudes and personal information that may be relevant—in stepping up the urgency of your notices.

Reminders are usually sent between three and ten days after the payment has become due. The request should then follow between ten and fifteen days thereafter, in order to maintain the essential persistent consistency. A knife, to cut effectively, must remain sharp. So too must your collection system maintain its razor's edge. Continue to observe the effectiveness of your system, and make changes where you observe slow payers waiting to receive final notices. And remember that by using a system of rotating demands, you'll be able to upset the preconceived concepts your customer may develop regarding your delinquency follow up.

THE PAYMENT REQUEST

The payment request is most frequently referred to as the number-two letter. It is also most predominantly created in a form design. However, this is perhaps the first neutral approach you might employ in your arsenal of correspondence. When writing the payment request, however, the best advice to follow is to treat your customer in a dignified and intelligent manner, and to write your letter as you would talk to your customer. The collection letter is as much an ambassador of good will as any other representative of the company. There is always a danger that as a creditor you will "lose your cool" when payment is not made, and will let the customer know your real feelings as they will show through in the correspondence. Try to avoid this. It is extremely important, as the collection effort increases in its intensity, to maintain a positive attitude in a courteous businesslike manner.

The following examples of effective collection correspondence representing the reminder, the request, the appeal, and the demand can easily be used as a complete cycle in a form-letter series. The general nature of the correspondence gives it universal appeal. However, to be most effective, regardless of the correspondence used, you should never go dunning in the dark and direct your correspondence to the Accounts Payable department, payment supervisor, or customer. Remember that *people* are responsible for payment; and addressing your correspondence to the attention of a decision-maker or the person responsible for the indebtedness will invariably produce the greatest result. Many companies have found that including a stamped, self-addressed envelope with a payment request increases the likelihood of a reply—and payment.

EXAMPLES OF EFFECTIVE COLLECTION LETTERS—REMINDER, REQUEST, APPEAL, DEMAND SYSTEM

Routine Reminder

1. Dear *Mr. Reed: DID YOU MAIL YOUR PAYMENT, or

    Did you overlook your account with BBB? We all slip up occasionally and let an invoice fall past due!

    If your check has already been mailed, please accept our thanks. If not, a self-addressed envelope is enclosed. Please mail your check today.

                    Very truly yours,

2. Dear *Mr. Reed:

    In the rush of today's business environment, invoices can easily be overlooked. Your check today in the mail would be appreciated. Please accept our thanks for your immediate attention.

                    Very truly yours,

Request

3. Dear *Mr. Reed: HAVE YOU PAID THIS BILL?

    As a customer, we know you appreciate being reminded when your bill is due. This one, however, is past due. So if you did overlook this invoice (copy enclosed), we request your check for payment.

    If payment has been sent forth, please accept our thanks. If not, a self-addressed envelope is enclosed. Please mail your check today.

                    Very truly yours,

Appeal

4. Dear *Mr. Reed: DID YOU FORGET TO TELL US YOUR PROBLEM?

We should like very much to help you place your account in a current state. If there is a problem with the payment due, please tell us now. You do agree that something should be done now, don't you?

Please advise and mail the balance due today. A self-addressed envelope is enclosed; we are counting on your cooperation.

Very truly yours,

Demand

5. Dear *Mr. Reed: THIS IS NOW URGENT.

This is your final notice. Your account is seriously past due. By ignoring our prior requests for payment, you must know you are forcing us to consider further action.

However, facts are necessary to make any decision. So here they are: when we take action to collect dollars you owe us, both of us lose. We, for example, may lose a customer and you lose a supplier.

Please consider the benefits of paying today and avoiding the costly alternatives ahead if we are forced to proceed. A self-addressed envelope is enclosed. Please mail your check today.

Very truly yours,

(*Person responsible for payment)

Of course, there are thousands of variations to each of the above, limited only by one's imagination. In addition, there are letters for skipped invoices, adjustments to invoices, unauthorized discount deductions, clarification requests for duplicate invoices, and proofs of delivery. Form communications could also be developed for late charge explanations, freight charges, held orders, disputed situations, request for credit line reviews, broken promises, cancelled checks, part-payment follow-ups, notice of "stop shipments," NSF checks, unsigned checks—and notices that the account will be placed for collection if payment is not forthcoming.

Additional Ways To Generate Replies

The use of colored paper and size variations on the letter and envelopes can also be an effective motivator for payment. Credit executives report that pink letterheads or return envelopes generate the greatest result. Bright orange and yellow are next, followed by salmon, green, and blue. Most experts involved in the collection effort indicate that when changing from white collection letters to colored ones, there was increased reaction and response in dollars, replies, and swiftness of response.

Also, where a response is required, sending a letter in duplicate, asking for a handwritten answer on the second copy, gets a quick result and appears to be the most effective way to generate replies (although not necessarily the best way to generate checks). People in business are often too busy to write letters or address envelopes—and are tempted to put such requests aside. As you provide this service to your customer, you may proportionally increase your results.

A letter library should be built so that the collector can handle the largest volume in the most routine fashion as possible. The contents of each letter can be reviewed periodically, so that stilted language can be updated, and words and phrases made more relevant as times change.

Finally, when a customer does promise payment, place the account for follow up (if large enough, note it on your calendar), on the date payment is due. If a promised check is more than a week away, consider sending a reminder five days before it is to be sent forth. It will serve you well. If the check doesn't come in on time, continue with your persistent consistency!

HOW TO GET THE MOST FROM A "PAYMENT APPEAL" LETTER

Astute Collection Managers overcome customer resistance by discussion and persuasion. This task is often made easier if a collector can learn why payment is being withheld. It is for that reason that the #3 letter is often referred to as "an appeal for payment." The collector acting as a correspondent in this stage strives for an explanation as to why payment has been withheld, in addition to trying to obtain payment.

Up to this point, the collection correspondence has become more and more insistent. It is because of this that some Collection Managers eliminate the "appeal" aspect of the program. Their feeling is that a mild letter providing the customer with an opportunity to fabricate his own reason for non-payment will undo much of the good created by the cumulative effect of the prior written demands. However, where there is an appeal to pride, fairness, good credit reputation, honor, fear, future business relations, etc., the value of an appeal in the correspondence sequence should not be underestimated.

THE FINAL DEMAND

In the final stages of collection correspondence, of course, persuasion moves towards coercion. *The final demand,* usually the last in the series of sequenced correspondence, is most likely to point out to the customer the seriousness of the delinquency and the unpleasantries that are sure to ensue if payment continues to be neglected. It is at this stage that the collector must balance the good will his company desires to maintain with the customer, with the strategy that must be employed in collecting in the quickest and most economical way. After all, if the bill is not paid, there's not only loss of good will but loss of a customer—as well as the money. A study of techniques of many experienced Credit and Collection Managers clearly indicates that at this point practically no idea or theme should be ruled out as the basis for an effective demand letter.

The length of time between the intermediate and final stages of collection differs from one business to another. Industry custom, economic conditions, customer mix, terms of sale, competition, and personal preference play a large role in determining your own best collection cycle. However, somewhere between the 60th and 90th day, if your account still remains unpaid, you will have undoubtedly reached the final stages of collection. It is at this point that you should match the credit file with each of the remaining delinquent accounts and carefully review it, to make certain that the latest information is available, and that all useable information is being considered in your collection approach.

At this point, the customer who has evaded your collection cycle probably: (1) has the ability to pay, but does not intend to; (2) is unable to pay all of his obligations and is only paying those who are exerting the greatest pressure, or whose business service or merchandise he needs; or (3) simply lacks the ability to pay any of his creditors, and may be on his way out of business. Of course, there are other possibilities. There's a problem with your account; you have been trying to communicate but the communication has been going astray, or you have not been able to reach an appropriate decision-maker. But the main objective of your final collection effort—like all others—is to motivate the customer to pay the account. Your final demand correspondence will undoubtedly point out in very specific terms that further delay cannot be tolerated, and that a definite commitment or immediate arrangements for payment must be made, if the costly alternatives are to be avoided.

In constructing your final demand, force is obtained by use of short, crisp and punchy sentences, each one building on the next so as to engender the response that you desire. To provoke response further and prod your customer towards payment, many organizations have their final written demand signed by a Senior Officer or the Corporate Credit Manager.

How Getting Tough Can Sometimes Save A Customer!

In many instances, a customer's endless array of excuses may seem unwarranted, and when you reach the final stage of your collection correspondence, customer good will may become secondary. Your principal objective is to salvage payment of the account receivable for your company. But by doing that, you may very well salvage your precious customer. After all, having just paid the account, your customer is very likely to place a new order, recognizing that he's re-established his credit. In effect, by resolving the account, you are helping your company to bring back a customer—and helping the customer to maintain his good relationship with you.

Going Beyond The "Last" Step

This final stage in collection *correspondence* should not necessarily be confused with the final stage of the collection *effort*. Additional impact may also be obtained by writing a personal letter to the highest authority involved in commercial indebtedness, i.e., a personal letter to the Chief Executive Officer of your customer's corporation may be especially productive.

Often collection attempts get bottlenecked in lower levels of management, and you may wish to advise the Chief Executive Officer that previous payment demands have been fruitless. It is on that basis that you request his direct assistance in attending to the matter personally. (In dealing with a consumer-debtor, you might wish to send a Certified Letter, as that kind of correspondence always suggests greater urgency; and a signed acceptance will prove that you've reached the proper party.)

TEN USEFUL TIPS FOR CREATING EFFECTIVE COLLECTION LETTERS

The following ten tips on how to write result-getting collection letters will not only aid you in the preparation of new correspondence, but will enable you to revise and rejuvenate some of the pulling power of your existing letters.

Be Brief—Break it to them gently; but do it in your first sentence. Highlight that sentence so that it stands out from the rest of the letter. By keeping your correspondence down to between 40 and 60 words, you can be tactful and polite without being wordy. Eliminate words in excess of three syllables. You want payment now, but don't forget to make the demand polite and businesslike. Don't threaten; promise, and be certain to keep your word.

Be Specific—Don't forget to ask for payment, and be specific as to dates and amounts of your request. Always specify the amount of money you want. Take it for granted that the merchandise or service rendered was satisfactory—and that there's no dispute about this. Collection philosophy is based on the fact that the customer is obligated to pay, and that you as a creditor have a right to collect.

Tell How and When—Don't assume that the customer will mail you a check simply because you mentioned the account is past due. Ask for the money, suggest a definite plan for the customer to act upon, and tell your customer both *how* and *when* to pay.

Be Persistent—Increase the pressure with each additional letter at agreed-upon intervals. This will build up a crescendo of urgency.

Be Clear—Employ basic language and use familiar terms. Use words the customer will understand so that there's no ambiguity. "Please pay now; mail your check today" is ideal.

Be Confident—Let your customer know you think he or she is honest and wants to maintain good credit standing. Keep in mind that your customer is important. As you write, think of the impact your letter will have on the customer.

Know Your Customer—Understanding necessarily precedes advice and guidance. In order to be effective and strike that responsive chord, you should choose the right appeal—and the right time to make it (as noted earlier).

Put Yourself In Your Customer's Place—Try to anticipate your customer's reaction to your communication. Place yourself in the background, and put the emphasis on the customer. Persuade the customer to see things your way. Make subtle use of all available appeals—such as customer benefits by paying now, credit reputation, credit standing, self-esteem, pride, cost of not paying now, courtesy, cooperation, good intentions, sympathy, fear, and justice.

Play It Straight—People react to hostility with hostility. Humor sometimes works, but it must be simple and straightforward. Avoid double-entendres, puns, and be certain to resist the temptation to be sarcastic. Stick to simplicity and sincerity. Use the "kiss" philosophy "Keep It Simple and Sincere."

Follow Up Promises—Make the most of any promise you obtain, and hold your customers to their word. The fact that you want payment is not enough; you must motivate the customer to pay. And be sure *not* to combine the "promise confirmation letter" or a "payment reminder" with a "what happens if you default" letter. If you tell customers in advance that you expect them *not* to keep their word, they may very well do just that.

What About The Use Of Humor?

There's nothing funny about owing money. Despite that fact, however, many companies resort to humorous reminders in their collection efforts. While collectors are human beings and as such are expected to retain a sense of humor, most delinquent customers are not in a very joking mood. Collection letters are designed to make people pay, not make people laugh.

Some collection managers have successfully used puns, humorous anecdotes, and even cartoons. As a general rule, though, customers are very touchy, maybe even worried and nervous about meeting their obligations, and a letter suggesting that their obligation is something to joke about may prove to be the most self-defeating thing that could have been sent.

SPECIAL REQUIREMENTS FOR RETAIL
COLLECTION LETTERS

Many retail merchants use charge accounts in order to increase business. The charge account is a great convenience; it allows customers to buy more freely than they otherwise would—without being too concerned about their current financial state. It also allows them to be more comfortable, since—in the event something that's purchased turns out to be defective—nothing is owed until the defect is cleared up.

From the company's standpoint, retail credit has become an important sales tool. Retail collection letters are not generally designed to engender the same type of early payment as is found in commercial transactions. Basically a retail account involves the use of a revolving credit balance, where minimal part payments are made against the monthly statement, and a service charge is applied to the unpaid balance. In many respects, the consumer credit grantor is not only selling a product but is selling credit services as well.

Many retailers recognize that their customer is likely to be a member of the local community. People frequently shop in close proximity to their residence. This also means that extending retail credit is likely to involve a more personal experience than you would expect in a commercial setting. The customer will often visit your place of business, so it's far more difficult to be impersonal.

Keeping The Appeal Personal—And Friendly

Strickly speaking, a collection letter is a collection letter; and regardless of the type of customer you are pursuing, for the most part your object is the same: to get paid. Nonetheless, when you are involved in a consumer transaction, it's not likely that your customer is sophisticated in matters of business. So it is even more important to keep your language simple and straightforward.

Use Retail Collections To Sell More

While every collector's role is partially that of a good-will ambassador, in the retail field it is not uncommon for new promotional sale items to be included with the monthly statement. That pretty well puts the collection manager betwixt and between. In effect, he's trying to collect his balance, and at the same time trying to promote his company and create the next obligation.

Who Is Your Customer?

Because of the large volume in retail business, very polite form letters are commonplace. The variety of people that you encounter in your collection effort is so vast that form letters must be kept very general in content, so as to assure the greatest range of appeal and acceptance. Tact and politeness, expressed most frequently by "We appreciate your business, but . . ." are more frequently found in the consumer than in commercial correspondence. Primarily this is because the decision-maker and customer are usually one and the same. While that's occasionally true in a commercial setting, it's rare to find a company with one employee that does everything. In business-to-business collections, you will more than likely be dealing with bookkeepers, treasurers, controllers, financial managers, etc. But you must remember that the past-due consumer, if offended, is likely to be the same person that buys next door from your competitor.

How To Strike A Responsive Chord

If only you could know what motivates individuals to pay and could determine what's in their minds—and in their banks—at the time they open their mail and read your letter, you could prepare and frame the perfect collection demand. You can't, of course—but you can come close.

Many retailers experience collection difficulties because of their preoccupation with trying to avoid offending customers. But this can't always be avoided. A collection demand produces results because it strikes a responsive chord—sometimes an irritating one.

Consumer appeals, however, must be carefully worded so as not to injure one's pride or sense of fairness. If you hurt somebody, you're likely to create ill will and aggressiveness—and even anti-company sentiment. Sometimes, even major accounts wonder what would happen if they don't pay on time. If you see people on your delinquent list that you're not accustomed to seeing, it's possible you're being tested. A customer might be wondering how long it will take you to respond, and just what that response will be. Don't ignore such a test. And once you've decided on the program and discipline necessary to preserve your receivables and maintain your sales, stick to it.

What To Do In The Final Stages

In the final stages of your collection correspondence, you're likely to abandon any hope of maintaining customer relations, and to opt to collect at all cost. Having reached this final stage, you now must consider the variety of alternatives that are available to you. You can promise to refer the matter to a lawyer or to a collection agency if the account is not paid. Or you can just promise to proceed without stating specifically just what you have in mind. This, of course, hints of further, stronger, more effective collection methods. It adds the pressure of silence, in that the customer is not sure just what your intentions are. This sometimes carries more weight than actually spelling out what you're going to do.

At this stage, you should be *promising* only what you intend to do, and not *threatening* in any way. Many companies will try, often for the first time, to suggest part payments or a schedule of payments. There are many firms that try a personal approach in the form of an appeal, giving a customer a final ten-day notice before actually taking any dramatic action.

While there are a variety of letters that can be used in this situation, you just cannot—and should not—continue to carry on an endless array of correspondence. There has to be a point beyond which you will not go. In keeping with your specific company's collection policy, it is not likely that you will have sent more than four or five written demands without having received some type of response or payment.

You can probably increase your recovery by providing self-addressed or even pre-paid self-addressed envelopes. It is also often advisable, if you think your customer may dispute you or make some complaint, to send your letter in duplicate, and ask that the customer merely return a copy with an outline of his position. As previously suggested, varying the color of the return envelope in this final demand stage may also prove effective, creating an apparent urgency that may otherwise not appear. Try pink, deep orange, salmon or blue. They have been proven most effective as attention-getters, and have gotten results.

Getting Down To The "Hard Facts"

The final demand provides sufficient variety and flexibility to enable you to handle most any situation. In some respects, this no-nonsense collection stage is psychologically easier for the collector to deal with because the pressure of trying to remain friendly, maintain customer relations and to collect is lifted. Your appeals to fair play, good credit, and your expressions of surprise and lack of understanding have already been exhausted; and now, having reached the point of "pay or else," you can show your impatience and get down to the business of hard-core collection.

The major objective of your letter is to communicate to the delinquent your goal; to get paid. If you were able to tell that to the customer face to face, it's unlikely that you'd be able to take the time to plan each word carefully as is the case in your written demands. However, while the best letters are those that communicate in language that you would use in your regular conversation, when committed to paper, they often don't seem quite as effective. As a result, a collection letter in this stage should create a sense of natural conversation—so that it sounds as if you are talking and explaining to your customer as it is being read. This would truly be the art of communicating. You may even find that you are most effective in designing what's best for you, by listening to yourself on the phone and remembering just how you'd say it.

COLLECTING FROM PROFESSIONAL ACCOUNTS

Doctors, lawyers, accountants, business consultants and other professionals face a unique difficulty in the handling of their collection accounts. It has been customary in the past for professionals to extend credit on a purely personal basis. While they are, of course, free to maintain the motto, "In God We Trust; all others pay cash," generally speaking credit is extended.

When people are in need, as in the case of a doctor's patient, it is often viewed as the professional's duty to provide relief. Ethics dictate that the physician is to heal, with financial considerations being suppressed. But when a professional extends credit liberally, he is in fact at risk. Many of the obligations may be far beyond the ability of the customer or debtor to pay. However, the fact that a professional's patients may be his friends also adds to the complexity of the collection problem. Knowing a patient or client personally, increases the difficulty of demanding payment. And many clients (as opposed to customers) who have a personal relationship with their creditors, do not expect to have payment demands made upon them.

How Best To Ask For Payment

There are several other reasons why professional accounts are not generally handled in the same aggressive manner as are consumer installment indebtedness or commercial receivables. Just how demanding the collection effort should be, is a matter of subjective judgment. Because of the rather personal friendly relations that probably exist between professionals and clients, pressing for payment is not usually the tactic employed.

The usual way is to send perhaps a half-dozen reminders, rather than a letter series increasing in intensity until the final demand. However, somewhat surprisingly, the reminders are often effective, just because of the personal relationship.

The Right Appeal

The most frequently used appeal for collecting professional accounts is the need of money. A commercial business would rarely if ever appeal to its own financial need, while with the professional this is the most frequently raised issue. In fact, professionals are expected to have a high standard of living, thus adding further credibility to their appeal for payment. On the other hand, even professionals must observe a discipline. There is a point beyond which reasonable people should not be pushed. If the client desires it, you can wait until your services are needed again. However, the chances are that the person indebted to you may feel some embarrassment, and it's likely that because of this embarrassment he may purposely stray and seek assistance from some other professional. In a very real sense, the best thing you can do for both your client and yourself is to bring the account current.

In the area of professional collections, lawyers naturally have the greatest advantage, since they need not refer the matter to counsel—it's already there. But they may, of course, seek assistance from a professional collection agency.

WHEN TO USE TELEGRAMS, MAILGRAMS, OR OVERNIGHT LETTERS

The telegram is one of the more effective methods of communication. Its power and success are largely the direct result of the fact that in the mind of the recipient, it is usually reserved for matters of great urgency. The same message sent by regular mail may prove meaningless, while the telegram appears extremely effective.

Telegrams should be firm without being belligerent. They should contain short, jolting messages. However, in considering the use of telegraphic messages, you should remember that you're moving into an area of collection where more caution is necessary than would be employed by phone or letter. This is because telegrams are not necessarily private communications. The information contained therein may be observed by people who cannot protect its contents. The real problem, of course, is that something might be included in the telegram which may be construed as libelous. Threats of any kind should be avoided, since the information is being delivered by a third party. Generally speaking, however, the privacy of a telegram is acknowledged.

Types Of Telegrams

There are three major types of telegrams. The universal method is to call a Western Union central phone bureau giving your message to the operator. It is then transmitted to the central computer, and from there to the nearest Post Office. A telegram can also be sent from a telex or a computer system. In addition, messages in bulk can be backed up on to tape and then sent to a Western Union computer center, where they are sent by computer to the customer's area for overnight delivery.

Because telegrams are used only in the latter stages of collection, they are not generally considered to carry messages of good will. However, many companies wishing to step up their initial collection efforts, have the facilities to back up on tape hundreds or thousands of their accounts, and substitute a Mailgram for perhaps their second or third form letter. It is generally agreed that the telegram, because it interrupts your customer, implies urgency and commands attention, is more effective then a Special Delivery, Registered Letter or Certified Letter sent under similar circumstances.

The Right Wording

When constructing a telegram, you can imply a great deal by choosing your words carefully and keeping your message short, say, under 20 words. However, you must exercise great care in determining just what you will say, as this wire is likely to be the last written communication between you and your customer. As is the case with the letter, try to determine the best timing and just what type of motivator will have the right impact on your customer.

Essentially, telegrams are composed of the same words and phrases that you would use in your form letters or dictated personalized correspondence. In effect, the same rules apply, but your message is substantially abbreviated. You will, of course, identify yourself and specify the amount of payment required. While it's easy to assume your customer knows about it, it's not recommended that you put his memory to the test. Then, of course, comes the provocation. You are determined to elicit a response by motivating—not threatening.

The telegraph company will gladly furnish you upon request a pamphlet that outlines telegraphic messages that are permissible. However, because of the variety of circumstances you are likely to be confronted with, it is advisable for those in the Collection Department of any organization to prepare in advance a number of sample messages, and have them cleared by competent counsel before making them available for company-wide use.

In addition to considering the telegram as a collection tool, the telegraph company itself can often act as an extension to a collector's own department. By adding information such as "Deliver to addressee only," and "Report address to which message was delivered," you are adding extra impact to your payment demands, and no doubt suggesting that your account should take priority in the mind of your customer.

In many cases, the cost of using a telegram may appear excessive when comparing it to other notices or even the telephone. But in fact, the cost of using telegrams will vary with the type of transmission and delivery. If one pictures a representative of the Western Union company knocking on the door at your customer's place of business or residence, hand delivering a message in rural America, it's conceivable that the cost would be exorbitant. On the other hand, many messages are delivered by telephone, and an equal number by overnight mail.

Because cost is undoubtedly a factor, many companies use the telegram on larger accounts or in the final stages of a collection effort. Depending on the balance due, even the Post Office overnight mail or special courier service may be warranted; and no technique should be ruled out in the backdrop of substantial dollars that need be collected. When other methods do not produce the desired result, accounts can often be salvaged with proper use of the telegram.

The following represent a sampling of wires that can be used in the collection of your accounts receivable.

- FUTURE BUSINESS DEPENDENT UPON GOOD CREDIT. MAIL PAYMENT OF $750.00 NOW.

- YOUR ACCOUNT WILL BE SENT TO OUR ATTORNEY BY MONDAY, MAY 15th, UNLESS BROUGHT CURRENT. MAIL $458.00 AT ONCE TO PREVENT POSSIBLE LEGAL ACTION.

- YOUR ACCOUNT IS PAST DUE. MAIL PAYMENT $500.00 NOW TO AVOID BEING ASSESSED COSTS IF WE PROCEED FURTHER.

- SEND $400.00 PAYMENT DUE ON INVOICE MAY 25th, #1000. MUST HAVE CHECK NOW OR WILL PROCEED TO ENFORCE PAYMENT. (To enforce payment optional.)

- PATIENCE AT AN END. MUST HAVE CHECK NOW. MAIL $300.00 TO PREVENT POSSIBLE LITIGATION.

- YOUR INSTALLMENTS, JANUARY, FEBRUARY NOT PAID. MARCH PAYMENT DELINQUENT. TO AVOID BREACH ACCELERATION AND LITIGATION, MAIL $300.00 WITHIN SEVEN DAYS.

- MUST HAVE YOUR $500.00 PAYMENT BY FRIDAY, 4/25. OUR ATTORNEY ON STANDBY WILL PROCEED. MAIL CHECK NOW.

- CREDIT IS A PRIVILEGE. DON'T TAKE ADVANTAGE. MAIL $650.00 TODAY. AVOID COSTLY ALTERNATIVES.

- PROMPT PAYMENT WILL ASSIST US AND PROTECT YOUR CREDIT. PLEASE MAIL YOUR CHECK TODAY.

- YOUR CHECK FOR OUR PAST DUE INVOICE IN THE AMOUNT OF _____ DATED _____ WILL BE APPRECIATED.

- REVIEWING CREDIT LINE, HOLDING ORDERS, MAIL YOUR CHECK NOW, URGENT. VITAL YOUR CHECK REACH US IN SEVEN DAYS. LAST CHANGE TO MAKE GOOD. MAIL TODAY.

- CONDITION OF YOUR ACCOUNT UNACCEPTABLE: MAIL CHECK IMMEDIATELY FOR $500.00 PAST DUE. MUST HAVE PAYMENT TODAY. PLEASE COOPERATE.

- DEMAND FOR IMMEDIATE PAYMENT, DUE US $1,000.00. MAIL CHECK TODAY.

HOW TO HANDLE NSF CHECKS

Every collector is likely to experience receipt of a bad check. While the reason for non-payment can vary from uncollected funds to "account closed," so do the intentions of the customer vary—from unintentional to deliberate. For the most part, however, the customer should be given every opportunity to make good on the check. A letter should immediately be written, pointing out that receipt of such a check is unacceptable and undoubtedly risks jeopardizing future business and friendly relations.

While checks for uncollected funds may be routinely redeposited, and checks for insufficient funds are sometimes redeposited, it is a good idea to place a call to the customer and send an appropriate written demand *simultaneously*. These should notify the customer of your intentions to either redeposit, or your request for a replacement check to clear the account.

Here are two sample letters that will "fill the bill" nicely:

Redepositing Insufficient Funds Check

Dear (Decision Maker):

Your bank has notified us that your check # _____ dated _____ in the amount of $_____ has not been honored because of insufficient funds.

We are redepositing this check. Please make arrangements immediately for its payment.

We are certain that you will want to cooperate and resolve this immediately in an amicable fashion.

Very truly yours,

Insufficient Funds Check—Request For New Check

Dear (Decision Maker):

Your check number _____ in the amount of $ _____ dated _____ has been returned to us by your bank with a notation "Refer to maker" ["Account attached," "Account closed"].

We consider the return of a check a very serious matter. It is now essential that you provide for its immediate replacement in guaranteed funds. Please mail to us a Cashier's Check, Money Order, or Certified Check immediately.

Upon receipt of your replacement, we will return the original check to you. At that time, we will discuss with you restoration of your good credit standing.

Please give this matter your immediate attention and mail your replacement check today.

Very truly yours,

UNUSUAL COLLECTION SITUATIONS

Occasionally during the pursuit of a consumer debt, you will encounter a particularly paternalistic, protective employer—the Civil Service or the Armed Forces, for example. Such an employer may be eager to have its employees keep an impeccable credit reputation. In each case, when you communicate with such an employer, you must remember you are asking for a favor—for their assistance in your collection effort. You should be encouraging in your tone and approach, and appreciative in your conclusion. In the case of the employer *not* involved in government service, you might even go so far as to say that you wish to avoid the possibility of garnishment (provided such action is authorized in your local jurisdiction). You may further say that you are "hoping to avoid embarrassing and unnecessary action" by having the employer ask his employee (your customer) to make satisfactory arrangements to clear the account.

Armed Services organizations have always maintained a public policy of good relations with local community service groups, and businesses in general. A sample letter to an employer or Commanding Officer in a polite and respectful manner therefore, is likely to get good results, as follows:

We are writing to ask your assistance in the handling of an account we have with one of your (employees) (servicemen), employed at _____ (stationed at) _____. This requires his attention. The (serviceman) (employee) is named _____ (if serviceman, add rank and serial number).

The present balance on the account is in the amount of $ _____ , which remains past due from _____ . This debt is based upon _____ .

We have contacted (name of person) without results.

We realize that you have many pressing responsibilities, but we are sure that (as part of the Armed Services) (as a member of the business community) it is your desire to render assistance in maintaining good relations between your employees and other (civilian, community) business organizations.

We would therefore appreciate your advice (to the name of the employee) in regard to his obligation.

Thank you for your efforts on our behalf.

Very truly yours,

Here are two further letters, worded slightly differently, but conveying the same message:

To An Armed Forces Officer

TO: COMMANDING OFFICER (NAME)

Subject: Name:
Rank:
Serial No.
Balance Due:

Dear Sir:

(Name), is indebted to us in the amount $ _____ for (merchandise invoice) (services rendered) (contract). All normal efforts to resolve the balance have been unproductive, and the account is now seriously delinquent.

Recognizing that the position of the Armed Forces in such matters has always been based on the desire to cooperate with the civilian population, we would appreciate it very much if you would counsel the individual regarding his responsibility to honor payment of the obligation.

It is not our intention to use your command as a collection service, but we do request that you bring this matter to the individual's attention. We're confident that it will work to our mutual benefit.

Thank you for your cooperation.

Very truly yours,

To An Employer

Dear ———————:

May we inquire of you if it is consistent with your company's policy to counsel employees concerning their indebtedness?

(Name) incurred an obligation with our company based on ———. All efforts to collect in an amicable fashion to date have been unproductive. The account is now seriously delinquent.

We are not asking that you act as our collector, and do not want the fact that your employee has failed to take care of this obligation to in any way effect his employment status with you. However, if it is part of your company's general policy to counsel employees in such matters as good credit and their standing in the community, we would appreciate your cooperation.

May we count on receiving the appropriate reply?

Very truly yours,

WHEN TO USE SIGHT DRAFTS

While the sight draft is used less frequently than in the past, it can still be an effective collection tool during the more serious stages of delinquency. In many respects, the sight draft is similar to a note or check. The difference is that the collector prepares it, and in doing so, requests that the customer's bank contact the customer for payment on the account. This puts the bank in the position of having to act as agent for the collector. And what collector couldn't use a bank on his side!

The customer whose bank is being asked for help does not want the bank to believe he's experiencing difficulty; so he or she is likely to authorize payment or to arrange to have payment made direct to the creditor. Thus, there is considerable moral pressure on the customer to pay his obligation.

Sight drafts are frequently most effective in obtaining payment when dealing with small balances, or where a large account has been reduced substantially. On the other hand, many large accounts can also be prodded toward payment by a sight draft. When successful, the customer's bank will charge a small fee for handling the draft, and mail the proceeds of the paid draft directly to the demanding creditor.

A sight draft, where you literally try to extract funds from the customer's account is not to be confused with the sight draft used in a letter of credit transaction, where the seller retains title to his merchandise and the draft is attached to a negotiable bill of lading and other documents. On page 134 is a sample of a sight draft that can be used along with the appropriate letters to the customer and the bank. Model letters follow beginning on page 135.

Exchange for

AMOUNT

DATE _____ 19___

—AT SIGHT—

of this **SECOND**

of Exchange (First unpaid) pay to the Order of

CREDITOR'S NAME
AMOUNT WRITTEN OUT
PAST DUE ACCOUNT

Value received and charge the same to account of

To CUSTOMERS NAME
CITY & STATE

No

BANK NAME
CITY & STATE

DRAWER OF DRAFT

FILE # _____ DATE _____ COLL. # _____

134

To Bank

Re: Creditor (name only)
Vs: Customer, City and State
$: Amount

Gentlemen:

Please present the attached draft for collection. Remit the proceeds to us, less your fee for your service, if collection is made.

If you are not able to collect or elicit an answer from your account customer within seven (7) days, please return the draft. A business reply envelope is enclosed for your convenience.

Very truly yours,

To Debtor (Customer)

Re: Creditor

Gentlemen:

We are drawing a sight draft against your bank
_____ _____, in the amount of $ _____.
(name)   (city and state)   (balance)

Please make arrangements with your bank to see that it is promptly paid. We are counting on your cooperation and trusting you to resolve the balance due us now.

Very truly yours,

Proof Of Delivery

Whether the result of habit, tradition or custom, the burden of supplying *Proof of Delivery* seems to be falling more and more on the shoulders of suppliers. Oftentimes this flies in the face of logic, since title usually passes at the time of shipment (FOB, Free On Board).

In spite of the fact that title may pass to your customer as soon as it leaves your factory, customers in increasing numbers are alleging that they've had no control over the carrier and no relationship to the carrier; and that therefore it's the creditor's responsibility to prove receipt! According to the UCC, there is a nine-month limitation from the date of shipment on filing claims against freight carriers.

Since a request for Proof of Delivery may not be made for weeks or months from the time you begin your collection effort, you can't afford any delay when finally attempting to obtain the proof. Sometimes there's more than one carrier involved, and by the time all the paperwork is done, you can get pretty close to the nine-month limitation. Therefore, the best way to protect yourself is to be sure that your Proof of Delivery request simultaneously indicates your intent to file a claim if Proof of Delivery is not provided. This intent foils the statute and enables you to file a claim after the nine months have elapsed. A sample letter to notify the freight company of your intent follows on page 137.

Request For Proof Of Delivery

To the Carrier
Att: Tracing Department

Gentlemen:

Please furnish us with Proof of Delivery for the following
shipment(s):

Date of Shipment
Number of Cartons
Bill of Lading Number
Bill of Lading Date
Invoice Number
Invoice Date
Amount
Weight

A copy of our original bill of lading is (enclosed). This
merchandise was consigned to _____.

We would appreciate your prompt attention in furnishing
the requested delivery receipt within the next 28 days. If we are
not in receipt of your reply, please consider this request our
formal claim filing for the full amount of our loss. Thank you for
your cooperation.

Very truly yours,

WHAT ABOUT E-COM SERVICE?

To give added spark, life and attention to your collection correspondence, you can now have your computer work to your advantage and deliver letters to the Post Office effectively and efficiently, as well as economically. Designed to transmit computer-generated letters quickly, *electronic computer-originated mail* (E-Com) provides two-day delivery within the continental boundaries of the United States. This method of collection can relieve your company of the burdensome and expensive task of printing, enveloping, stamping and mailing. With E-Com service, all you do is have a certified carrier transmit your computer letters to the Postal Service—or you can become certified to send E-Com letters directly.

For smaller companies without computer facilities, carriers acting as agents will assist by providing consolidation of letters from companies unable to achieve the required minimum of 200 letters.

E-Com service generates a letter of up to two pages in hard copy, puts it in an envelope, and sends it to your customer by First Class mail. Delivery is enhanced because you are bypassing your own internal mail department and transmitting these letters directly to the Postal Service. In addition, you have the added advantage of sending the correspondence any time you want. The lines are opened 24 hours a day, 7 days a week.

All E-Com letters are delivered in highly visible, blue-streaked envelopes that are similar in format to Mailgrams. In addition, the correspondence can be sent in these three formats.

1.   Variable text letters, which have a unique text for each customer.

2.   Common letters, which enable you to send the same letter to numerous customers.

3.   Personalized letters, which have a common text as well as variable texts that can be inserted as the individual situation warrants.

Companies interested in the E-Com service, however, must contact the Post Office or private company E-Com service center in their area and 1) establish an advanced deposit account for which there is an annual fee; 2) format their correspondence accordingly to specific requirements; 3) provide for the computer hardware equipment (CRT and Modem apparatus necessary to dial up); and 4) have sample letter text approved in format, substance and content.

When used in bulk quantities, this approach can be extremely effective, and enable you to handle quantity correspondence with minimal cost.

(For a sample of actual collection letters—appropriate to virtually any situation—see Chapters 2, 4, and 8.)

2

Model Collection Letters: Reminders, Requests And Appeals

Table of Contents

PAYMENT REQUESTS

Action Approaches:

PAYMENT APPEALS

Action Approaches:

2

Model Collection Letters:
Reminders, Requests
And Appeals

This chapter offers a wide variety of letters—twelve reminders, twenty requests, and twenty-two appeals—for use in the early, friendly stages of the collection process. These letters have been tested and have proven effective in hundreds of situations; and each one is easily adaptable to a number of specific situations.

Reminder: You've never met anyone whose name is "account" or "payable." So, for best results, personalize your letters. Write to a decision maker *by name,* and you're far more likely to get a response.

REMINDER

Action Approach: Let's Be Brief

Balance Due: _____

Dear Decision Maker:

Our idea of an effective collection letter could be summarized as follows:

A. It should be friendly
B. It should be brief
C. It should be successful

This letter is friendly; this letter is brief, but it's success rests with you. Please mail your check today.

Very truly yours,

REMINDER

Action Approach: Did You Forget?

Balance Due: _____

Dear _____ :

JUST A ROUTINE REMINDER . . .
. . . that your account with us has not been paid. Routine, because you likely overlooked this matter.

If that is the case, please do mail your check today. If your check has already been mailed, please accept our thanks.

_____
Collection Department

REMINDER

Action Approach: Customers Tell Us They Like To Be Reminded

Balance Due: _____

Dear _____ :

MANY CUSTOMERS SUGGEST . . .
. . . that they like a reminder when their account with us is past due.

If payment was mailed, please accept our thanks.

But, if you did overlook this, we request you mail your check for the balance today.

_____
Collection Department

REMINDER

Action Approach: Little Things Are Often Overlooked

Balance Due: _____

Dear _____ :

IT'S THE LITTLE THINGS THAT ARE OFTEN OVERLOOKED.

That's probably what happened to the _____ charge of $ _____ shown on the attached statement. We will appreciate your mailing a check now.

Very truly yours,

REMINDER

Action Approach: In The Rush Of Business

Balance Due: _____

Dear _____ :

In the rush of business, small charges are frequently overlooked.

Your check now will be appreciated.

Very truly yours,

REMINDER

Action Approach: You Probably Overlooked Us

Balance Due: _____

Dear _____ :

You probably overlooked our (November) balance of $ _____ when sending your check last month.

This happens to all of us at times. We believe, however, that you will want to take care of it now.

Your check for $ _____ to clear the balance due will take care of this. Please mail your check today.

Thank you.

REMINDER

Action Approach: Has Your Payment Gone Astray?

Balance Due: _____

Dear _____ :

HAS YOUR PAYMENT GONE ASTRAY?

This is to remind you that we have not received payment of your past-due account.

If your check is not already in the mail, will you please use the enclosed envelope and mail it to us today.

Very truly yours,

REMINDER

Action Approach: List Of Invoices Enclosed

Balance Due: _____

Dear _____ :

This reminder requests your cooperation in sending us your check to credit your account.

Our records indicate the following invoice(s) remain open on your account:

INVOICE NUMBER   DATE   AMOUNT

Please accept our appreciation if your payment has been sent, or use the envelope enclosed and mail your payment today.

Very truly yours.

REMINDER

**Action Approach: Statement And Invoices
Enclosed**

Balance Due: _____

Dear _____ :

HAVE YOU OVERLOOKED OUR ACCOUNT?

Attached please find a copy of a statement of your account and copies of all invoices listed as past due.

Kindly process these invoices for payment and mail your check today.

Your cooperation is greatly appreciated.

Very truly yours,

Collection Department

enc.

REMINDER

Action Approach: Please Cooperate

Balance Due: _____

Dear _____ :

WE REMEMBERED YOU; PLEASE REMEMBER US.

Attached please find a statement of your account showing a balance due us of _____.

We would appreciate your cooperation and attention.

Please mail your check today.

Very truly yours,

_____

Collection Department

REMINDER

Action Approach: In Case You Forgot

Balance Due: _____

Dear _____ :

IN CASE YOU FORGOT.

The enclosed invoice(s) appear(s) past due on your account.

Please put these items in line for payment.

Kindly return this letter with your check today in the prepaid, self-addressed envelope attached.

Very truly yours,

_____

enc.   Collection Department

DATE   INVOICE NUMBER   AMOUNT

REMINDER

Action Approach: Keep Your Account Current

Balance Due: _____

Dear _____ :

WE FEEL SURE YOU WILL WANT TO KEEP YOUR ACCOUNT IN CURRENT CONDITION.

Your business is sincerely appreciated, and your account is current except for $ _____ on your _____ statement.

Will you please send us your check within five (5) days to clear that portion of the account.

Thank you.

Very truly yours,

PAYMENT REQUEST

Action Approach: Won't You Agree, Pay, Or Advise?

Balance Due: _____

Dear _____ :

WON'T YOU AGREE THAT . . .
. . . we have devoted time, effort, and attention to your account.

We must have payment ten (10) days from today. At that time, if you do not respond . . . we must take other steps to protect our interests.

Two courses are open to you:

1. Mail your check in full today.

2. Reply, on back of this letter, with your payment today.

_____
Collection Department

PAYMENT REQUEST

Action Approach: We Tried To Help; Do Your Part

Balance Due: _____

Dear _____ :

WE HAVE TRIED TO HELP . . .
. . . in mailing reminders and statements detailing your account. Even so, it has reached a past-due condition.

It is now up to you to do your part—one of two things—today:

1. Mail your check in full.

2. Notify us when your check will be mailed.

Today . . . for certain . . . do give this matter your prime attention.

_____

Collection Department

PAYMENT REQUEST

Action Approach: We Are Surprised Not To Hear From You

Re: Invoice Date
Invoice Number
Invoice Amount

Dear ————————— :

We are somewhat surprised at not having received the courtesy of a reply to our previous correspondence regarding the above past-due invoice(s).

Since we have not heard from you to the contrary, we now assume that the item(s) is in order for payment, and we must insist upon receiving your check immediately.

Thank you.

Cordially yours,

PAYMENT REQUEST

Action Approach: We Are Concerned About Your Past-Due Balance

Balance Due: —————————

Dear ————————— :

With deep concern, we again request you to clear up your past-due balance with us.

In servicing your account, we help your success. When you do not pay, then there can be no joy for you or for us.

It is our desire to work with you again. To that end, we'll keep doing our part. Please do your part; mail your check in full today.

Today . . . please.

PAYMENT REQUEST

Action Approach: Do Not Forget; Pay Today

Balance Due: _____

Dear _____ :

Recently we asked you to look into the overdue balance shown. But, as of yet, we haven't heard from you.

Please. . .before you forget. . .we solicit your cooperation in bringing your account up to date.

Kindly mail your check today.

Very truly yours,

Credit Manager

PAYMENT REQUEST

Action Approach: Protect Your Credit

Balance Due: _____

Dear _____ :

A statement was mailed to you showing your past-due balance. It may have merely been overlooked, so here is another copy. Protect your credit today; tomorrow it may be important to you. Today, this is important to us.

Were our positions reversed, you would expect no less. So that we may keep your account the way you want it to be—current, please mail your check today.

(enclose photo of statement)   _____

PAYMENT REQUEST

Action Approach: Pay Entire Past-Due Balance

Balance Due: _____

Dear _____ :

We do not understand your failure to send us your check or reply to our letters of (dates).

Inasmuch as our invoice(s) (as listed below) of (date) for (amount) is (are) now way past maturity, we trust that your check will be mailed to us today to cover the entire past-due balance of _____ on your account.

INVOICE(S)

Very truly yours,

PAYMENT REQUEST

Action Approach: Future Credit Approved, But Past-Due Balance Must Be Paid Now

Balance Due: _____

Dear _____ :

We have approved credit for your future orders. However, in reviewing your account, we note that there are invoices that are past due. These were detailed on your last monthly statement. So that the shipment will not be delayed on your new orders, please mail your check clearing the past-due items today.

Very truly yours,

PAYMENT REQUEST

Action Approach: Good Credit Is Priceless

Balance Due: _____

Dear _____ :

That time has come on your account. The amount is $ _____. It is urgent that you take care of this now.

Your good credit standing is priceless. Just place your check in the enclosed envelope and mail it today.

Very truly yours,

PAYMENT REQUEST

Action Approach: Straight-Forward Request—Pay If Statement Correct

Balance Due: _____

Dear _____ :

"INVOICES DUE NOW."

Our records indicate the invoices listed are past due. If correct, we trust that you will mail us your check.

Thank you for cooperating.

Very truly yours,

Credit Department

DATE   INVOICE NUMBERS   AMOUNT

TOTAL: _____

PAYMENT REQUEST

Action Approach: Pay Or Advise Why Not

Balance Due: _____

Dear _____ :

Your account continues to run overdue, and our previous notices appear to have been ignored.

It is imperative that we receive either your check or the reason for non-payment, immediately.

_____
Credit Department

PAYMENT REQUEST

Action Approach: Advise If There Is Any Problem

Balance Due: _____

Dear _____ :

Your account is now seriously past due. The delinquent balance totals $ _____.

If you have any questions, or find any discrepancies, please do not hesitate to call. We require payment now.

Your attention in expediting immediate payment of this balance will be greatly appreciated. If your check has already been mailed, please accept our thanks. If not, please mail your check today.

Very truly yours,

PAYMENT REQUEST
TO BE SIGNED BY COLLECTION MANAGER

Action Approach: Clear Balance Before Year-End

Balance Due: _____

Dear _____ :

Your account has recently been brought to my attention because of the continuing past-due balance. We will appreciate your giving this matter your personal attention.

We are making a special effort to ask you to clear your overdue balance(s) before our fiscal year-end.

Please send your payment now to bring your account up to date. Your check should be mailed by _____ to reach us before our fiscal closing.

Thank you for your cooperation.

Very truly yours,

Collection Manager

PAYMENT REQUEST
(SEASONAL OR HOLIDAY)

**Action Approach: Be Eligible For Cash Discounts
By Clearing The Way Now**

Balance Due: _____

Dear _____ :

    We realize you've been busy during the pre-holiday season. Perhaps that's why we haven't yet received payment of the past-due items checked on the attached statement.

    We know that you want to earn and receive cash discount on all your purchases in the new year. Why not clear the way now by bringing your account up to date with a check for $ _____ today.

Very truly yours,

REQUEST FOR PART PAYMENT

Action Approach: Protect Your Credit; It's Good Common Sense

Balance Due: _____

Dear _____ :

PROTECT YOUR CREDIT TODAY! YOU MIGHT NEED IT TOMORROW!

IT'S JUST GOOD COMMON SENSE.

Facts are necessary to make any decision. Here they are:

A check for at least $ _____ now and $ _____ more by _____ will keep the account on a reasonable basis. It is up to you.

Perhaps you have it in the mail. If not, it is urgent that you mail it now.

Your account with us is dangerously near the point of hurting your credit standing.

Continuation of the account, therefore, will depend upon your cooperation in restoring it to a current condition.

Please mail your check today.

Very truly yours,

PAYMENT REQUEST

Action Approach: Avoid Possible Acceleration Of Your Contract

Balance Due: _____

Dear _____ :

The contract that you signed with us contains a stipulation that permits us to declare the entire balance due and payable in the event that any one payment of the installment is delinquent. To prevent acceleration of your indebtedness, it is essential that you clear up the past-due portion of your account now.

We are counting on your cooperation and understanding, and ask that you mail your check today in the self-addressed envelope enclosed.

Very truly yours,

PAYMENT REQUEST

Action Approach: Avoid Penalty And Interest Charges

Balance Due: _____

Dear _____ :

Your last chance for payment will be Tuesday, May 31st, at which time our office will be open from 10:00 A.M. to 4:00 P.M. After that date, the money must be paid to our Collection Department—plus penalty and interest.

If full payment has already been made, please disregard this notice.

If you are unable to appear personally, please mail your check today.

Thank you.

Very truly yours,

PAYMENT REQUEST

Action Approach: Cash Discount Taken Improperly

Balance Due: _____

Dear _____ :

This will acknowledge your letter (check) of October 24th about a cash discount. We sincerely wish that we could comply.

However, we are hesitant to discuss an exception for two reasons. First, this might be construed by other customers as unfair to them. Second, if we did make an exception, you, whose confidence we certainly want to keep, might wonder a little whether someone else, using pressure, might get still better terms.

We are confident that you will understand and cooperate.

Your check for the small difference will clear the remaining portion of your account. Please mail your check today.

Very truly yours,

PAYMENT REQUEST

**Action Approach: Please Reimburse Us For
Discount**

Balance Due: _____

Dear _____ :

Cash discounts are earned by prompt payment pursuant to terms of sale; otherwise they would serve no purpose. If there were no premiums for promptness or penalty for lateness, then why be prompt? That as you know, is the principle upon which a cash discount is designed.

Thank you for understanding. Please mail the remaining balance today in the envelope enclosed for your convenience.

Very truly yours,

PAYMENT REQUEST

Action Approach: Maintain Normal Business Relationship

Balance Due: _____

Dear _____ :

Upon reviewing your account, we find that Invoice No. _____ and _____ in the amounts of $ _____ and $ _____ are now seriously past due.

The merchandise represented by these two open invoices was shipped to you in good faith, on terms which you accepted. Therefore, we can no longer accept a further delay in payment, and we look forward to receiving your check by return mail in full payment of the account, in the enclosed envelope.

We look forward to your cooperation so that normal business relations between our two companies can be maintained.

Yours truly,

PAYMENT APPEAL

Action Approach: If We Are Wrong, Please Explain

Balance Due: _____

Dear _____ :

DID WE DO SOMETHING WRONG?

If so, please explain. We would like to hear from you.

But if all is OK, do mail your check for the balance due today.

Thank you for cooperating.

Very truly yours,

PAYMENT APPEAL

Action Approach: We Trusted You, But . . .

Re: Invoice Date
Invoice Number
Invoice Amount

Dear _____ :

WE HAVE TRUSTED YOU, BUT . . .

Our most recent statement of your account reflects that the above-noted invoice(s) remains past due.

We would appreciate receiving information regarding any possible discrepancy that may exist. If, however, you find these items to be in order, please forward your check by return mail today.

Thank you.

Cordially yours,

PAYMENT APPEAL

Action Approach: How May We Help? Advise Or Pay

Balance Due: _____

Dear _____ :

HOW MAY WE HELP YOU?

Your account is overdue and we have not heard from you. When you run into unusual problems, we stand ready to assist provided that you let us know why there is going to be a delay.

We would appreciate your check now.

Cordially,

PAYMENT APPEAL

Action Approach: Was Payment Overlooked? Let Us Hear From You

Balance Due: _____

Dear _____ :

PERHAPS THIS WAS OVERLOOKED . . .

According to our records your account shows a past-due balance. Statements containing details have been mailed to you.

Another possibility is that there is some good reason why payment is being withheld. In either case, we should very much appreciate hearing from you at this time. Please advise or mail payment today.

Cordially,

PAYMENT APPEAL

Action Approach: Why Haven't You Paid Us?

Re: Invoice Date
Invoice Number
Invoice Amount

Dear _____ :

We do not appear to have received a reply to our previous correspondence regarding the above past-due invoice(s).

We would be most happy to receive information regarding any discrepancy. Therefore, unless we hear from you to the contrary, we will assume the item(s) are in order for payment; and, accordingly, we request your check by return mail.

Thank you for your cooperation.

Cordially yours,

PAYMENT APPEAL

Action Approach: Advise Why Payment Is Being Withheld

Balance Due: _____

Dear _____ :

SO YOU WOULDN'T FORGET . . .

We recently sent you a reminder regarding the past-due invoice(s) listed below.

To date, we have not received either your payment or reply. If there is any reason payment is being withheld, please inform us now. However, if your records agree, we request that you mail a check to us today.

Very truly yours,

PAYMENT APPEAL

Action Approach: Straight-Forward Appeal To Call Us

Balance Due: _____

Dear _____ :

We have no record of receiving payment on the invoice(s) listed below. We must have immediate payment or advice as to why payment has not been made. If you have any questions concerning this matter, call me at_____. If not, please mail your check today.

INVOICE #	INVOICE DUE DATE	INVOICE AMOUNT

Very truly yours,

PAYMENT APPEAL

Action Approach: Please Advise Of Any Discrepancy

Re: Invoice Date
Invoice Number
Invoice Amount

Dear _____ :

Our most recent statement of your account reflects the above-noted invoice(s) as being past due.

Please advise us if there is any possible discrepancy that may exist. If you find this item(s) to be in order, won't you please mail your check, or let us know when we may expect payment.

Thank you for your attention.

Cordially yours,

PAYMENT APPEAL
TO GOOD CREDIT

Action Approach: Check It Out

Balance Due: _____

Dear _____ :

HAVE YOU HAD A CHANCE . . .
. . . to check our statement and process the items for payment?
We mean the statement we reminded you about a short time ago.
If you have not as yet done so, won't you please review it and
forward payment right away, or advise if there is some reason for
the delay.

Your promptness will be appreciated. Good credit is an asset.

Amount due: $ _____. Please mail today.

Very truly yours,

APPEAL FOR SUBSTANTIAL
PART PAYMENT

Action Approach: Restore Trust, Faith, And Confidence

Balance Due: _____

Dear _____ :

Credit is confidence—mutual trust and faith. It is more precious than money because it enables you to get what you want when you want it, and pay at a more convenient time.

Your account is considerably in arrears; and every day adds to the seriousness of the situation. Will you please send us one-half (1/2) on account now, and your plan for paying the balance.

Very truly yours,

APPEAL TO FAIRNESS

Action Approach: We Serviced You Promptly; Please Pay Us

Balance Due: _____

Dear _____ :

When you requested our services, they were immediately made available. The same promptness on your part in retiring this obligation is fair. Don't you agree?

Your (month) account is still outstanding. Won't you send us your check for $ _____ before we are forced to proceed further.

Please mail your check today.

Very truly yours,

PAYMENT APPEAL TO GOOD CREDIT

Action Approach: Please Pay. Good Credit Is A Privilege

Balance Due: _____

Dear _____ :

PLEASE TELL US . . .

. . . why we have not received neither a payment nor a reply. We are once again calling this past-due balance to your attention.

To carry your account on a current basis, we need your check for $ _____.

Please help us by mailing your check today. Good credit is a privilege.

Very truly yours,

PAYMENT APPEAL FOR GOOD CREDIT

Action Approach: Has Our Account Escaped Your Attention?

Balance Due: _____

Dear _____ :

HAS OUR ACCOUNT ESCAPED YOUR ATTENTION?

Our previous reminder(s) advised of the following unpaid invoices(s):

INVOICE #   DATE   AMOUNT

Please send your payment by return mail, or advise us promptly of any special reason why payment has been withheld. We're counting on your good credit reputation for action.

Very truly yours,

PAYMENT APPEAL

**Action Approach: Invoices Listed; For Your
Immediate Attention**

Balance Due: _____

Dear _____ :

A review of your account indicates a past-due balance of
$ _____ comprised of the following invoice(s):

INVOICE #   DATE   AMOUNT   P.O.#

Should there be any reason why the above has not been paid,
we would appreciate a reply. Otherwise, we will be expecting your
check by return mail.

Thank you in advance for your cooperation.

Very truly yours,

PAYMENT APPEAL

Action Approach: Why Don't You Tell Us The Problem? What Is Causing The Delay?

Balance Due: _____

Dear _____ :

Your account is long overdue, and we have not heard from you as to why. Whenever there is some good reason why you cannot take care of your bills as they fall due, we are always ready to help you—provided, of course, that you help us by letting us know what is causing the delay.

If you do not write and let us know why, we feel it is fair to insist that you pay within terms. In keeping with this, we will look for your check in full to clear the invoices shown on the enclosed statement.

Very truly yours,

PAYMENT APPEAL

**Action Approach: Explain Why Account Is Unpaid,
Or Pay Within Ten Days**

Balance Due: _____

Dear _____ :

    The enclosed invoices are long past due. Please process them for payment.

    Should there be some reason why payment is being withheld, please notify us immediately. Otherwise, we expect payment within the next ten (10) days.

    Thank you for your cooperation.

Very truly yours,

enc.

FINAL PAYMENT APPEAL

Action Approach: Follow Up, With Request For Immediate Explanation Or Payment

Balance Due: _____

Dear _____ :

WE EXPLAINED OUR POSITION; PLEASE EXPLAIN YOURS.

We recently wrote and showed you the exact breakdown leading to the above delinquent balance. We felt sure you would respond at once, by explaining your position . . . or by mailing a check to clear up your account.

Your account is now seriously past due. Please remedy the matter by mailing your check in full today.

Today . . . please.

_____

Credit Department

FINAL PAYMENT APPEAL

Action Approach: From Credit Manager Or Higher Authority: Let's Talk It Over

Balance Due: _____

Dear _____ :

You have been a customer for several years, so you can imagine my surprise when the Manager of our Collection Department placed your account on my desk. There must be some special reason why we have not received payment for your account of $ _____.

Perhaps if we could talk it over, we would have a better understanding—and both of us would benefit. You can count on our doing our part. Please do yours.

Won't you please let us hear from you today.

Very truly yours,

FINAL PAYMENT APPEAL

Action Approach: Write Or Call Right Away

Balance Due: _____

Dear _____ :

Your account is long overdue. We are always ready to listen—provided, of course, that you help us by letting us know what is causing the delay. But we have not heard from you.

If you do not write or call, we feel it is fair to insist that you remit within terms. In keeping with this, we will look for your check in full in seven (7) days to clear the invoices shown on the enclosed statement.

Mail your check today in the enclosed self-addressed envelope. We urge you to act now and avoid the costly alternatives.

Very truly yours,

SEASONAL PAYMENT APPEAL

Action Approach: Start The New Year With A Clear Account

Balance Due: _____

Dear _____ :

     Having received no response to our request for payment, we are becoming concerned.

     You are now approaching one of the busiest and most profitable times of the year. We know that you will want to start the new year with a clear account.

     It is important for your account to become current as soon as possible. Will you please use the enclosed envelope to mail your check for $ _____ to my attention now.

     Thank you.

Very truly yours,

PAYMENT APPEAL TO GOOD CREDIT

**Action Approach: To Maintain Our Service And
Your Credit, We Must Hear From You**

Balance Due: _____

Dear _____ :

Your account is the best possible proof of our confidence in you.

In your own interest as well as ours, we urge you to keep your account in good standing.

Your credit card was issued because of your "prompt pay" record. There must be a good reason why your account is still unpaid.

Won't you send us a letter—or, preferably, a check—promptly?

Your check by return mail will enable us to maintain the good service you deserve.

Very truly yours,

SUPER PAYMENT APPEAL

Action Approach: Preserve Your Good Credit And Good Name

Balance Due: _____

Dear _____ :

Consistent promptness in meeting your obligations has earned you an excellent credit record—and valuable friendship and good will, besides. You will certainly want to protect these assets.

Your good name should not be on our past-due list; but it is.

Since it is generally not your policy to allow these old items to appear open on your account, please make certain your check is mailed today. I know you will want to take care of this.

Very truly yours,

3

How To Get The Jump On Marginal And "Problem" Accounts

Table of Contents

3

How To Get The Jump On Marginal And "Problem" Accounts

While there are a number of instances where improper credit decisions have resulted in bad debts or collection problems, more often than not subsequent deterioration of an account is the real culprit. In fact, when proper credit procedure is followed, there really is no such thing as a bad risk, as—if the customer does not prove worthy—no credit should be extended. Actually, if as much attention were paid to an account *before* credit was extended as *after,* there would be far fewer collection problems.

HOW BEST TO HANDLE MARGINAL ACCOUNTS

Accounts that will most likely turn out to be collection problems are generally considered "marginal" accounts at the time of sale. Traditionally, creditors have been wary of them. However, an increasing number of companies are viewing such accounts as an important part of their overall growth. Such accounts, in fact, often show the greatest promise of future growth themselves. Thus, there may be many a situation where you pretty well know you're starting out with a potential collection problem—and have the responsibility of taking effective action to assure payment—but will decide that the risk is worth taking.

What Is A Marginal Account?

A marginal account is generally defined as one that has a weakness in the basic "C's" of credit, capital, capacity and collateral. One could even say a company is marginal if it is likely to be more affected by general conditions of the country. (Conditions of the country, from economic or any other external influence, constitute the fourth "C" of credit.)

Which Accounts Are Likely To Be Marginal?

The graph on page 305 labelled "Risk Analysis by Customer Classification" is a clear indication of how you can zero in on what types of customers should or should not be given credit. At the point where fixed and variable costs exceed expected revenue, any attempt to conduct business with that category of clientele will result in a loss. (This, of course, assumes equal sales volume with equal fixed costs.) It's likely that the costs of investigating and maintaining marginal accounts, as well as the collection costs associated with slow paying and special term accounts, will increase the costs associated with marginal account customers. You'll have to take them into account, too.

In the graphic example illustrated, if sales in Class D were $50,000 for the year, and it was estimated in advance that 15% of the customers in Class D would not pay, that would leave an expected revenue from sales to Class D at $42,500. If the fixed costs of production in selling amounted to $35,000, and the variable costs including the additional collection costs amounted to $5,000, there would still be a $2,500 profit before taxes.

EVALUATING MARGINAL ACCOUNTS

The following factors should be taken into consideration in evaluating—or collecting from—marginal accounts.

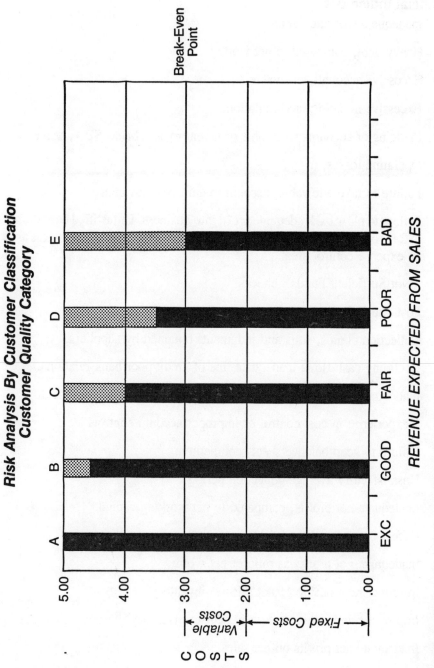

Risk Analysis By Customer Classification
Customer Quality Category

Break-Even Point

COSTS

5.00
4.00
3.00
2.00
1.00
.00

Variable Costs
Fixed Costs

A — EXC
B — GOOD
C — FAIR
D — POOR
E — BAD

REVENUE EXPECTED FROM SALES

Anticipated collection problem and/or bad debt potential

Actual revenue from sales

I. Financial Indicators

- Inadequate working capital.

- Heavy debt, compared to net worth.

- Excessive accounts receivable.

- Excessive inventory accumulation.

- Pledging of accounts receivable or inventory to a bank, SBA, or Factor.

- Operating losses.

- Failure to take allowable discount to gain cost advantages.

- Failure to plow back adequate profit into business. Unjustified cash drain in form of large salaries. Absence of Tax Planning in a growth business as an expense control area.

- "Not Sufficient Funds" checks.

- Post-dated checks.

- Collection claims, suits and judgments obtained by suppliers.

- Declining cash flow; inadequate line of credit/poor bank relations.

- Inadequate and declining sales volume and dwindling order backlog.

- Inexperience in cost control or improper account controls.

- Failure to keep balance sheets competitive.

- Unsatisfactory average collection period.

- Inadequate net profits, compared to net working capital.

- Excess current and total debt, compared to net worth.

- Inadequate net profits as ratio of net worth.

- Improper relationship of net sales to inventory.

- Improper relationship of current debt to inventory.

- Inadequate net profits on net sales.

- Improper relationship of sales to net worth.

- Extraordinary compensation.

- Placing relatives on retainer to do inactive jobs.

- Overtrading (trade buying in excess of capital).

- Disclosure of false or misleading financial statements

- Refusal to share financial information:

  A. Repeated delays in releasing data.
  B. Partial rather than complete information given.
  C. Partial or unaudited information given.

- Increasing volume, but steadily declining profit.

- Abrupt or frequent change of banks.

- Partial and erratic "payments on account."

- Request for a moratorium on payments until additional financing is arranged.

- Failure to maintain scheduled payments on debentures, mortgages, etc.

Financial Ratios, and What They Mean:

		Meaning of Result
1. Current Ratio	Current Assets / Current Liabilities	The extent to which liquid assets are available to cover short-term obligations.
2. Quick Ratio	Cash, Marketable Securities, Accounts Receivables / Current Liabilities	The availability of highly liquid assets to cover current obligations.
3. Debt Ratio	Total Liabilities / Total Assets	The capital structure of the company and the degree to which it is leveraged; the relative risk of the company's capital structure.

4. Receivables Turnover

$$\frac{\text{Net Sales}}{\text{Average Receivables}}$$

The average length of time that cash is tied up in receivables; also indicates the generosity of credit terms and the effectiveness of billing and collection procedures.

5. Inventory Turnover

$$\frac{\text{Cost of Sales}}{\text{Inventory}}$$

The average length of time that cash is tied up in inventory. Substantial movement upward over time and/or systematic deviations from industry averages may indicate the existence of slow-moving or obsolete inventory items.

II. Management Indicators

- Frequent management changes; personality problems.

- Previous inexperience or ineptitude on the part of management.

- Inaccessibility of management for interview.

- Excessive irritation at credit or collection contacts.

- Failure to train and motivate young management personnel.

- Refusal to respond to collection demands.

- Refusal to respond to requests for credit information.

- Reoccurrence of problems previously presumed to be solved.

- Lack of short- and long-range planning.

- Lack of back-up support.

- Poorly defined lines of communication, authority, and responsibility.

- Lack of coordination between levels of management.

III. Operations Indicators

- Auction of equipment; irregular disposal of assets.

- Overdependence on one or two major customers.

- Excess use of foreign materials.

- Failure to keep pace with industry prices.

- Shifting of supplies:

  A. Receipt of an order from an inactive or unsolicited account.
  B. Premeditated overbuying.

- Competitive weakness. Poor performance due to adverse economic conditions, such as throat-cutting competition from more established outlets.

- Imprudent extension of credit.

- Late deliveries on customer shipments.

- Inferior quality product.

- Products becoming obsolete, or lack of research and development on new products.

- Inability to adapt to changing conditions and methods of operation within the industry.

- Poor and deteriorating geographical location.

- Physical neglect of premises.

- Operation of the business as a "sideline."

- Purchases out of normal supply areas.

- Increase in frequency of trade inquiries.

- Slowdown of payments and following pattern of excuses:

  A. moving office
  B. rapid personnel changes
  C. modernization-mechanization of payables

    D. frequency of "lost" invoices
    E. vacations
    F. conferring with laywer

- Indiscriminate acquisition or too rapid expansion of policy, resulting in a lesser cash position and poor control of operations.

- Reverse diversification (selling off newly acquired units).

- Expansion into an area where the operator lacks experience.

- Notification denying responsibility for debts and advising certain acceptable signatures on purchase orders, etc.

- Periodic fire and theft losses not adequately covered by insurance.

- Lack of availability of information concerning a business through credit reporting agencies.

- Submitting of invalid trade references.

- Unethical marketing practices.

- Past record of bankruptcy or fraud.

- Reduced mercantile agency rating.

- Unearned discount suddenly being taken.

- Missing books and records.

- Costs of doing business:

    A. Are labor costs same as or higher than competition?
    B. Pays more for labor and materials (doesn't take advantage of quantity discounts or timely payment discount).
    C. Expenses; maintains excessive capacity.
    D. Product or service improperly costed.
    E. Overhead cost controls not in place.

- Untested speculative ventures.

- Loss of key product lines, perhaps from government regulation.

- Failure to upgrade and/or replace product, or service now obsolete.

- Excessive order cancellations or returns.

- Lack of quality control.

- Concentration of sales with too few customers.

- Declining sales volume.

- Poorly trained sales representatives or indifferent manufacturers' representatives.

- Insufficient production capacity to meet order needs.

- Poorly trained staff resulting in too many people employed or unnecessary overtime costs.

IV. External Influences

- Leases, higher wage demands by unions, defense contracts;

- Weather, floods, fire;

- Contingent liabilities, i.e., patent suits or product liability problems;

- Impending IRS problems (tax disputes, or potential adverse decisions which may also carry a penalty);

- Ecological pollution, environmental issues, or government regulations pending.

* * * * *

By classifying marginal accounts according to the degree of risk, you can make your efforts more effective and increase your profit from marginals.

SIGNS OF TROUBLE—AND WHAT TO DO
ABOUT THEM

Despite the most careful selection of potentially profitable accounts—and the most careful weeding-out of potentially troublesome ones—you're always going to encounter some situations that require immediate, protective action. You'll need to be able to recognize these, and to be prepared to respond. So we'll now consider some typical "problem" situations, what they mean, and how to handle them:

1. The Bulk Transfer (sale).

2. How to handle a "paid in full" check for less than the full balance on a disputed account.

3. The compromise settlement (providing *50 key questions* that when answered enable you to make the best decision).

4. Use of personal guarantees.

5. The late-payment service charge; how to implement the program, and its benefits and problems.

6. Dealing with customers who take improper deductions.

7. Protecting yourself by becoming a secured creditor.

WHAT TO DO ABOUT BULK TRANSFERS

A bulk transfer, as defined by the Uniform Commercial Code, Section 6-102, is "any transfer in bulk and not in the ordinary course of the transferor's business, of a major part of the materials, supplies, or merchandise or other inventory" to a third party. Creditors usually rely upon the visible assets of a business to insure repayment of debts. But if the customer's assets are transferred to another person or business, it may be for cash in an amount considerably less than its actual value. Although it happens infrequently, it's easy to see how creditors can be severely hurt. In order to protect creditors, laws have been designed to prevent the secret sale of certain types of company assets.

The main protection afforded to creditors is the right of *warning*. Article #6 of the Code contains a provision calling for notice and disclosure of a transfer about to take place. Failure to comply with the law would render the title of the buyer to such assets defective. Laws of particular states may vary to some extent in how they apply specific provisions of Article #6; but generally speaking, any sale transfer or assignment in bulk of part or all of a stock of merchandise or of furniture and fixtures—other than in the regular course of business—is void against creditors of the seller unless notice has been given.

The collection executive should consult with competent legal counsel to determine what provisions apply in his or her specific jurisdiction. In some areas, the purchaser must apply the proceeds of the sale to the claims of creditors. In still other areas of the country, as noted, failure to conform with the provisions of the bulk sales law renders the sale void. Where a creditor seeks to set aside the sale of goods as fraudulent, the burden of proof is on the debtor. The creditor must only show that the sale took place without conforming to the requirements of Article #6 of the Uniform Commercial Code.

There are a number of transfers that are exempt from the requirements of Article #6. For example, secured transactions are generally exempted (they are covered under the different provisions of Article #9 of the Uniform Commercial Code). Service businesses—and the transfer of accounts receivable, collateralized property, contracts, and promissory notes—are all exempted. Additional exemptions include sale of substantial amount of inventory or an entire business to a new buyer *who assumes responsibility for existing debts*.

What The Required Notice Consists Of

The following items should be considered essential to any notice of bulk sale: pursuant to Article #6, Section 105,* notice must be given to creditors of all bulk transfers ten days before the buyer takes possession or makes payment.

Article #6, Section 104 requires that a list of creditors be available, and a schedule of the property to be sold be kept available for inspection by creditors. Different states have different requirements for where the list must be filed. However, the list must be sworn to, and in sufficient detail, as to identify the property and give some indication of its value.

Note: In some states (such as California), publication of notice of sale in a local newspaper may constitute appropriate notice!

What Should You Do As A Creditor When You Receive Notice?

1. Immediately review your credit file and determine whether or not the transferor (seller) is incorporated. If the transferor is not incorporated, but rather a proprietor or partnership, liability remains and cannot be transferred along with sale.

2. Determine when the sale will take place.

3. Try to obtain a description of the property to be sold and its value, in an effort to learn whether or not it will be sold for its fair market value. In addition, obtain the list of creditors and the amounts owed, so that you can verify whether your balance is properly reflected.

4. Determine where you must file your claim, and what remedies are available to you if you wish to object to the sale:

    A. If you did not receive notice, consult with your attorney to determine what rights you have against the buyer or seller.
    B. If you have received notice and wish to object to the sale, do so only after consulting with counsel—who can verify whether there was improper compliance with the law—or after evaluating the merchandise to be sold, and determining that there was improper consideration (money being paid) for the inventory being transferred.

5. Review the notice to determine whether the debts are to be paid in full from the proceeds.

From time to time, creditors become outraged because, as part of the notice of sale, they observe that principals of one corporation are selling to the same principals of a new corporation; and it appears that the entire transaction is done for the purpose of deceiving creditors. Once again, the matter should be discussed directly with your attorney, who can then determine whether or not one corporation is simply the alter ego of another, and whether or not legal action would be economically feasible and legally advisable.

Suppose You Haven't Received Timely Notice?

Occasionally, you as a creditor may not receive notice because you would become a creditor after the notice was sent out, but before the sale was to take place. In that situation, you lose the major protection (the early warning) afforded other creditors. Under such circumstances, you must act especially promptly and file your claim *before the sale occurs*. According to Article #6, Section 111, you do have six months to effect your claim against merchandise sold in bulk sale—unless there's been an allegation of fraud and concealment. In that case, additional time, up to one year, may be provided. Usually actions may be started up to six months after alleged fraud has been discovered.

Although the foregoing assumes that you're an unsecured creditor who has not taken any other action, and that the bulk sale comes as a surprise, it's just as likely that you may have been involved in a lawsuit or brought your account to judgment. If that is the case, your attorney may be able to levy and issue execution on the property to be transferred, so that you can intercede and prevent the sale. In other jurisdictions, you may be able to file garnishment proceedings after taking legal action, or file an attachment on other grounds. Or you may be able to apply for the appointment of a receiver, or for an injunction, or participate with other creditors in stopping the sale by filing an involuntary petition in bankruptcy. Each of these situations provides a dramatic remedy in its own right; and you should consult with counsel to obtain the proper advice and guidance, and to see that your interests are properly protected.

Notice From A Creditors' Committee

Occasionally you will receive notice of a bulk sale from a company, as a result of creditors' committee negotiations with that company. This is as it should be. But one of the most frequently observed objections voiced by creditors who receive a bulk sales notice is that their debtor/customer did *not* consult with them first. After all, if a company has a negative net worth, creditors would appear to have greater equity in the business than its principals. So the least the customer could have done was to consult with creditors as to what course of action to take. Perhaps other buyers could have been found that would have bid more for the items to be sold! Or perhaps an ongoing liquidation would have produced greater recovery. The possibilities are limited only by your imagination; but they emphasize the importance of receiving notice of sale. When it's done with the supervision and encouragement of the creditors, this can be of real benefit.

It was probably not the intent of Congress to create a Uniform Commercial Code, Article #6, Bulk Sales Law for the purpose of using it as a vehicle for insolvent companies to settle their debts. However, it has been used as a tool in exactly that fashion; and for the most part it is viewed as an effective way to bring into line those objecting creditors that would otherwise litigate and even attempt to block the sale.

Remember, act swiftly and decisively to protect yourself whenever you receive a notice of a bulk sale, or learn that a sale is contemplated or has already occurred. The laws as designed afford minimal protection to creditors, and are not designed to prevent customers from selling their lot to others. The notice you receive may be your first and last chance to act.

HOW TO HANDLE A CHECK MARKED "PAID IN FULL" ON A DISPUTED ACCOUNT

All too often, a customer who has a dispute with a supplier about the specific amount of money owed will try to settle the matter by sending a check marked "payment in full," or with other words with the same meaning and intent. This, of course, presents the creditor with a particularly troublesome dilemma. Cashing the check may risk losing the remaining portion not yet paid; but sending the check back to the customer may risk losing the entire balance. Customers generally believe that if their supplier endorses and cashes the check, any dispute based on that transaction is wiped out, and that "Accord and Satisfaction" have been reached.

Naturally creditors are not very happy with this scenerio, and all too often they search out a possible alternative that will enable them to keep the money and pursue the balance. Most often they are advised to refer to the Uniform Commercial Code 1-207, providing that "a party who with explicit reservation of rights performs or promises performance or to perform in a manner demanded or offered by the other party does not thereby prejudice the rights reserved." If that is the basis for their action, creditors will proceed to write on the back of the check words such as "Without prejudice," "Under protest," or "This check is deposited without prejudice and with full reservations of all rights reserved to proceed on the balance pursuant to provision of UCCI-207." Having endorsed the check in such a qualified fashion, they can then of course proceed to cash the check.

What Action Should You Take?

Does all this action taken by creditors in such sensitive situations actually avoid the release of all claims? In some jurisdictions it will, and in others it won't. There is no single rule to follow, and generally speaking, decisions are based on the extent of prior correspondence and documentation.

Still other creditors try to *have it both ways*. They certify the check and set the funds aside, while attempting to resolve their dispute. Courts in many jurisdictions, however, have ruled that certification of a check constitutes acceptance by the payee. Therefore, despite the fact that the Uniform Commercial Code allows the payee to reserve his rights, if certification takes place there may be nothing to proceed with—because "Accord and Satisfaction" have already been reached.

If you get a check which suggests that acceptance would constitute payment in full, the overwhelming opinion seems to be that acceptance would constitute "Accord and Satisfaction," and that no condition of protest or attempted reservation of rights could materially effect that position. To be safe, consult with competent legal counsel. There are specific opinions both for and against the feasibility of taking action.* But generally speaking, if a creditor could reserve his rights to proceed on checks designed to release obligations and duly marked "paid in full," a very convenient device for the resolution of disagreements in the business community would be seriously impeded.

In view of the foregoing, a collector must conclude that the law regarding accepting checks "paid in full" on disputed accounts remains unsettled. Therefore, a decision regarding accepting or rejecting a customer's check must be made on the basis of other economic considerations such as: size of the difference, size of the balance, stability of the customer being pursued, and cost of the potential action. Only when all aspects of the proposal are considered, can a collector truly make an informed judgment regarding acceptance or rejection of such a check.

THE COMPROMISE SETTLEMENT

As is the case with unauthorized discounts, it is unfair to your other customers for you to accept less than what is due—except in the most deserving of situations. To do so is to allow a particular customer/debtor to buy from you at a lower cost than your other accounts. But there are times when you may have little choice.

---

*In New York, the First Dept. has stated that an endorsement "without prejudice and with full reservation of rights" did in fact preserve a creditors' rights under Section 1-207, thus precluding Accord and Satisfaction. However, the Second Dept. reached a different conclusion. The negotiation of the checks constituted an Accord and Satisfaction under the common law, and the words "without prejudice," it held, were of no lawful effect. (*New York Law Journal;* October 13, 1982.)

Whether or not to compromise indebtedness is among the most difficult problems you're likely to encounter. It places you in a position of having to sit in judgment on your customer-turned-debtor, while at the same time having to evaluate the customer's position and weigh it against your responsibility to preserve your company's assets.

Advantages Of Settling Out Of Court

There is justification for a voluntary out-of-court settlement. This settling of differences by mutual concessions, when weighed against the rule of absolute priority that might prevail in the distribution of assets after bankruptcy court liquidation, often appears economically attractive. The cost of administering a bankrupt estate may be saved. And often recovery for unsecured creditors, usually last in line, can be achieved. If the assets are valued on a going-concern basis, a settlement provides for possible payment to that group of creditors—whereas forced liquidation of those assets might not. The cost of receivers, trustees, attorneys, accountants and of priority claims and administrative expenses can also be avoided, or at least minimized.

The additional advantage of voluntary settlement is the fact that it is rather straightforward and simple. Such settlements generally take one of two forms: an offer that comes directly from the debtor or debtor's attorney, either by mail or in person; or an offer that comes as a result of a meeting of a creditors' committee called to negotiate the best available arrangement. After having conducted a complete investigation into the matters relating to the compromise and after extensive negotiations with the customer, the committee will often make a recommendation. This voluntary means of settlement is usually the most effective, least expensive one; and it provides creditors with the maximum possible return.

Creditor-controlled compromise settlements in general provide the honest debtor an excellent form for meeting his creditors, openly discussing his problems, and sharing all the information.

Suppose Settlement Isn't Voluntary?

Compromises negotiated by the debtor without creditor support should be viewed very cautiously, because of the strong possibility that preferential treatment may be afforded to some creditors. Those that accept right away may get more (or less) than those that hold out! Without creditor control, the task is extremely difficult.

On occasion, the situation is purely an economic one. If the liquidated value of the assets exceeds the offer, rejection is essential. On the other hand, if you are convinced of the debtor's honesty and can see a way out of his financial difficulty, there's a reasonable basis for supporting the company.

Occasionally, the collector must weigh the advantage of a composition cash settlement from an honest debtor, compared with a moratorium and a protracted repayment over a long period of time—although the latter might yield an amount greater than the cash offer. (The net return, however, if you were to take the cash and invest it, might still be the same.)

There are no hard-and-fast rules that can be laid down for dealing with some accounts, as each has its own peculiar problems. A compromise offer should be weighed in light of the following Model Settlement Work-Up fact sheet, which provides a complete guide to justify acceptance or rejection.

A MODEL SETTLEMENT WORK-UP

It is all too common to learn that a customer may offer to settle for less than 100% of the money that is due. The following is a comprehensive list of questions that should be answered in order to make an intelligent decision about accepting or rejecting an offer.

1. Balance due? _____

2. What caused the problem? Limited capital, rapid expansion, act of God, poor health, marital problem? Other? _____

3. Percentage offered? _____

4. Is it too cheap to accept? _____

5. Is the offer fair and feasible? _____

6. For 10¢ on the dollar, maybe we should automatically reject? _____

7. How was the % figure calculated? On what was it based?
_____

8. Status of our collection effort? _____

9. What is the character of the debtor company?
Corporation? _____
Partnership? _____
Proprietorship? _____

10. Do we have guarantees, subordinations, agreements, collateral, security? _____

11. Were any goods recently shipped? _____

12. Is any merchandise in transit? _____ Can we get it back?
_____

13. Do we have financial information in the credit file that will enable us to make an informed judgment? _____

14. Do we know whether the financial statement was false in any way?
_____

15. Can we obtain full financial disclosure at this time to support and substantiate the feasibility of accepting the offer? _____

16. Did the company keep good records? _____

17. Will the company stay in business? _____

18. Was the company managed properly? Will it be? Will there be new owners or a new business entity? _____

19. Does the company deserve our cooperation and rehabilitative efforts?
_____

20. Are we dealing with honest people? _____

21. Is there a legitimate basis for the debtors' request to compromise?
_____

22. Is there evidence of fraud, concealed assets, or misrepresentation?
_____

23. Are there any irregularities whatsoever? _____

24. Was merchandise purchased or services rendered on a high or low profit margin? _____

25. What is our cost of goods sold on this account? _____

26. Was this debtor previously a good customer? _____ For how long? _____

27. What is customer attitude "wise guy—take it or leave it," or cooperative? _____

28. Will we benefit by selling the account again? _____

29. Is there evidence of a prior dispute? _____

30. If yes, did we try and resolve it? _____

31. Does the trade report indicate that the customer has a history of going in and out of business often? _____

32. Where personal liability is involved, are personal assets included in the financial information submitted, and are they being taken into account in the decision-making process? _____

33. Can we properly document our balance to support totally what is owed in the event we elect to take alternative action? _____

34. Can we supply a witness if necessary? _____

35. What are the costs of legal action; the economics or alternatives if we elect to reject the offer? _____

36. Did other creditors accept the offer? _____ How many? _____

37. How many creditors must accept before distribution will take place? _____

38. Are all creditors in each class being treated equally? _____

39. Will we be paid promptly the moment we accept? _____

40. Do we know of any preference payments to the trade or insider deals being made to officers or relatives? _____

41. Do we have reason to believe that a secured creditor may have improved its position during the past 90 days, and obtained a preference? _____

42. Will there be a bulk sale as a ploy to force creditor acceptance? _____

43. Is the offer a result of an orderly liquidation? _____

44. Is the liquidation guided by creditor control? _____

45. What is the source of the funds that will be used for payment? _____

46. Does the offer exceed the estimated liquidation value of the debtor's assets? _____

47. Would acceptance therefore be in our best interest? _____

48. Has all information having material bearing on the offer been taken into account in this decision? _____

* * * * *

49. Should we accept or reject the offer? _____

50. Why? _____

51. What error was made, if any, on this account to lead us into this situation? _____

52. How can we prevent this in the future? _____

53. What can we learn from this experience? _____

HOW TO USE PERSONAL GUARANTEES SUCCESSFULLY

Any person or company that places itself in a position to answer for the payment of a debt, or the performance of a duty of another, is in a position of a "guarantor."

Collectors of both consumer and commercial indebtedness frequently find themselves in a position where they have to collect from such a third party. The guarantee is customarily given early, to provide additional collateral or security in consideration for the extension of credit. However, just as frequently, for an extended repayment program, a personal guarantee may be obtained by a collector in the *latter* stages of a collection effort, when that appears necessary or desirable.

Guarantees may be used in many special circumstances. A guarantee can be requested, for example, because of weakness on the part of a company or person who wishes to become your customer as additional security for a loan. Or when property or assets that a company or individual possesses are jointly owned, a guarantee may be sought from the other owner of that property as additional collateral. Also, with thinly capitalized corporations or new businesses needing credit, personal guarantees of the principals are frequently requested.

From time to time, a husband may be asked to guarantee the debts of a wife or vice versa, or a corporation may be asked to guarantee the debts of its subsidiary or vice versa, or a third party unrelated to the business may be asked to guarantee the debts of the business or its principal.

Guarantees can help; but they also have the potential for adding to any problems—by involving a third party in a dispute.

Types Of Guarantees

Guarantees really fall into two major categories: those that guarantee payment on an account, and those that guarantee collection on an account. The heart of the difference is whether or not a guarantor acts as a co-promisor with the principal customer and is jointly liable, or whether the guarantor's liability arises only after attempts to collect from the original customer have failed. One is a guarantee of *payment,* and the other the guarantee of *collection*.

The holder of a guarantee of payment is generally pursued either individually or simultaneously with the customer, regardless of whether attempts to collect from the customer have failed. In effect, payment guarantees put the guarantor in a position of being jointly responsible for the entire indebtedness. On the other hand, a collection guarantee will only become due if it can be proven that attempts to collect from the original customer have failed. (If you're involved in any dispute concerning a letter of guarantee, consult with competent legal counsel for specific advice about surety and payment guarantees.)

When dealing with partnerships or corporations, you must determine for certain whether or not the guarantor has sufficient authority to bind the partnership or the corporation. Often corporations have language in their charter that specific resolutions must be passed in order to bind the corporation. So you'd do well to obtain corporate resolutions before accepting such guarantees.

Elements Of A Guarantee

Whether you have a "down-stream" guarantee where a parent guarantees the debts of its subsidiary, or an "up-stream" guarantee where the subsidiary guarantees the debts of its parent, it is very important that you be sure—

1. That it is a written guarantee.

2. That it defines a specific indebtedness both current and future (if any).

3. That it's a guarantee of payment or a guarantee of collection.

4. Whether there's any limit as to liability or expiration date.

5. If it will include any interest or attorney's fees or expenses incurred should you attempt to collect in the event of a default.

6. How and when it is to be renewed or revoked.

7. What exceptions there are, if any, to the guarantee.

8. That the makers and endorsers jointly and individually waive presentment for payment, protest, notice of protest, and notice of nonpayment.

It is common for collectors to pursue recovery on accounts with guarantees. The strategy used to collect from them is the same as with regular collections.

How To Improve Your Position

A collector may also try to obtain a guarantee on an account that otherwise has none. By attempting to extract a guarantee in consideration for payment terms, forebearance, a debt adjustment, or for any reason whatsoever, a collector may be able to "take the temperature of his customer," and determine how committed the customer is to repayment of the obligation. It's human nature to have more confidence in a company whose principals are willing to provide a guarantee than in a company whose principals are not.

If a customer needs extra time to pay off an obligation, that person's willingness to issue a guarantee may help to convince a collector to go along. The reasoning is very similar to that used in attempting to obtain a promissory note, or a post-dated check. The attempt is very worthwhile. Just by "sounding out" the customer, you may learn how much confidence it has in itself. Of course, if the customer agrees to provide a personal guarantee, you've further improved your position.

Forms Of Guarantees

There are various pre-printed guarantees frequently used at the time credit is extended, and the forms can be easily obtained. Or—if you prefer—you can ask your attorney to prepare one for you.

As a general rule, be sure to notify all guarantors—whether they are co-signers, co-makers, accommodation endorsers, corporate guarantors, husband or wife, etc.—concerning any change in payment terms or company dealings. They should be notified of a sale of collateral, sale of merchandise, change in payment terms, extension agreement, or anything at all that could materially effect the guarantor. Even a simple extension may have an unfavorable impact on the liability of guarantor, unless notice is provided.

The following is a personal guarantee in the simplest form. A collector can use it without terrorizing the potential guarantor with a lot of legalese.

Note that—even though the words, personally and individually, are capitalized so that the purpose is crystal clear—caution is urged. A collector should not permit the person signing the guarantee to use the corporate name or his title, i.e., President, Vice President, etc.

For the purpose of extending _(Debtor's)_ time to pay the existing debt of $ _____ , presently due and owing to _____(Creditor)_____ , and in consideration thereof, I the undersigned PERSONALLY and INDIVIDUALLY guarantee that I will pay the _(Creditor)_ the above debt of $_____ , or any balance due on account of said debt.
Dated:

_____

_____
                 Name

_____
            Residence

What To Do About Customer Reluctance

If you are having trouble getting your customers to sign a guarantee, have your company attorney prepare for you a standard guarantee form. Then have it printed. Psychologically, customers are more inclined to sign pre-printed material and less likely to go running to their lawyers, than would be the case with individually typed guarantee agreements that look like legal contracts.

LATE-PAYMENT INTEREST AND SERVICE CHARGES

Interest may be loosely defined as "the cost to the seller of having to replace or provide monies, as the result of the customer's failure to make timely payment."

Service charges in a commercial or business setting may be "any sum upon which the parties in an arm's-length transaction" agree, or as may be reflected in their prior dealings or trade custom or usage.

Interest, while normally subject to a state's usury law, may be applied at a rate higher than the state's usury rate because of the commercial nature of the transaction, if all parties agree.

Interest must be contrasted with a "service charge." A service charge is a specific sum that is assessed against a customer solely because of his failure to make payments in a timely manner. It is a sum above and beyond the amount ordinarily due in the event of timely payment, and is normally equated with a reasonable additional cost of maintaining the account (because of additional employee time and overhead).

Service charges are negotiated and placed in writing prior to a sale, delivery and invoicing. If a service charge is not in writing, the right to recover the service charge may be questioned. It is a matter of custom, usage or prior relationship with the customer. The further removed such a charge is from expressed written agreement, the more difficult it may be to impose.

If a customer fails to pay a service charge, here is a letter that might be sent, asking for it:

Balance Due: _____

Dear (Decision Maker):

Thank you for your recent payment clearing the past-due portion of your account.

However, you did not include our service charge in the amount of $ _____. Now, in order to maintain your account in good standing, please mail your check today.

Very truly yours,

Such correspondence is typical of what you would send to a customer that has accepted your policy of imposing a service charge for late payment. Although imposition of interest is common in both consumer and industrial installment credit imposing a service charge on overdue commercial accounts is something that many companies find very difficult to implement. But imposing a service charge on delinquent accounts can play a significant role in encouraging such an account to pay promptly. In addition, it serves to compensate you for the lost revenue and lack of available use of a customer's money. Of course, the amount and type of penalty imposed will vary from company to company as well as from industry to industry.

Considering the cost of doing business, which includes the cost of borrowing, customers may not like the idea of being penalized for late payment; but they certainly should not dispute the need for such charges. In fact, when a company does not properly police its accounts receivable, and permits its customers to pay late without penalty, it's giving an unfair competitive advantage to those customers—permitting them to operate on borrowed time and money.

The Creditor Isn't A Banker

Most customers associate interest charges and late-payment charges with bank borrowing. However, the relationship between customer and supplier is usually not the same as a relationship between a bank and its customer. The supplier supplies merchandise and service, while the bank supplies money. The supplier is not in the business of lending money—and it shouldn't be expected to do this. That's why a supplier charges a *service charge* for late payment, while a bank may charge *interest*.

Other Side Of The Coin

Despite the benefits of implementing service charge penalties, many companies do not use such programs. They feel that, while they desire to reduce their bad debts and certainly don't wish to increase their collection expenses, they still desire to accommodate customers and preserve their good will. Fear of losing customers to competition who do not charge such service fees plays a major role in some companies' reluctance to impose such late-payment charges. Still other companies don't believe their customers will pay the charges, but believe in imposing them. They may even feel that such charges increase the cost of collection in an amount that's disproportionately high.

The Robinson-Patman Act was set in place to prevent unfair trade discrimination, and it specifically outlaws discriminatory pricing practices. Corporate attorneys caution companies that imposition of service charges would require that all customers be assessed similarly, so as to stay totally clear of any potential discrimination. Each company should therefore seek competent legal counsel before instituting any service charge program.

PROVIDING FOR YOUR RIGHT TO IMPOSE A SERVICE CHARGE

The right to impose a service charge should be clearly set forth on your customer's request for credit. In addition, a notice should appear on each statement and invoice, so that there's no misunderstanding as to its application. Putting such arrangement in writing, early on in a relationship, establishes the customer's acceptance, and makes the charge far easier to collect.

How Much Should It Be?

Among the most important considerations in setting up an internal service charge program is *what rate to charge*. If you're trying to get people to pay on time, a high rate is a good inducement. And by increasing the penalty, you will probably decrease the number of people to which it applies. On the other hand, if the rate is not high enough, you could be encouraging customers to pay late. Customers may prefer to pay your late payment charge than to pay the bill on time. The penalty for late payment must therefore be *in excess of the prevailing market rate for borrowing funds*.

However, many companies find that policy too costly and too difficult to enforce, and feel that customers would object to such a severe penalty. They reason, therefore, that they would rather have two out of three customers pay 6% than one out of three customers paying 10%!

Applicability In Commercial Credit

The concept of service charges originated in the retail industry, and today is still widely used in consumer sales. Implementation of service charges in commercial transactions, however, has taken place at a much slower pace. But customer's acceptance and understanding is becoming more widespread as the cost of carrying late payers has become more substantial. Companies are not likely to continue to tolerate much longer the investment in accounts receivable that are caused by the late payer. To date, we've seen prices rise and the cost of bad debts, in turn, added to the purchase price.

The most common service charge of 1% to 1½% per month of the unpaid balance, is already built in. It is clear that imposition of service charges is only one more bullet in the collection arsenal for maintaining, containing, and disciplining slow-paying accounts. But it can be a very effective one.

HOW TO DEAL WITH IMPROPER CUSTOMER DEDUCTIONS

Customer deductions can be defined as "shortages taken by a customer on a check for amounts other than cash discounts, for which there is no open credit to be applied." The deduction may or may not be applicable against the specific invoice listed.

A deduction could be taken on a disputed item, or a pending adjustment on a customer complaint. Regardless of how deductions come about, however, the growth of unresolved balances poses a serious problem for collection efficiency, operating costs, and customer relations. The processing, evaluation, and ultimate resolution are taking far too long. As these transactions age, the documentation needed to investigate is less likely to be available; and thus the chances of collecting the full amount are significantly diminished.

It is for just those reasons that further attention is being focused on the development of better methods and procedures to reduce the size of customer deductions, and to resolve them more promptly. After all, the longer it takes, the greater the cost to your company, and the less likely it will be collected.

Deductions fall into a variety of categories, but the following are the most common: (1) *freight claims,* which include lost shipments, shortages, damages, refused items, discrepancies on freight bills, disputes over who's to pay them, incorrect routing, failure to follow proper shipping instructions, weight disputes, and shipping insurance charges. (2) *Quantity* differences concerning overcharges or shortages, or differences between the number of items and the amount actually invoiced; shortages could occur within boxes, or could be counting errors or if cartons were actually lost by a carrier. (3) *Pricing* and billing errors, covering a wide variety of deductions, which could also include taxing or mathematical errors or incorrect terms, or misstated due dates. (4) *Quality* disputes involving differences between the quality of the product purchased and that received, which could also involve returns, order refusals, replacements, restocking charges. (5) *Participative advertising* and promotional allowances, which often involve disputes where volume activity has not yet qualified the customer for the discount, or appropriate documentation has not been submitted to justify the deduction.

There really is no "garden variety" of deduction. Imagination often plays a role in how the situation arises, and on many occasions customers will compound the problem by failing to indicate exactly why items are being deducted from a payment. This creates a double cost burden on the company and a double burden on the collector, who must now trace the events that led to the reason for the payment differences. In effect, he must contact the customer all over again for the same amount previously due.

It is not only the magnitude of the deduction build-up that gives it significance, but the fact that many deductions are really the result of legitimate claims by customers, nearly all of them eventually settled by issuing a credit. Consequently, it is mutually beneficial to resolve customer deductions as quickly as possible. The longer it takes, the greater the risk of offending a good customer and destroying an important relationship.

Added headache: As the dollars involved in the deduction category increase, and claims continue to remain unresolved, there is the potential for distorting the total invested in accounts receivable. But a credit memo or write-off would reduce reported earnings, ultimately providing your company with some tax benefit. That's sometimes a point to consider.

What to do about it: When attempting to resolve deductions, a collector should take a straightforward, quick approach. Keep the costs of carrying the receivable deduction at a minimum, reduce taxes if the item has to be written off, and in some cases, absorb small expenses rather than conducting expensive investigations to determine whether or not the customer is justified. All too frequently, the cost of investigation is greater than the amount of the deduction.

Naturally your attitude in this situation is governed by company policy. But one of the greatest preventive measures a company can take to minimize its deduction problem is to be certain that customers *know* your company policy. Such policy may be disseminated through sales personnel, on your order forms and invoices, and in all customer communications. When all the information is clearly understood, confusion and unauthorized deductions are likely to be minimal. Nonetheless, this shouldn't be taken for granted—and the size of a deduction, in any case, has no bearing on its legitimacy.

Where excessive returns seem to be a problem, more effective quality control before shipment, with monthly reports to management can help. Permitting sales personnel on-the-spot minimal authority to adjust minor complaints is likely to reduce paperwork and processing, while substantially increasing customer satisfaction. Using reputable and responsive transport carriers that provide efficient and reliable service will help to reduce traffic claims and shorten the time between detection and solution.

Pricing errors are occasionally the result of carelessness, but just as often the result of poor communication between sales and billing. Being certain to advise staff—before customers—about price changes can reduce errors still further. A random spot check of pricing will usually provide the necessary control to keep such errors at a minimum.

Successfully Handling Unauthorized Discounts

A real headache—which really is almost self-imposed—is the result of having cash discounts backfiring, when the customer takes the cash discount but doesn't pay on time. If you're contronted with this situation, take a hard look at your terms. Be certain that your customers know the meaning of the discount, and be certain that there's no misunderstanding as to when the discount period expires. Overlooking cash discount violations is tantamount to not enforcing your terms of sale—which could tend to increase the entire collection problem. Preventing such abuses by chiseling customers is critical.

How Important Are Unauthorized Discounts?

Discounts usually do not seem very large, and therefore collectors may be tempted to overlook them. But a collector should not permit this attitude to flow through to the customer in either his written or verbal communications. The collector must maintain the terms of sale and enforce policy in a consistent but courteous way. So as to minimize discount disputes, a grace period may be provided beyond the discount date up to a maximum of five days, depending on the original terms and the proximity of the customer. This will prevent many crosses in the mail, which account for most of the cash discount disputes.

Explaining The Problem To A Customer

In the handling of discounts, it is rather common to prepare courteous letters carefully identifying the problem, and again explaining the basis for your request for payment. A disagreement then could arise over when to "start the clock ticking" for discount eligibility. Date of invoice, date of shipment, customer receipt of goods upon receipt of the invoice, when the invoice is paid, the date of the check, the date it was mailed, the date it was received, the date it clears—all should be considered. There should be no doubt regarding what you expect the customer to do.

Generally, companies will set maximum dollar figures—beyond which there *must* be a follow up. Most companies will also set up minimum figures, which in their opinion are too low to be worth pursuing. In that category would be items where the collection cost would exceed the amount to be collected. However, there is danger that this information is likely to become public after a while. Therefore, such figures should constantly be subject to change, and should remain proprietary information.

When attempting to finalize a customer's deduction, timing becomes the most important aspect of the situation. After all, following the audit trail can be an expensive proposition. Usually you have to inspect customer files and accounts receivable records, and check with other departments. You may have to review correspondence which has brought the deduction to light, credit memos, purchase orders, shipping documents and invoices all to verify price, billing quantities, volume discounts, and promotions—and to verify that what was ordered was actually shipped, and that the service requested was actually performed. Copies of checks usually have to be obtained, or check stubs which might further explain in detail the customer's deductions.

The interaction with other departments, such as sales, advertising, accounting, or traffic distribution, is frequently required, making this research even more time-consuming and tedious. But nonetheless, it's absolutely necessary if verification is to take place.

Keeping Customers Happy While Inquiries Are Being Made

Despite the fact that unresolved deductions tend to pyramid, a simple solution is not possible while the collection executive has the prime responsibility of resolving the problem. The cure often lies in coordinating with sales, service, advertising, and customer relations. While a simple solution is not possible, you should be certain that your policy is clearly documented and understood by customers. In addition, you'd be well advised not to leave unresolved deductions in the accounts receivable total. Such items belong in a "disputed reserve" or "miscellaneous" account which could be budgeted yearly to absorb all deductions, and not distort the actual accounts receivable records and projected cash flow.

How A "Special Account" Can Help

As deductions are processed and collections effected, cash can be debited to the account just as easily as claims are credited to the account.

The internal processing is similar. By isolating the deductions to a specific new account, you pave the way for the possible transfer of that account outside of the credit and collection department to an adjustment department. Items can quickly be removed from customer ledgers or statements, thereby immediately improving customer relations.

Where research indicates a chargeback is required, the item can be cancelled from the special account, and once again charged back to accounts receivable. This special account also provides the mechanism through which an individual person can be given authority to coordinate all departments involved in the adjustment process.

By putting into place the recommendation that a special account be created, a more accurate picture of the actual income and sales volume can be observed. All customer deductions can then be charged against sales income. Sales personnel could advise their customers as a last resort to deduct whatever is necessary, and inform the adjustment people as to the nature of the complaint and deduction.

In the end, this method of handling complaints will minimize customer excuses for withholding payment. It further allows for the elimination of the item from accounts payable, for a faster investigation.

Merits of pursuing deductions notwithstanding, proceeding or not proceeding to enforce the collection of deductions remains an open question. It requires cost consideration, extensive communication and full cooperation with sales. A collector in this role is likely to find his patience tested to a point of exasperation. Yet he must still expect to perform as a professional, even-tempered collection expert.

PROTECTING YOURSELF BY BECOMING A SECURED CREDITOR

It is very common for a collector to attempt to make his (her) position more secure by obtaining a security interest in either property or particular assets owned by the debtor—as spelled out in Article 9 of the Uniform Commercial Code, entitled "secured transactions." Then, if the debtor becomes insolvent, the validity of the security interest is of critical importance. "The perfection of a security interest" in collateral, then, becomes a special responsibility of a collector.

"Filing" means giving public notice of your security agreement. Individual states have different rules as to where financing statements must be filed, although the form most constantly used is the UCC-1 form. However, you may file the actual security agreement itself. The financing statement on the security agreement must contain a description of the collateral, indicating exactly what is covered. Furthermore, it should contain a clause specifically indicating that the creditor will be entitled to the proceeds of the collateral in the event it is sold. Where the specific property may be accounts receivable or inventory, it is essential that the agreement contain an "after-acquired property" clause.

While the common place for filing the security agreement is with the Secretary of State as well as the debtor's county (and the county where the property is located), you'd be wise to consult with counsel to be certain that there is no defect.

(For further information on Article 9 of the UCC, see Chapter 7 on "special collection situations.")

Summary: Marginal and even "problem" accounts can be profitable. But you must get the jump on them—early—and take steps, drastic ones if necessary, to protect your interests. Only then can these accounts be really worthwhile.

4

Model Collection Letters: Demands That Get Attention And Action

Table of Contents

PAYMENT DEMANDS

Action Approaches:

4

Model Collection Letters: Demands That Get Attention And Action

This chapter, like Chapter 2, contains model letters, thirty-two of them, that you can easily adapt for your own use. These, of course, are for far less friendly situations—when your reminders, requests, and appeals have been overlooked or ignored—and your intent must be made unmistakably plain. These, too, should be directed to the attention of a decision maker.

Here are the no-nonsense, *demand* letters:

PAYMENT DEMAND

Action Approach: Make Your Payment In Five Days

Balance Due: _____

Dear Decision Maker:

We are still counting on you, but if your check does not reach us within five (5) days, we will have no choice but to turn your account over to our attorneys.

It is up to you to relieve the present critical condition of your account by mailing your check today.

Very truly yours,

PAYMENT DEMAND

Action Approach: We've Been Patient Too Long. Pay In Seven Days

Balance Due: _____

Dear _____ :

Your account is still unpaid. There has been no acknowledgment to previous requests for payment. The oldest invoice is long past due.

We think you will agree that we have been most patient, and that you cannot expect us to carry your account any longer. We must ask that you send a check in full within seven (7) days. Otherwise, you will leave us no alternative but to consider other means to enforce collection.

Very truly yours,

PAYMENT DEMAND

Action Approach: Prevent Complications By
_____ Problems

Balance Due: _____

Your firm's account _____ remains past due. The
delinquent balance totals $ _____

Statements are sent at the end of each month listing the
specific charges involved. In addition, several letters have been
sent reminding you of this disturbing situation.

Your check must be received immediately to prevent
complications. If there are any problems that we are not aware of,
or if there will be any further delays, please contact me directly.

As we are sure you would want to cooperate, we would
appreciate your check today.

Very truly yours,

PAYMENT DEMAND

Action Approach: Last Chance To Respond Amicably

Balance Due: _____

Dear _____ :

Your file has been reviewed and we find the above-stated balance to be unpaid and seriously past due.

This will be your final chance to resolve the matter amicably. Full payment must be mailed to this office within seven (7) days.

Failing to receive a satisfactory response, we will have no alternative but to proceed with the necessary action to effectuate payment.

It would be in your best interest to clear this obligation immediately. A self-addressed envelope is enclosed so that you can mail your check now.

Very truly yours,

PAYMENT DEMAND

Action Approach: Balance Of Payment Overdue

Balance Due: _____

Dear _____ :

Here is your _____ statement. There's been no subsequent payment. The age of the invoices and your lack of response make this a very serious situation.

If arrangements to clear this balance are not made within seven (7) days, we will have no alternative but to consider outside means to enforce collection. We certainly hope this will not be necessary. Mail your check today.

Very truly yours,

PAYMENT DEMAND

**Action Approach: To Preserve Business
Relationship; Pay In Seven Days**

Balance Due: _____

Dear _____ :

Until now our business relationship has been pleasant.

However, you have not replied to our letters about your overdue account, and obviously we cannot allow this balance to remain unpaid indefinitely.

Therefore, as much as we would dislike to take any steps to enforce this collection, you will leave us no other choice if we do not hear from you within seven (7) days. We must have a check in full now.

For our mutual best interests, please do not delay in answering this letter. Mail your check today.

Very truly yours,

PAYMENT DEMAND

Action Approach: Phone Us At Once To Arrange For Payment

Balance Due: _____

Dear _____ :

Your account has been reviewed and we find the above-stated balance to be seriously delinquent.

This will be your final notice. Full payment must be mailed to this office immediately, or a reasonable plan of payment arranged. It is important that you contact this office at once. Call _____.

If we do not receive a satisfactory response, you will force us to take further action to protect our interests.

Very truly yours,

PAYMENT DEMAND

Action Approach: Future Relationship In Doubt

Balance Due: _____

Dear _____ :

Your account is seriously past due on the referenced outstanding invoices. We have received neither payment nor a reason why payment has not been made.

Credit was extended with the expectation you would pay in accordance with the agreed invoice terms. You have not kept this commitment. Should you continue to ignore this obligation, it will have an extremely negative effect on our ability and willingness to do future business with your firm.

The time has come to act. We must have your check in seven (7) days. We're counting on your concern.

Very truly yours,

PAYMENT DEMAND

Action Approach: Promise Not Kept

Balance Due: _____

Dear _____ :

The seriously past-due stage of your account requires that you clear that account now.

You promised to mail a check to clear your past-due account, but no payment was received.

Even though we have reminded you of your commitment, the account is still unpaid.

Please give careful attention to this most serious matter, and mail your check today.

Very truly yours,

PAYMENT DEMAND

Action Approach: Repeated Promises Not Kept

Balance Due: _____

Dear _____ :

Because of your broken promises of payment, your file has been referred to me for final disposition.

Unless we receive your check on the account as previously promised in the enclosed envelope by seven (7) days, we will be compelled to assume it is not your intention to settle the account amicably, and will therefore place your account with an attorney without further notice.

Collection Manager

PAYMENT DEMAND

Action Approach: Keep Promise Today

Balance Due: _____

Dear _____ :

When you promised to mail your check, we accepted you at your word without a second thought. Yet now we find that your payment has not been received.

The above balance is seriously delinquent. Since you have previously promised to clear it up, please do not delay. Mail that promised check today.

Very truly yours,

PAYMENT DEMAND

Action Approach: Distributor Agreement May Be Cancelled

Balance Due: _____

Dear _____ :

Your attention has been previously called to the need for honoring the sales terms under which all our direct distributors are sold. Your account is now seriously past due.

Because of your continued disregard of these terms, and the excessive collection effort required by your inaction, we are considering cancellation of your direct buying privileges.

Before you are removed from our list of direct distributors, you may wish to send us your written assurance that future invoices will be paid within our normal sales terms. This, and receipt of your check for $ _____, by_____ will allow us to defer cancellation of your Retail Distributor's Agreement.

Mail your check today.

Very truly yours,

PAYMENT DEMAND

Action Approach: Send Certified Check

Balance Due: _____

Dear _____ :

    Your check # _____ issued to our order for the amount of
$ _____ has been returned to us dishonored a second time.

    Your bank has indicated the reason for dishonor to be
_____.

    Please send us a certified check or money order by return
mail immediately, for the amount of your dishonored check.

    Your failure to comply by (10 days) will leave us no
alternative but to refer the matter to our Legal Department, with
instructions that they take the necessary steps to protect our
interests.

Very truly yours,

PAYMENT DEMAND

Action Approach: We Sent Documentation To Support Balance

Balance Due: _____

Dear _____ :

When you asked for a breakdown of your account, we promptly responded. We were quite confident that you should respond as well and mail your check.

However, no check has been received. And your account is in a serious state.

It is most urgent that you clear your account at once. Please . . . mail your check in full today.

Very truly yours,

PAYMENT DEMAND

Action Approach: Call And Tell Us Your Problem

Balance Due: _____

Dear _____ :

The check which you promised to send has not as yet been received, despite your assurance that it would be mailed.

Your account with us is seriously past due. If a temporary problem has developed, call me upon receipt of this letter. Otherwise, I expect your promised payment by return mail.

I'm sure that neither of us would prefer the costly alternatives.

Please use the enclosed envelope and mail your payment today.

Very truly yours,

FINAL DEMAND

Action Approach: After Several Calls And Letters

Balance Due: _____

Dear _____ :

　　We have tried to reach you by telephone to discuss this account, about which we previously wrote to you, because this matter must be pursued to a prompt conclusion.

　　Your file, therefore, has been referred to me for final disposition. Since we cannot discuss this account with you, we must now advise you that unless we have your check on this account by _____, we will assume it is not your intention to settle the account amicably. We will then have no choice but to place your account for collection without further notice.

　　　　　　　　　　　Very truly yours,

FINAL DEMAND

Action Approach: Do You Realize What Can Happen?

Balance Due: _____

Dear _____ :

Although you have remained unresponsive to our previous payment demands, we wish to give you one more opportunity to clear your account before we proceed. Do you realize the potential impact of a legal action? Do you know that a legal action becomes a matter of public record? Are you aware of the impact that such negative information will have on your credit standing?

We sincerely believe that it is in your best interest to resolve your account now. We will allow you ten (10) days time in which to make your choice. If we do not hear from you within that time, we will take the steps necessary to enforce payment.

Very truly yours,

FINAL DEMAND

Action Approach: You're Leaving Us No Alternative

Balance Due: _____

Dear _____ :

We regret to see that there has been no reply from you about your overdue balance.

Your account can no longer be carried on this basis. You leave us no alternative. If payment in full is not received immediately, the matter will be placed with our collection agency (attorney) for immediate action.

Mail your check today.

Very truly yours,

FINAL DEMAND

Action Approach: Sight Draft Will Be Drawn

Balance Due: _____

Dear _____ :

We are drawing a sight draft against your bank, in the amount of $ _____.

If this draft is not paid, we will have no alternative but to have a local attorney take immediate steps to enforce payment.

Very truly yours,

FINAL DEMAND

Action Approach: Last Opportunity To Pay

Balance Due: _____

Dear _____ :

Your account has been sent to my office for final disposition.

We have attempted to reach you by telephone to discuss this account, but you have not been available.

Normally, we would proceed without further notice to you. However, because you were not able to discuss this matter by phone, we thought it would be advisable to offer you this last opportunity to send us your check.

Now, unless your check is received in seven (7) days, we will—without further notice to you—proceed to refer this account to an attorney.

Very truly yours,

FINAL DEMAND

**Action Approach: Pay Now Or We'll Proceed
Further**

Balance Due: _____

Dear _____ :

I have been advised by our Collection Department that the
above amounts are seriously past due. We have been promised
checks on several occasions, but to date payment has not been
received.

As of today, therefore, all pending orders will be held.
Further shipments will be made only when your account is
brought to a current status. Furthermore, if we do not receive a
check by return mail, we will have no alternative but to take
further steps necessary to protect our interests. Please mail your
check today.

Very truly yours,

FINAL DEMAND

Action Approach: Part-Payment Received; Mail Balance

Balance Due: _____

Dear _____ :

When we received your check for part of your seriously delinquent account . . . we thanked you and reminded you of the remaining balance.

Actually, we were quite certain that you would act by mailing a check to clear your account in full. However, that payment has not been received.

We must now advise you that unless your check is received within the next ten (10) days, you leave us with no alternative except to place your account for collection. Please eliminate the necessity of this costly pursuit, and mail your check today.

Very truly yours,

FINAL DEMAND

Action Approach: Pay In Seven Days

Balance Due: _____

Dear _____ :

By ignoring our many requests for payment of your past-due balance, you must know that you are forcing us to consider retaining an attorney and taking legal action. When we do this to collect the money you owe us, both of us lose. We lose a customer, and you lose a supplier.

Please don't force our hand. This is your last chance to pay. If your check is not received within seven (7) days, your account will become actionable.

Don't lose another minute. Do mail your check today.

Very truly yours,

FINAL DEMAND

Action Approach: Wire Money To Avoid Third-Party Action

Balance Due: _____

Dear _____ :

    Your overdue account has been referred to me with the recommendation it be given to an attorney for action.

    We would like to avoid this action, but you have neither sent a check or word when payment can be expected.

    Please wire your check to my personal attention by _____ to avoid third-party collection action, or mail your check today.

Very truly yours,

_____

Collection Manager

FINAL DEMAND

Action Approach: Requested Information Not Supplied

Balance Due: _____

Dear _____ :

Although you were provided, as requested, with the necessary information to identify this account, we have not received your check or a reply to our most recent letter.

Your file has now been referred to me for final disposition.

Unless your check is in our office by_____, we will assume it is not your intention to take care of this matter amicably, and we will without further notice forward this account for collection.

Very truly yours,

FINAL DEMAND

Action Approach: Pay In Five Days Or Face Attorney Action

Balance Due: _____

Dear _____ :

Your continued silence leaves us no alternative except to refer your account for collection—a step that we would sincerely regret. So won't you respond to this final appeal for your cooperation, and avoid a procedure that can only mean embarrassment, inconvenience, and additional expense to you?

Unless we hear from you within five (5) days, your account will be transferred to our attorney for immediate action.

Very truly yours,

FINAL DEMAND

Action Approach: We Can't Wait

Balance Due: _____

Dear _____ :

Every effort to conclude this account amicably has been made, without success. We cannot wait any longer. This matter must be pursued to a prompt conclusion.

Your file, therefore, has been referred to me for final disposition. In view of your prior payment, we felt it would be advisable to offer you this last opportunity to send us your check on this account by _____.

If your check is not received by that date in the enclosed envelope, we will assume it is not your intention to settle your account amicably, and we will place your account with our collection agency without further notice.

Very truly yours,

_____
Collection Manager

FINAL DEMAND

Action Approach: You've Ignored All Appeals

Balance Due: _____

Dear _____ :

Your account is seriously past due. Letters have been sent and calls have been made, but so far we have heard nothing from you. Even a partial payment would have been a welcome sign that you are working to get this cleared up.

Normally we would place your account for collection. But we hesitate to take a step so damaging to a relationship. It was our desire to do business with your company that prompted us to open your account in the first place.

Please let us hear from you now, so that it will be possible for us to avoid taking unpleasant and drastic action to protect our interest.

Act now!

Very truly yours,

FINAL DEMAND

Action Approach: Advise At Once When Account Will Be Paid

Balance Due: _____

Dear _____ :

    We have not had the courtesy of a reply to our prior appeals for payment. Your continued silence in this matter is very disturbing.

    We again point out that the balance is $ _____ now _____ days past due. Payment of this account cannot be overlooked any longer, and we would appreciate your immediate payment in the enclosed envelope.

    If there has been any reason for nonpayment, it is equally important that you contact this office immediately. Since we have not heard from you to the contrary, we now assume that the account is in order for payment. If we don't hear from you at this time, we will have no alternative but to assign your account for collection, which may cause you additional expense and inconvenience.

    Please avoid this situation by mailing your payment today.

Very truly yours,

FINAL DEMAND

Action Approach: Pay Now To Avoid Costly Court Proceedings

Balance Due: _____

Dear _____ :

THIS IS YOUR FINAL NOTICE FROM THIS OFFICE.

Because you have failed to recognize your responsibility involving your debt, we are focused to send you this FINAL NOTICE.

The total amount of your past-due account is $ _____.

Please forward a check for this amount to my personal attention within ten (10) days. Failure to do so will result in referral of your account to our legal department for appropriate court proceedings in the amount of your debt, plus court costs, disbursements and interest.

If legal action is started, it would be a matter of public record. In addition, credit agencies are likely to be advised.

To avoid this, please mail your payment today.

Very truly yours,

FINAL DEMAND

Action Approach: Avoid Unpleasantness

Balance Due: _____

Dear _____ :

Our efforts to arrange a mutually satisfactory payment plan of the past-due balance on your account have proved fruitless. Therefore, unless your check for $ _____ is received by _____, your account will be referred to our collection agency.

Your cooperation in mailing your check in the enclosed envelope will allow us both to avoid the added unpleasantness and expense of potential legal action.

Very truly yours,

FINAL DEMAND

Action Approach: Pay Or Face Attorney Action

Balance Due: _____

Dear _____ :

Your account has been turned over to me for handling because of your failure to answer our prior written requests for payment.

We attempted to reach you by telephone to discuss this account, but you have been unavailable.

Normally, we would proceed without further notice to you. However, since we have not been able to speak with you on the phone about this account, we offer you this last opportunity to send us your check.

Unless your check is received by _____, we will have no alternative but to proceed and refer this account to an attorney for collection.

Very truly yours,

_____

Collection Manager

5

Tested Telephone Collection Techniques That Control The Conversation—And Get Results

Table of Contents

5

Tested Telephone Collection Techniques That Control The Conversation—And Get Results

At one time, when postage, paper, and labor were relatively cheap, telephone calls were rarely used in the collection effort—because they were not deemed to be "cost effective." A firm, however, cannot do today's business with yesterday's methods and procedures, and expect to be in business tomorrow. Today, wide area telephone service is available from a variety of sources, and makes telephoning even the most remote customer competitive with letter writing.

The average cost of sending a collection letter is in excess of $4.00, which doesn't include the time it takes to create or dictate the letter (if any). Accordingly, you can determine the cost effectiveness of using the telephone in your collection effort by applying the following formula: $\frac{AR \times D}{365} \times C$

Average accounts receivable per individual customer times the number of days you're able to accelerate the payment divided by 365, times the cost of borrowing for your company on an annual basis. If that figure is greater than your average total cost per phone call, then a call is clearly justified.

For example, let's say a $10,000.00 customer average is maintained, and that as a result of a call you were able to improve the customer's payment habit by 10 days. If borrowing money costs you 17%, each call would therefore be worth $46.58. Whenever the value of the accelerated payment exceeds the cost of the call, use of the telephone makes good economic sense. ($10,000 $\times \frac{10}{365} \times$ 17% = $46.58), even for a balance of $1,000.00, the saving = $4.66.

Demo Is Better Than Memo

Getting faster payments from even the most chronic delinquent accounts can be accomplished by demonstrating a personal interest. Even the best letters are often passive, one-way communicators creating monologue, not dialogue, and may not be seen by the people you want to reach. Traditionally, the customer is more conditioned to expect a letter or two about an unpaid or overdue obligation. A telephone call early on in the collection effort, however, has the advantage of surprise.

If you're finding your written demands unproductive, break the silence and electrify your collection effort by telephoning a decision maker in the customer's firm. This direct approach makes it practically impossible for a customer to ignore you. In addition, it emphasizes the importance of your account, and enables you to resolve by phone in a few minutes a problem that might take weeks to solve by letter.

MAKING EFFECTIVE USE OF PRE-CALL
REMINDERS

In order to derive the best results from each call, the following series of pre-call reminders can aid you. Before you make the call, check the credit file (if available) to be certain you have the right company or person. If the sale was a new account, check to see if there is any previous information or clue as to whom to approach. Look for guarantees, subordination agreements, UCC-1 filings that would secure your position on merchandise or equipment. Try to determine the character of your delinquent account, whether it is a corporation, partnership, proprietorship, or an individual consumer. Think about the nature of your customer's operation.

For example, if it is a business, determine what type it is. Would the customer more likely be available in early A.M.—such as a contractor or self-employed person—or in the late P.M. (an individual doing business from his home)? This will produce more direct contacts and more timely recovery and results. Also, be on the alert for alternative phone numbers and different addresses where principals can be reached.

What Approach Is Best?

Once you have your facts, you'll need to have a firm, no-nonsense, businesslike attitude. You should speak in a natural tone of voice and be sure to avoid using a "canned" monotone message. Furthermore, do not use self-defeating expressions—a word or phrase in a tone of voice that might offend the listener. Remember, if your approach is a "turn-off," you're likely to turn off the flow of funds as well.

To begin, it is important first to identify yourself and your firm, and then state the reason for your call. You should prepare an opening statement and ask a question, such as: "Has the payment been put in the mail?" This transfers the onus of further discussion to your customer. Then you should pause, allowing the customer time to answer. Always be positive in your approach, and be pleasant, confident and relaxed in your tone.

What to Include: The following fact-finding questions should be part of any collection call:

ESSENTIAL FACT-FINDING QUESTIONS FOR PRE-CALL PLANNING

Your Six Helpers:

WHO .... is calling?
owes the money?
should I talk to?
is the key person?
is the decision maker?
can sign the checks?
authorizes payment?

WHAT .... is the past payment record?
is the pattern of delinquency?

is the frequency of lateness?
(Evaluate the trend of past
   performance.)
is the prior collection effort?
(Letters, calls, visits; results thereof.)
can you pay?
do you offer?
is the problem (dispute)?

WHY .... can't you pay now?
do you need more time?
is the account disputed?

WHEN .... can you pay?
will you mail the check?
will the owner be in?

WHERE .... is the check promised?
is the owner (or principal)?
was the check sent?

HOW .... much are you short?
can you pay?
can we help you to pay on time?
have we failed you?
are we at fault?
(Review records. Were payments
applied; merchandise returned;
correspondence answered;
complaints answered?)

SHOULD YOU PLAY DEVIL OR DIPLOMAT?

No skill is needed to make a harassing phone call; but a great deal is needed to make a *"successful"* one. Your conversation and collection dialogue must turn people on and motivate them to pay. "Turning people off" cuts the lines of communication, and can only antagonize an already-strained relationship.

When you dial a phone number and speak with your customer, you become the voice of the firm you represent. The customer judges your company on what you say. This suggests that there is far more to a successful collection effort than just taking a pile of statements, listing your accounts receivable, and asking for payment. A sales representative canvassing for new customers for your company can fail—but that failure would mean not getting new accounts. A poorly trained inexperienced yet well-meaning collector, on the other hand, could conceivably lose your company's existing clients if he or she was permitted to run-a-muck and ruin customer relations!

There should always be a definite purpose for your call; and the significance of what you say and how you say it should never be underestimated. The impression you make on your customer may have a lasting effect. Thus, common sense mandates that you recognize the importance of each call, and treat it individually, with enthusiasm and intelligence.

How To Promote Good Will

Collecting money, while being a collector's primary objective, is only part of a collector's function. In the early stages of a collection effort, where the greatest majority of accounts are resolved, a collector is in the best position to provide effective and economical advertising for his firm. In addition, a collector is in the best position to create company good will that will help to maintain customers as active accounts and to promote repeat business.

The collector in fact may be the only contact the customer has had with your firm, with the exception of the sales rep. Hence, the image projected and the impression left by you as a collector will be viewed by the customer as a *company* image.

The collector's manner can sometimes alienate a customer, or can create animosity. This can ruin a relation with a perfectly good customer—thus possibly creating a slow-paying or no-paying account.

That's why it is necessary to have properly trained people for the position in the collection department of any company. There is too much at stake to leave it to people who are unqualified. The telephone and the collector's voice are good collection tools. But much like the auto, if abused they could become dangerous weapons.

HOW TO TAKE CONTROL OF THE CONVERSATION

When telephoning to ask for a payment, always remember that you have the advantage position. The person you are talking to owes the money, and there's nothing for you to be apologetic about. You are doing the job delegated to you by your company, and the customer should be on the defensive. Don't permit the customer to turn the tables!

What to do: Get your message across swiftly, with no hesitation. Make your statement, control the discussion, and lead the customer to the conclusion *you want* him to draw. When you ask for the payment, leave no room for doubt: you are expecting it. Delinquent customers usually recognize timidness quickly. A sign of weakness will be used against you.

In addition, make sure that the delinquent customer you are phoning is the individual who is responsible for payment; or that he or she is the owner, partner, or officer of a business indebted to you. That enables you to address him or her by name. Don't ask what the decision maker is going to do. Tell him or her what *you* want to be done. Remember, in the majority of cases, your prior demands have been ignored. If the customer has failed to deny your account or complain about it to date, it is not necessary at this point to ask if the account is correct. You can just assume that it is.

When To Be Flexible

Many delinquent accounts are also prone to bargain. Beat them to the punch. Hold them taut, and impress on them that you expect your request for payment to get results.

There are some cases, however, where more will be accomplished by a display of leniency. If you sense that a customer is responding too eagerly (suggesting that he's momentarily strapped), give a little time by saying that you would be willing to wait a week if necessary. Never question a customer's intentions. To the contrary, let him know that you are well aware he wants to pay, and that you wish to be of assistance.

Beware Of The "Ready Promiser"

Beware of the fellow who says "Yes" to everything (and probably doesn't mean it). When dealing with that type, leave no room for doubt. Make it clear you will wait only until the date you specify, and no longer. Also, be aware of the type who says, "I've been sick," etc. Most, when pressed, will admit that they have not been sick for the three, four, or five days, or weeks or months, since the account has been past due. And beware of the type who attempts to becloud the issue. If the customer argues, complains, and disputes, it's usually in order to buy time. So you should ease into your plan for repayment with a transition statement, such as, "I have an idea that can help you, a plan that will help us resume normal relations."

Always ask for full payment. But when that is not possible, strive for as much as possible as fast as possible. This is where the unskilled collector can lose control of the conversation. When you can't get it all today, guide the customer to specific performance, arranging for payment on specified dates in specified amounts. But don't give too much. If the customer tells you he will have to have more time—two or three or four weeks—point out the age of the account, and suggest an immediate reasonable payment on account with two or three weeks extension on the balance. This usually will work.

Obtain a specific commitment. Pin down your customer to a definite amount to be sent at a definite time, such as: Tuesday, March 23rd—not "some time next week," or "within 10 days," or "at the end of the month." It's better to accept less money for a specific date and amount than to hope for a larger, unspecified amount at some unknown time in the future.

Remember: In your approach be positive, and determine a payment plan that is both doable and reasonable. You must learn to develop the art of doing what's possible. Unreasonable demands and expectations will only create unnecessary default. But reasonable ones can be met—if you insist on it.

What About "The Account Has Been Paid" Excuse?

If a customer alleges that the account is paid, ask for a copy of the cancelled check. An honest customer will be happy to give you the exact amount and date, and send you a copy if necessary. But beware of put-offs, particularly from someone who's not really responsible. If you cannot talk with the person responsible, you should talk to someone who knows something about the account. Impress upon that person the importance of verifying the payment, and find out—now or in a subsequent call—details on the alleged payment.

TWO KEYS TO IMPROVED TELEPHONE EFFECTIVENESS

Keep The Collection File Current

In reporting on the results of telephone efforts, stick to the facts. Never say anything you don't *know* to be true. Usually you only know what the debtor alleges. You do not know the merchandise was defective. You only know that the debtor *claims* that to be true.

Adoption of the "Collector's Worksheet Code" (Figure 5-1) will help enable you to maintain uniformity and continuity in your collection calls and follow-up. The abbreviations listed will help you to document your efforts quickly and accurately. They will enable others to comprehend exactly what has taken place.

COLLECTOR'S PERSONAL WORKSHEET CODE

D/O	— Debtor Out	Fa/Pa	— Father
L/M	— Left Message	H	— He
D/A	— Doesn't Answer	Hsb	— Husband
Disp.	— Disputed	L/P	— Last Payment
C/L	— Can't Locate	Ltr	— Letter
Ins.	— Insolvency	M/I/L	— Mother-In-Law
O/C	— Other Claims with Attorney	Ml	— Mail
N/P	— No Phone	M/O	— Money Order
P.D. Prom.	— Post-Dated Check Promised	M/RMdse	— Mail Returned
Prom	— Check Promised	N/A or D/A	— No Answer
N/C	— No Contact	Nb	— Neighbor
N/Coop	— No Cooperation	NSF	— Not Sufficient Fund
D/Prom	— Defaulted Promise	N/W	— Not Working
C/P	— Debtor Says Can't Pay	Pa/P	— Payment Plan
O/O	— Others Owed	Par/P	— Partial Payment
Bktcy.	— Bankruptcy	Pd	— Paid
Assig.	— Assignment	P/D/Ck/Pd	— Post-dated check
L/MT/CB	— Left Message to Call Back	PIF	— Pay (Paid) in Full
Bal	— Balance	Pmt	— Payment
Bk	— Bank	S/I/L	— Sister-In-Law
B.P.	— Broken Promise	Sis	— Sister
Bro.	— Brother	T(Tel)	— Telephone (d)
C/M	— Certified Mail	Tmr	— Tomorrow
Ck	— Check	Tdy	— Today
Dau	— Daughter	Wf	— Wife
Dtr	— Debtor	Wk	— Week
Div	— Divorce	W/Ph	— Will Phone
		WCB	— Will call back

Figure 5-1

Ask Questions That Will Get The Response You Want

By asking questions correctly, you will further enhance your telephone collection efforts. There are always several ways to ask a question; be sure you use the one that is most advantageous.

Questions should be designed so that the answer to the question you pose must confirm what you wish your customer to accomplish. For example, you should be sure to ask, "When will you put the payment in the mail?" That question implies that you are asking the customer to make a *commitment* to pay. The customer must either deny he plans to pay your bill, or commit to the date or dates of payment. By putting your question this way, you are leading the customer to the point of making the commitment you want.

ACTION WORDS THAT GET RESULTS

Always ask for payment in full. You should say, "May we expect you to mail your check in full today?" or "Will you mail a check in full today?" This is better than the often-used "Can you mail a check?" Of course, the person will answer "Yes," but that is not a promise to pay. He (or she) merely says he *could*—didn't say he would!

Be sure to use action words that are picturesque. Mail brings to mind a mail box, stamped envelope, etc. "Send us a check" beats "remittance," and "today" beats "now" or "immediately," as only "today" represents an undisputed time frame understood by all. Nearly every customer, if handled properly, will respond to these action words.

Keep in mind: You are collecting—or attempting to collect—an entire account. So, do not permit a customer to tell you that he (or she) will mail a check for a portion of the account, without getting specific arrangements to resolve the balance of the account. Don't be a partial-payment collector.

Collection "Salesmanship"

Collecting is largely salesmanship. "Sell" the customer on what he (or she) should do and how to settle, and see if he will respond.

The following "buzz phrases" will assist you in formulating an effective collection dialogue:

- How much are you short?

- Will you mail a check in full today?

- Will you mail a check . . . today . . . to bring your balance current?

- Mr. Reed, you promised I would have your check today. But you did not mail that check. Now, I appreciate that things can happen between the promise and the action. But *you* must appreciate that we cannot continue to keep an unpaid balance on the books. Let's call this "one more chance," Mr. Reed. Now . . . will you be *sure* to mail that check today?

- I'm sorry Mr. Reed is not at home right now. Because this matter is most urgent, will you tell me where might I reach him now?

- If we did make a mistake on your account—well, we don't do it often; and we are only human, Mr. Reed. Tell me, exactly what is wrong?

- When you pay your balance, Mr. Reed, you are buying something of great value. You are buying the right to use your credit again.

- We know that you are honest, Mr. Reed. That will never be a problem between us. Now let's work out your payment arrangement. Will you work it out with me now?

THE IMPORTANCE OF A GOOD DELIVERY

No matter how good the script, it's the delivery—the actual conversation—that makes or breaks the recovery. Tone, timing, sincerity, and pace are all critical ingredients. Talking too fast causes misunderstanding; talking too slow can cause customers to get impatient. And unfortunately the telephone tends to exaggerate a poorly paced message. Generally 150 words per minute is ideal. Friendliness must also be conveyed by a person's voice. Despite the business-like manner, a collector should be trained to smile while talking. Be careful not to be any of the following:

1. *UNTRUTHFUL*—one false statement will cast doubt on the validity of the entire call. Gimmicks invite disbelief, suspicion and rejection, whereas straight-forwardness commands attention and customer respect.

2. *OVERPOWERING*—the customer must be allowed time to digest the information, particularly at the beginning. The purpose of the call should be stated simply and directly. All questions should be handled intelligently. Vagueness will also meet with rejection.

3. *DISCOURTEOUS OR IMPERSONAL*—treating people as people, not numbers, will get better results. Be courteous even when encountering rejection.

4. *LONG-WINDED*—telephone collection people must make efficient use of, and conserve, their time. Once an agreement is reached, the conversation should be concluded. A longer conversation opens the door for customers to back out, or for misunderstandings to creep in.

5. *THE BAD LISTENER*—the art of collection, after all, is the ability to win a customer's cooperation by getting him or her to pay. Try to grasp the customer's problem first, before you give any statements of advice or guidance. It is imperative to listen in order to evaluate the customer's needs properly. You must listen to gain understanding as to what the customer is trying to say. This helps to build good will.

6. *DISTRACTED*—collection people must be trained to concentrate their full attention on the customer. Remove all distractions from the desk, such as radios, newspapers and other memos, etc. Trainees often fail in their collection efforts because they feel uncomfortable on the phone to begin with, and thus are distracted from listening.

7. *ARGUMENTATIVE*—you may win the argument, but lose the ability to communicate further. Thus, you may lose the collection and the customer. The collection technique must flow with purposeful continuity. After all, tact is the ability to make a point without making an enemy. Successful collectors must adjust their personality and approach to fit the individual and company with whom they're dealing.

A good telephone collection technique is outlined in the following chart. Once you have mastered the concepts, you will be a more successful collector. A good technique, even in the hands of an inexperienced collector, will perform well—but a poor technique, regardless of who delivers it, will not produce any favorable results.

TELEPHONE COLLECTION TECHNIQUES: WHAT TO DO OR NOT TO DO

DO

- Gather all the information you will need for a complete, accurate and intelligent answer
- Confront the customer with the facts
- Resolve—remember "obligation" means "in debt to"
- Pre-Call Plan—decide what you *can* and *cannot* do in advance
- Choose your approach carefully
- Choose your "appeals" so they influence your customer's self-interest
- Present alternative choices
- Get through to key people—companies owe $, but people pay bills
- Propose a definite plan of payment
- Show willingness to cooperate
- Get letter of commitment—acknowledgement of debt
- Admit mistakes willingly
- Let them "save face"—give a debtor space
- Offer to raise the credit line under certain circumstances after payment
- Suggest borrowing at a bank
- Ask for post-dated checks/notes
- Say "you may be right, but . . ."
- Develop art of doing the possible—"do-ability"
- Reward Performance:

Protect credit reputation
Avoid suit fees
Take discounts
Insure future orders
Pride

- Withhold future shipments

- Take a positive attitude: We will consider shipment when you pay

- Ask for payment in full

DON'T

- Contradict

- Belittle, be condescending, rub it in

- Be sarcastic/threaten

- Ridicule/lecture

- Yell, scream

- Say "you are wrong; we are right"

- Dun in the dark

- Harass/argue

- Try to hurt a person's pride

DEALING WITH EVASIVE CUSTOMERS

Sometimes you may encounter a situation where you telephone a customer four or five times over several days and get no response. Do not despair. It usually indicates that your customer prefers not to make false promises or excuses for nonpayment. There is a good reason to feel frustrated, but you must grin and bear it. Should such activity continue, though, you can vary the approach.

If calling direct, station-to-station, try person-to-person. Secretaries are less likely to reject the calls, and the company is not charged for incompleted calls or time spent waiting for the person to answer at the other end. Placing such calls through the phone operator, in fact, adds to the apparent urgency. You should also consider directing calls to another decision maker. They will usually try and give you an explanation as to why the party you called has not responded, and may even offer assistance in having the matter resolved in an amicable fashion without delay.

ADD URGENCY AND IMPACT TO YOUR PHONE DEMANDS

You can also add a sense of urgency and impact to your phone demands. Have a call transferred from a company officer to a bookkeeper, or Treasurer to Controller, or President to Controller or Accounts Payable Manager. This creates the impression that the person in higher authority has approved of your call, and maybe your request for payment as well. When higher-ups take an interest in your particular account, the people involved in handling your account on a regular basis usually take care to see that you get special treatment.

Once contact is established and the dialogue begins, however tempting, do not put the customer through a grand inquisition as to why your prior calls were ignored. That would only prove to be a source of common irritation, and not a good basis to begin a collection dialogue towards recovering your money.

Obtain A Specific Commitment

Tell your customer exactly what you require. Usually you will know by your customer's reaction whether you will get paid. "If not you, who is responsible for payment?" and "If not now, when will the account be paid?" are questions frequently asked by a collector. Do not be satisfied with a vague, "I'll send you something some time next week," or "I'll review the account and get something out to you later this week," or "I'll send as much as I can as soon as I can; give me a few days."

Pin down your customer to the exact amount to be sent and at a specific time, such as: Tuesday, March 23rd. Take advantage of the opportunity to get a definite personal commitment on the dates and amounts. You should avoid any ambiguity whatsoever. ''I'll see what the weekend receipts are like, and send a good chunk of money'' is just not good enough. Keep in mind, it's better to accept less money for a specific definite amount if you can agree on a date and amount—than to hope that the larger unspecified amount will be sent at some unknown time in the future.

Show A Passion For Payment—But Keep It Under Control

Avoid complacency and practice humility. These are necessary for a successful recovery. Remember that success itself can be destructive. Any collector who has enjoyed several successful calls must be careful not to appear and act like a know-it-all. Many people in such situations seem to develop hearing defects when it comes to listening to what others have to say, and their complacency takes the place of questioning and listening.

By always trying to grasp the debtor's problem first, before giving statements of advice and guidance, you will be certain to maintain your humility, help build his good will and have a better understanding of his point of view. And you'll be able to pursue payment with even greater confidence and assurance that the arranged commitment will be adhered to. Your passion for payment must always be blended with superb tact.

USES OF COLLECT CALLS AND TOLL CALLS

Undoubtedly every company has a set policy regarding the use of collect calls. While such policy must be adhered to, consideration should be given, if appropriate, to placing toll calls collect to customers. After all, you are calling to discuss business with the particular customer about his (or her) specific account. Thus, the customer should absorb the cost of the call if possible. Obviously, it will save you money and enable you to maintain effective price levels for your customers on merchandise or service rendered.

Even more importantly, a collect call can make the customer dramatically aware of his indebtedness. Since the customer is to pay for the call, he'll likely handle it himself and quickly get down to business. It is also probable that the customer will regard his account in a more serious light if the contact costs money. Of course, there is also an advantage to the customer to keep any commitment made, since in the event of a default, there is an implication that future calls could prove even more costly. Less obvious is the fact that customers, not wanting to appear evasive or financially strapped, will often accept the collect call just to let their suppliers know that everything is okay.

In addition, the fact that you as a collector were concerned enough about the customer's account to place the call has impact in itself. Even if the call is refused, the customer may react and send the payment. By demonstrating personal concern and imparting that concern to the customer, you're sending a clear message. The ball is now in the customer's court. You are expecting a reply. The customer will be judged by his reaction.

What Choices Does The Customer Have?

Naturally, the customer has choices. He can accept the call, or refuse the call and pay the account, or refuse the call and call you back, or even write to you at a more convenient time. The real benefit is the sense of urgency that is created. After all, it is not likely that your customer is as enthusiastic about paying your bill as you are about collecting it. This gives you the initiative.

However, when more than one call is refused and the account is not yet paid, the collector should take it upon himself to call direct, and pay for the call. In the event that no response to either type call is obtained, a personal letter—in the midst of the collection effort, to maintain momentum—is an alternative to consider between the collect and paid-for phone call.

What Choices Do You Have?

In the handling of collect or toll calls, there are alternative choices that have to be dealt with such as, should the call be person-to-person or station-to-station? If collect, the customer pays if he accepts, so it really doesn't matter in that instance. Under those circumstances, it's usually best to go person-to-person if you know who is in charge—the name of the decision maker with whom you wish to discuss the account. That way, if the call is refused, it may be refused by the very person you're trying to interview. That being the case, you can call right back, station-to-station direct, and be certain that the party you now wish to talk to is more likely to be available.

These techniques can be invaluable as long-distance collection tools. However, because of the relative ease and accessibility of the telephone to all, there is always temptation to overdo a good thing. A collector must be mindful of his role and not abuse the system.

How To Use Long-Distance Calls

Toll calls to a customer, whether they are person-to-person or station-to-station, can take on all the advantages of collect calls—with the exception of the cost advantage that a collect call has.

While many companies have wide area telephone service (WATS lines), and still others use such private companies as Western Union, RCA, and MCI to reduce costs of long-distance calls, some companies still are without such cost-effective apparatus. A collector must therefore be ever mindful of the cost of a phone call.

Long-distance telephoning can be very expensive, and therefore should be watched and carefully regulated within the scope of a company's collection policy. Keep calls short, and call as many customers as you can during lower-priced time periods. This is not to suggest that making as many calls as you can is the right way to go. Be certain that your customer is still available, or the call—even at less cost—may be for nothing. You must always remember that it is *customers* who owe money, and that money may be an impersonal item on the balance sheet; but *people* pay bills, and it is people that must be motivated to live up to their obligations.

THE IMPACT OF THE INITIAL CONTACT

Without question, the first call is the most important. An inept presentation usually results in an indifferent response from the customer—or none at all.

What are the things you should strive to accomplish with the first call? Among them are:

— Firm control of the facts: review customer's account before, not during, conversation to avoid fumbling for dates, names, background, etc.

— Positively confirm that you have the correct party or firm. The customer may have a number of people calling him for payment. Therefore, it's important that you clearly distinguish yourself from the crowd. After all, if you make the call, you certainly would not be happy to learn that, mistakenly, someone else had received the payment.

— Identify and contact the person authorized to pay bills.

— Inform the customer as to the nature and purpose of your call. At this state, it isn't necessary to push or motivate the customer. The call actually follows a pattern similar to the pattern established by your letter cycle: Reminder, Request, Appeal, Demand.

— Make a *professional pause*, after your opening statement. This shifts the burden of conversation to the customer. It gives the customer a chance to volunteer an explanation and offer to pay now. By ending your opening statement with a question, you can set up the pause.

— Proceed on confident assumption that the account is correct (to do otherwise invites the customer to raise a ''smoke screen'').

— Tell the customer what's expected.

— Secure a firm commitment.

— Summarize agreement.

— Supply the mailing address.

Often the principal will not be in. When this happens, the key is to leave a message geared to get him or her as an incentive to return the call. A routine message, delivered in a boring monotone, will not do! No one approach will be the ultimate answer, of course, but let's review some approaches geared to stimulate a response—either on the first call or follow-up ones:

— ''Tell him it's urgent that I speak with him right away! He can contact me at _____.''

— ''Please have him call me immediately. Time is of the essence.''

— ''Tell him Tim called. He'll know who it is.'' (A personalized approach evokes curiosity.)

— "This is a matter which can't be put off any longer. Have him (or her) call me right away."

— "He (or she) is very familiar with this problem and will want to talk with me at once."

— "This is a top priority, but he may not know it unless you say so." (Create a sense of urgency.)

— "Didn't he get my earlier message(s)? I'm sure he'll be very upset since this is quite important. Please see that he gets this one! By the way, what's your name?"

— "If I don't hear from him, I'll be forced to proceed. . . ."

— "I'm sure he wants to cooperate. It would be in his best interest to return the call immediately."

Naturally, there are as many variations as there are collectors with imagination. Just remember: don't be ludicrous, don't overstrain for effect, and stay away from references to attorneys or legal action.

When the contact is finally made, the collector must be assertive and command the customer's respect. Some knowledge of the facts must be evident. Stumbling, mumbling or hesitancy is a sure way to lose control of the conversation.

You must absolutely convey an expectation of prompt payment, get quickly to the point, make and confirm arrangements, then get off the phone! Time is money, and money is made by moving rapidly from call to call. Besides, just as in sales, *too much talking* can weaken your chances for success.

Be Assertive, Not Aggressive

You should be assertive, not aggressive—encourage the debtor to perform, i.e., say "I'm counting on your cooperation. I'm sure that by working together we can resolve this amicably." Even when discussing items that may be disputed, it is much better to say, "You may be right, but . . ." than "You are wrong." "You are wrong" is often interpreted as a challenge, and may be viewed as too aggressive an approach by your customer. With this approach, the debtor may feel compelled to defend his position.

Furthermore, you should be constructive—not destructive—when handling rejections or disputed items. Believe in people; be careful not to sound cynical. Encouragement can go a long way toward instilling confidence and getting your customer to adhere to a commitment. By saying, "You may be right," you are not only avoiding a dispute, but you are also reminding yourself that the other person may be at least partially right. This approach will help you to be a better listener—and collector. Keep these guidelines in mind:

1. You, as an assertive person, *do not answer every question* or respond to every topic raised by customers.

2. You, as an assertive person, should stay on the topic and *not be drawn into any side issues*.

3. You, as an assertive person, rarely allow yourself to become aggressive. When others are reduced to screaming insults, *you are often able to get your needs met while speaking in a calm manner*.

4. You, as an assertive person, *use a persistent pattern of communication—* if necessary. This is done with the same short sentence repeated frequently in the conversation. No explanations, no accusations—just the "broken record" message. This enables many people to maintain their self-respect, while reminding them about the real purpose of the call. It obliges debtors to behave in a manner that will be cooperative.

The Telephone As A Reminder

In the early stages of your collection efforts, if you are really trying to "get the money in," sometimes even before the bill is due, you can use another very effective collection and counseling technique. You can call to emphasize thanks for the past order, offering to help, explaining any company policy that is not clear (such as payment terms), and reminding him of the due date on the invoice just to be sure he doesn't overlook paying on time. Without coming right out and saying so, this tells the customer you expect him to pay promptly.

FOLLOWING UP ON BROKEN PROMISES

Whenever your customer has made a commitment to pay and doesn't, a fast, forceful follow-up on the first broken promise is essential. If handled properly, the customer becomes impressed with your reluctance to tolerate stalling, and, realizing he has got a fight on his hands the moment he defaults, is more apt to pay to get you "off his back." Whatever the payment proposal, when part or full payment is expected, call when payment is due, time permitting. If a customer promises to mail a check Monday, call Tuesday to be certain the check has been sent. Naturally, time shortage and volume can often delay follow-ups. But you should call your "jumbo" exposures until the check is in the mail. Then allow extra mailing time for the money to arrive.

What Approach Is Best?

An overly aggressive follow-up schedule may be harmful to your firm's good will and image. On the other hand, an apathetic or too-routine follow-up often leads to further stalls, a breakdown of payment arrangements, and a lessened profit.

It is not too difficult to become mentally prepared for this type of call. If considering the reasons for a shattered promise, you must keep in mind the following possibilities:

- The customer has willfully misstated his intentions. In effect, he has deliberately lied.

- The customer wasn't sufficiently concerned to remember the commitment.

- You have a right to be upset. After all, as a sincere, businesslike individual, you have kept your promise—and you have a right to expect him to keep his.

- The customer isn't interested in paying.

- He made an honest mistake, and will pay.

While it is wholly unprofessional to become personally involved, emotions are often a useful tool. When purposefully used to attain a specific reaction from the customer, the results can be remarkable. For this reason, it sometimes helps to display a trace of faint anger, impatience, irritation, surprise or even disdain when reminding the customer of the default.

Thus, having set the stage, you can seize the initiative in the following ways:

— Remind customer of his broken promise(s).

— Act skeptical about taking another chance. Mention the specific date(s) the identical promise was made before.

— Remind the customer of the age of the account.

— Tell the customer this is strictly a courtesy call—you won't tolerate further delay.

— Tell the customer you're obligated to proceed as instructed, but thought it best to allow him a final opportunity to cooperate.

— Remind the customer that further action is imminent, and that it could well lead to further expense.

— Demand payment by a specific deadline.

— Point out the claim can be settled either the hard way or the easy way—which way does he choose?

Here again, your approach will vary with the different circumstances, the age of the account, past experience, special instructions, and intuition. In each case, your ability to persuade the customer to respond will help to bring the account to a successful close.

In some cases, it may be necessary to thoroughly question the customer. If so, don't take a tactic that will insult him, but try to appeal to his sense of decency, and make pointed reference to alternatives. Remember, your objective is to get the customer concerned enough to pay—now!

Finally, while becoming "buddy-buddy" with a customer can sometimes help, caution should be exercised not to undermine the basic collector-customer relationship. Customers often take advantage of a presumed friendship by stalling. The result is excessive follow-up, and frequently long and irrelevant conversations.

How To Ask For Part Payment

When asking for part payment, a collector, as pointed out, should avoid asking a customer, "How much can you afford to send?" Instead, the collector must say, "Your balance is $1,200.00; how short of paying the balance in full are you? Are you short $200.00? If so, we'll take $1,000.00 on account!'' By doing that, you'll average much better than letting the customer automatically fill in whatever amount he or she desires, or ''can spare.'' How much a customer would like to give you, and how much he can actually afford, may be two different figures. You should, of course, always opt for the higher number. You'll average much larger payments by saying ''How much are you short?'' instead of ''How much can you send?''

How Best To Handle NSF Checks

There was a time when collectors would use the above tactic in the handling of NSF checks. For example, if a check for $300.00 was returned for insufficient funds, you could get information from the customer as to how much he was short, and then make a deposit of your own for the amount of the shortage. If you learned that there was $240.00 in the bank account, you could make a deposit to the customer's account of $60.00 of your own money, and then attempt to get the check certified for $300.00. You'd then reimburse yourself the $60.00, and credit the account for $240.00! That way, you'd get at least a part of what was due—instead of nothing.

THE DOUBLE-TEAMING APPROACH

If a rapport develops between you and a customer which makes a tough approach awkward or unrealistic, the account should be transferred to another collector. This third-party technique is often very effective. A switch to more direct, vigorous and impersonal handling frequently stimulates the customer's checkbook.

What The "Third Party" Collector Should Do

If the customer's bookkeeper is stalling, go to the treasurer or controller (assuming you couldn't reach them initially), or even contact the president. Make sure that everyone in authority is fully aware of the consequences of non-cooperation. Get through to key people. Follow up—delays of a day, 5 days or a week are all too common, and when a company doesn't acknowledge a part payment, sometimes a month goes by! That type of follow-up will mean the need for an entirely new arrangement and additional costs. If timely follow-up is not enforced as a matter of collection policy, then your company loses its competitive edge. A third-party collector can help you maintain that edge.

This double-teaming approach is also used as a good guy/bad guy concept, with two collectors each handling the same debtor. This allows the customer to react to the good-guy approach, as the "good guy" saved the customer from the arrogant, pushy demands mandated by the "bad guy." Sometimes just a different voice at a different time will bring about better results.

HOW TO MAKE INSTALLMENT ARRANGEMENTS

A little pre-call planning is also necessary whenever you and your customer are attempting to arrive at a reasonable repayment program. If a customer needs extra time to pay, installment arrangements should be considered. However, whether a proposal is reasonable or not will depend on a number of factors:

1. *The size of the account*—if the balance is small and the economics of further pursuit are against you, then it's very logical to consider any arrangement that generates a paid-in-full result—even if it appears longer than what you would otherwise accept.

2. *Amounts offered*—consider the size of the initial downpayment and determine a specific date for the final payment. Will the payments be equal, or will there be a balloon payment at the end, calling for the greatest portion of the remaining balance to be made with the final check?

3. *Intervals*—consider both the intervals between payment and the time frame involved before the first payment will be made. Naturally, the shortest possible time should be allowed in each instance; and even if it means taking a lesser amount, it's much more productive to attempt to obtain weekly payments than monthly payments. You certainly would not want to find out a month after an account paid you that the check was returned and that the account was closing. Weekly arrangements allow you a closer monitoring of the account, and the information is worth the extra cost of follow-up and handling.

4. *Past history and experience* with the customer—these are undoubtedly going to influence your decision as to just how cooperative you wish to be, and whether or not the customer in the past was able to keep its commitment to "the negotiated terms."

Naturally, consideration has to be given to the cost-effectiveness of handling the account on a long-term follow-up basis. You may also want to consider whether or not your company's interests would be better protected if you were to take more dramatic action and seek the full amount due. Ask: ''Will I be able to get the matter to court and collect through litigation before I am paid off under the arrangement the debtor proposes?'' Assuming that your customer's proposal appears reasonable, it should be made clear that acceptance is subject to an immediate tangible demonstration of good faith. A strong request should then be made for post-dated checks or notes. A collector must be extremely alert and perceptive, however, in directing the customer towards a specific position. A customer objection to sending post-dated checks or promissory notes may be voiced as a combination of one or more of the items listed. Only a truly alert collector will be able to compose objections on the spot, and to shatter a customer's complacency in order to achieve the desired result.

WHAT ABOUT POST-DATED CHECKS?

Post-dated checks are accepted by most companies—and are commonly asked for, as part of a telephone collection effort.

A post-dated check is made out and signed by a customer in advance of its date. It is, of course, understood that the check is to be held by the creditor until the date it is due. Then it will be presented at the customer's bank for payment. Generally speaking, failure to cover the post-dated check is no different from failing to pay an invoice for goods sold on credit. Laws involving ''insufficient funds'' checks do not apply to checks made out as post-dated instruments.

There are a number of objections a customer may make, however, to a request for post-dated checks. You'll need to be aware of these, and prepared to give no-nonsense replies.

Here are some of the commonest objections—and the ways you might respond to them:

ANSWERS TO 16 COMMONLY RAISED
OBJECTIONS ABOUT
POST-DATED CHECKS

1. *What good is writing a check when I don't have money in the bank now?*
   It is true, perhaps, that you don't have the money now. But a post-dated

check is a promise to pay in the future. It's a promise that you are going to see that the money is in your bank on the due date.

2. *Don't you trust me?*
It isn't a case of whether we trust you or not. We don't know you personally, and we are not judging your honesty. We trusted you and sold to you on credit. To confirm this trust, you should declare your intention to pay and tie this matter down with a post-dated check (or checks) or note.

3. *I tried it once, and all I got was bouncing checks.*
If you keep a careful record of the checks you give us, there should be no difficulty. We are not going to ask you for checks of such large amounts that you can't meet them. You must think this over and come up with amounts that you feel certain you can meet on the due dates. But if by chance, you cannot meet a check on a particular day, if you call us the day before, we will hold a check a reasonable length of time (3 or 4 days) for you to cover it.

4. *If I give you post-dated checks, will you call me before you deposit each one?*
We handle too many checks in a day to call you. However, I will give you my name and telephone number, and if you need extra time, you can call me *the day before* a check is due. We will be glad to hold it a reasonable length of time (3 or 4 days).

5. *When I have the money, I'll pay. I've never given a post-dated check in my life.*
There are times when a person has to do something he has never done before to protect his interests. You would like more time. We would like to help you and give you the needed time, but we must have your promise to pay, covered by a post-dated check or check (or notes). A post-dated check indicates good faith on your part, and a positive willingness to pay on a specified date.

6. *I never know how much money will come in each week.*
You have certain obligations you have to meet each week, such as payroll, so you can also make this a part of your planning. You can generally approximate your income based on previous experience. Together, let's try to find an amount for each week or each month that

you feel you can definitely meet. This is your opportunity now to work out an arrangement that you believe is doable.

7. *I need time to pay.*
   We can undoubtedly give you time if it is reasonable. Tell me how much time you will need to pay in full? (Then, after the customer has given time and number of payments.) Fine, I think we can get that time or even a little more, if you can do one thing for us—we will have to have reassurance. This arrangement must be tied down with post-dated checks, or with notes. Which do you prefer?

8. *It's illegal to give post-dated checks.*
   It is not illegal to give post-dated checks. A post-dated check is simply a promise to pay in the future on a specified date, just as a note would be. How could a prominent concern such as ours recommend illegal procedures to businesspeople?

9. *My attorney won't let me give post-dated checks.*
   I'm sure if your attorney knew that there was a pending action against your firm, he would want you to do something to stop it. Why don't you call your attorney and discuss it with him? Or, you can have your attorney call me and we can discuss this. Maybe we can come up with a plan to help. Since the giving of post-dated checks or notes is generally accepted in the business world, your attorney could have no objections to it. Certainly, your attorney would not want you to jeopardize your credit standing.

10. *My bank won't let me give post-dated checks.*
    Your bank would have no knowledge of your giving post-dated checks, because they would be deposited on the due dates. It is true some banks frown on giving post-dated checks, because irresponsible people deposit them before the due date—causing the banks difficulty. But we have the facilities for handling these properly.

11. *My accountant won't let me give post-dated checks.*
    Your accountant would certainly want to be helpful. Why not discuss it with him, or have him call me to discuss it? Your accountant works for you, and it isn't your accountant who will suffer if this delinquency goes further. Surely, he would want us to come up with a plan to benefit you.

12. *This confuses my records or bookkeeping.*

It shouldn't confuse your records. You are setting the dates for payment. The checks will be deposited on those dates. Either have your bookkeeper do it, or you mark these checks on a calendar, or enter record in your checkbook or calendar desk pad. You will then enter the checks on these dates in your checkbook for deduction from your balance.

Admittedly, it does cause you some slight difficulties and extra work, but in order to get the extra time you are asking for, you will have to find a way to overcome your bookkeeping problem.

13. *I gave a post-dated check once to someone, and he deposited it before time.*

We will not deposit your checks ahead of time. We have the facilities for handling post-dated checks. The checks are not released until the due date. You are dealing with us and we are trying to help you. There would be no point in our making an arrangement with you, and then not holding to it.

14. *I'd be glad to give you the post-dated checks, but I'm refinancing and may change bank accounts.*

Any time you may refinance or change your bank account, you can be assured that we will exchange the checks you give us for new ones to be given in their place. Until such time as you refinance or change your bank account, we will make arrangements under your present financial setup and on your present bank account. If you find at a later date, you want to pay at a faster rate or over a shorter period, we will make a new arrangement and you can send us new checks to replace the ones originally given.

15. *If I default, I'll give you post-dated checks.*

If you default, there may be no later reconsideration. We may not be agreeable to any further proposals of a payment plan. As the matter stands now, you are already in default and you are seeking more time. You must *positively* show your good faith. Issuance of post-dated checks will indicate your willingness to pay.

16. *There is nothing wrong. Your company turned me in, now you can wait for your money.*

Your account is now due. We have every right to use whatever means we have at our disposal to collect this debt. We are not pressing you unjustly. I cannot take sides as to whether or not you feel we are being unfair. But we can stop this matter from going further. If you feel you want more time, give us a post-dated check to hold here until due. After all, if you won't bank on yourself, why should we bank on you?

PROMISSORY NOTES

Promissory notes may be agreed on in the course of a collection day. These generally provide for payment of a specified sum at a bank at a specific future date. Interest may or may not be included, at the discretion of the parties involved. Where interest is included, the prevailing rate charged by commercial banks to lend money to businesses would normally be the rate requested.

Here is a typical promissory note:

$	19
after date promise to pay to	
the order of	
	Dollars
at	
Value received	
No. Due	

AD 41

The Use Of Notes In Personal Collections

A note is a negotiable instrument promising to pay a specific amount at a specific future date. A note is similar to a post-dated check—with several significant differences.

1. **When Used**

   A. Refusal by debtor to issue post-dated checks.

   B. When creditor wants interest.

   C. On large accounts where debtor payment plan would extend over a long period of time (six months, for example).

2. **Types of Notes**

   A. A promissory or regular note is used when there is to be only one note to cover the account, or if the debtor will not give accelerated notes. (They can be interest-bearing.)

   B. Series or accelerated notes are used for a series of extended payments. Default on any one payment makes balance become due immediately. (See acceleration clause on small notes below.)

3. **Advantages**

   A. The note or notes are placed in bank ten days before the due date. Debtor is therefore notified by his bank that the note has been placed for collection. This eliminates the possibility of debtor saying he forgot the note was to have been met.

   B. Series notes: If one note is defaulted upon, the rest of the notes become immediately due.

   C. Interest is usually added to note at an agreed-upon amount.

4. **Disadvantages**

   A. The defaulted note usually cannot be put back in the bank. It must be replaced by a check or money order.

   B. The due date of a note cannot be held up if debtor needs a day or two, unless covered by a check.

CAUTION: When it is a large or extended series, try to confirm that your management will accept the arrangement before the notes are made up.

Information Needed From The Debtor For A Note

1. *Promissory Notes* (See example that follows of form currently in use):

   A.   Date(s) note(s) will be due.

   B.   Amount of each note

   C.   Value received (i.e., interest 8%)

   D.   Name, branch and address of bank note will be presented at

   E.   Full title of the debtor firm as the account would appear in the bank

   F.   Number of signatures required on the note

2. *On Series (Accelerated) Notes:*

   Accelerated notes need the same information as promissory notes—and more. Be sure, in addition, to specify the *number* of notes to be set up.

Here is a checklist of the information needed on a series of notes:

Date _____

Name of Payee _____

Name of Bank Where Payable _____

Address of Bank _____

Interest (Value Received) _____

Correct Name of Debtor Firm (Payee) (Maker)
(Name Bank Account is Under) _____

Number of Signatures Required _____

DATE DUE AND AMOUNT OF EACH NOTE:

Here are several forms of notes which are part of a series:

$............................ ....19......

....after date, for value received,..................promise

to pay to the order of...

....Dollars

at ....

with interest at.........................per cent.
This note is one of a series of.............................notes of even date herewith, aggregating $.............................
It is understood and agreed that in the event of the non-payment of any one of said series and such default continue for a period
of..............................days, then at the option of the holder of any of the said notes, all or any part of the remaining unpaid notes shall forth-
with become due and payable. The failure to assert this right shall not be deemed a waiver thereof.

No...................Due....................................

....

No. 1000N Serial Note—Julius Blumberg, Inc., 80 Exchange Place, New York

---

$ _____   _____19___

_____ after date_____ promise to pay to

the order of _____

_____ Dollars

Payable at_____

This note is No._____of a series of_____notes; that upon the default in the payment of any one of the notes the
remaining notes shall immediately become due and payable without notice.

Value received   _____

No._____Due_____   _____

NO. 484 JULIUS BLUMBERG, INC., LAW BLANK PUBLISHERS, 80 EXCHANGE PL., N. Y.

SAMPLE INSTALLMENT PROMISSORY NOTE

$ _____   _____, 19____

At the times and in the installments hereinafter stated, for value received _____ promise to pay to the order of _____

the sum of _____ Dollars, payments as follows:

$ _____ _____, 19____ $ _____ _____, 19____

$ _____ _____, 19____ $ _____ _____, 19____

$ _____ _____, 19____ $ _____ _____, 19____

$ _____ _____, 19____ $ _____ _____, 19____

$ _____ _____, 19____ $ _____ _____, 19____

$ _____ _____, 19____ $ _____ _____, 19____

$ _____ _____, 19____ $ _____ _____, 19____

$ _____ _____, 19____ $ _____ _____, 19____

$ _____ _____, 19____ $ _____ _____, 19____

with interest from date at the rate of _____ per cent per annum until paid, and in the event of default in payment of any amounts as herein provided, then the entire amount shall become due at the option of the holder hereof. Principal and interest payable in lawful money of the United States, at _____, and in case suit is instituted to collect this note or any portion thereof, _____ promise to pay such additional sum as the Court may adjudge reasonable as Attorney's fees in said suit. Demand, presentment for payment, protest and notice of protest are hereby waived.

_____

Witness: _____   _____

                                    Address _____

PROMISSORY NOTE

$ _____   _____ , _____
                                       (City)   (State)

                              _____ , 19 _____

On or before _____ , 19 _____ , the undersigned promises to pay to the order of _____ , at its principal office in the city of _____ , or at such other place as the holder hereof may designate, the principal sum of _____ Dollars ($), with interest on the unpaid principal amount owing at the rate of _____% per annum until maturity, while and so long as there exists no uncured default hereunder and with interest at the rate of _____ % per annum after maturity, and while and so long as there exists no default until paid, all without relief from valuation and appraisement laws and with reasonable attorney's fees.

The outstanding indebtedness described hereinabove shall be paid in equal installments as follows:

_____

_____

_____

_____

If there is any default payment of any one of the above-described installments, which default extends over a period of more than ten days, or if at any time the holder hereof deems itself insecure, then in such event, the entire amount of this note shall—at the option of the holder hereof— immediately become due and payable without notice or demand.

The makers, endorsers and all guarantors of this note severally waive demand, presentment for payment, protest, notice of protest, notice of non-payment of this note and also waive any and all defenses on the ground of any extensions or partial payments which may be granted or accepted by the holder hereof before or after the maturity of this note or any part thereof.

_____
(Signature of Individual)

_____
(Signature of Individual)

_____
(Corporate Signature)

By _____

_____
(Title)

OVERCOMING OBJECTIONS TO
POST-DATED CHECKS OR NOTES

There are a number of common customer objections to negotiating a payout with checks or notes. These objections usually hide the real reasons for not agreeing to pay now. So you should be alert to them. Keep these rules in mind:

1. To overcome objections, seek out a common ground. Stay flexible. You want to be paid. Assume also that the customer wants to pay.

2. Get agreement on the parts of the plan not objected to.

3. Isolate specific areas of disagreement. Get customer to reveal the real problem.

4. Narrow the issues, and confirm that acceptance of the entire program hinges on finding a solution to one major objection.

5. Present attractive alternative choices as solutions for that specific area of difference.

6. Close and confirm all areas of agreement and summarize. Does that sound familiar? It should; you probably do it all the time when dealing with customers' objections, but may not realize it. Think of yourself as a salesperson. Your job is to overcome objections and sell your product the "pay-out plan."

The Benefits Of Post-Dated Checks Or Notes

By asking your customer to sign a promissory note or post-dated check, you are really testing—but not necessarily questioning—his intentions. After all, if a customer promises payment 20 days from now, it's not unreasonable for a collector to say "Please date the check for 20 days from now, and mail it today." Should the customer respond with statements like "Well, how do I know I am going to have the money?" or "I am not sure I will be able to cover the check," then obviously you'll wonder why the customer promised payment on that date in the first place! Why should you wait 20 days, only to learn that no money was available? Better it should be known now.

Perhaps a new program should be arranged that appears more doable—a program based on the customer's willingness to issue notes or checks. Of course, the real psychology in this situation is the fact that you are asking a customer to *bank* on his commitment. Why should you have more faith in the customer than the customer has in himself? If you are willing to wait, why should the customer not be willing to send the check?

Watch this: According to Public Law 95-109, "The Fair Debt Collection Practices Act," the acceptance by a debt collector of a check or other payment instrument post-dated by more than five days may be considered an unfair trade practice—unless such person is notified in writing of the debt collector's intent to deposit such check or instrument not more than ten or less than three business days prior to such deposit.

In addition, the solicitation by a debt collector by any post-dated check or other post-dated payment instrument for the sole purpose of threatening or instituting criminal prosecution is forbidden. Some communities—such as New York City—have similar restrictions on use of post-dated checks for early deposit. However, most laws only apply to third-party collectors.

Offering Time In Exchange For Payment

You might also try offering customers a little bit more time in exchange for their cooperation and willingness in dating the check. For example, if a customer suggests that he is not certain funds will be available on the date you have required, you can either request the check for a week after that, or consider breaking the payment in two or three parts. That would provide the customer with a variety of alternative choices, a positive answer which should result in your being paid.

Once again, the tactics employed are similar to those that are used by salespeople. Have you ever heard a salesperson ask whether or not you prefer the large size or small size or the blue one or green one, or one dozen or two dozen? Does he (or she) ask you to sign a contract with your own pen, or does he offer you his? These types of choices are effective sales techniques. They can also be adapted for collections.

Checks Or Notes?

Post-dated checks are preferable if the amounts involved are small and the payments are closely spaced. Notes are preferable if the payments are larger and the balances are more substantial, or if payments are to be made over an extended period of time and with interest. You could of course have an extra payment made by check, if interest is to be paid on the account.

Both arrangements, however, provide for an acknowledgment of debt and, they enhance your position from a legal point of view. Also, it must be pointed out that since you are competing for payment with other creditors, you may be in an advantageous position if you hold the post-dated check. After all, if the customer owes you $1,000.00 and another creditor $1,000.00—and gives you a check for $1,000.00—it's only logical that your check will be paid before the customer decides to write another check to someone else. By employing the proper techniques and obtaining payment, even in post-dated fashion, you are certainly enhancing your position and will probably collect more, and follow up less.

Of the two arrangements, promissory notes have the advantage of providing an almost incontestable admission of liability. Further, when they're payable through the customer's bank, the bank, in effect, becomes your collection agent. For obvious reasons, a customer is generally unwilling to admit to his bank an inability to honor his obligations—so he'll make an extra effort to honor the notes.

On the other hand, notes are usually not as easily obtained as post-dated checks, and cannot be redeposited as can a check. The burden of making them out is usually on the collector. They also cannot be held beyond their due date, and require presentment to the bank several days in advance. They also need an "Accelerator Clause," which provides for the balance of notes to fall due in the event of default. Otherwise, you can legally make demand only for the sum of the note in default.

Naturally, it will not always be possible to get your choice of notes or post-dated checks. In any case, it is always a temptation to accept the first offer. But this is both easy and dangerous. Too quick acceptance may lead the customer to assume you will be happy with whatever he gives you, and to feel he can break promises with impunity.

Make The Customer Earn Any Arrangements You Agree To

If the customer feels he's been through a battle, he'll be wary about facing you again if there is a default—and thus will be less likely to do so. If the customer makes a proposal that's ridiculous, react in a businesslike manner.

This will often shame or pressure him into better terms. You should assume the customer is offering less than he really can afford. So you should insist on a sizable first payment, push for higher installments and try to compress the schedule. Finally, be sure to confirm arrangements promptly.

WHAT A LETTER OF COMMITMENT DOES

If, despite your best efforts, you can't obtain notes or post-dated checks, at least try to obtain a letter of commitment from the customer, acknowledging the obligation and spelling out the agreed terms of repayment—a specific schedule of dates and amounts. This letter of commitment acts as an acknowledgment of the debt and is an extremely valuable collection tool. It requires the customer to commit his intentions to written form, and makes the customer likely to take the commitment more seriously than a verbal promise would. Furthermore, obtaining admission of liability from your customer may significantly enhance your future legal position. Having previously acknowledged the liability to you, a customer would be hard-pressed to deny the debt later on.

HANDLING DIFFERENT CUSTOMER ATTITUDES

Some customers may immediately cooperate and give you all the information and money requested. Others may give only superficial cooperation, and when you probe further, they stop being cooperative. Customers may even "yes" a collector to death without any intention of making good.

Still other customers may plead ignorance as to the outstanding balance, and even deny responsibility for the entire debt—an excuse frequently used by both the old and new owners of a recently sold business. It is also a favorite excuse of a husband or wife after a divorce decree, or of a parent when referring to a charge by a son or daughter. Whether they are minors at the time is not even considered.

Customers may also have legitimate disputes regarding the service performed or the merchandise received, or the disputes could be nothing but a sham to avoid payment.

Some customers may even appear to be totally oblivious to your demands. When you ask for payment, you hear only silence. Frustrating, isn't it! Like talking to yourself. Even an angry customer is better than talking to yourself. Oftentimes a collector will encounter a customer that believes he or she is genuinely unable to pay even on an installment basis. If that occurs, suggest means of refinancing the debt as follows:

1. *Credit Unions*. Most companies have employees' credit unions. Find out if the debtor belongs to a credit union, and suggest applying for a loan.

2. *Employees*. Employers will often advance money to pay past-due bills of their employees. Explore this source.

3. *Banks*. Most banks have installment loan departments. Many people can borrow money or increase a present loan at the bank. Many automobiles are financed with the bank. Most people do not realize that they can refinance and obtain additional money before the present loan is paid off. Remind them.

4. *Loan Companies—Roll-Over or Consolidate*. Many customers already have installment loans outstanding. Get the name of the loan company they owe. Often, many loans can be *consolidated* into one. Customers may save money or interest, have a reduction of payment amounts, and get a reduction of the number of people they must pay. Also, many people have paid-up loans. They can return for another loan. Remind them.

5. *Insurance Policies*. Many people have insurance policies of long standing. They can borrow money at a very low rate of interest—much less than from a loan company or bank, because the policies have cash surrender value. Remind them.

6. *Relatives*. Many people can borrow from their relatives and keep their credit reputation strong. Explore this source.

7. *Homes*. Many people have been paying on their homes for years. They can refinance, get enough money to pay off your bill, and perhaps get a reduction of their home-loan payment amounts.

8. *Bank Credit Card*. Your acceptance of Master Card or Visa enables you to get paid while customer pays off the bank card on his (her) own.

CLOSING THE CALL ON A POSITIVE NOTE

Now that we have reviewed the essential techniques you should employ during your telephone conversations, and a variety of situations that you may encounter, it's important to get a good feel for just how to end the discussion.

Finishing up a conversation in the correct manner could mean the difference between obtaining payment, or facing a broken promise. By following a few simple guidelines, you can close the conversation with complete understanding and on a positive note.

So remember:

1. Be sure to speak clearly and distinctly.

2. Give the customer your mailing address, and have him (or her) read it back to you to be certain he's got it correct.

3. Leave your name; and ask the customer to be certain to send the check to your attention.

4. Make the customer feel that you are counting on his (or her) prompt attention and cooperation.

5. Above all, make sure your customer takes you seriously.

While call-backs are not generally desirable, if you don't have the customer's attention, perhaps it would be better to consider calling back at a more convenient time.

After you've completed the call, be sure to enter the nucleus and plot of the conversation in the work-note area on your file—information such as date and time called—using the abbreviations outlined earlier in this chapter, so that the other collectors can follow your efforts in your absence.

At the same time, be sure you have entered any helpful information on the face of your collection file, such as a payment plan agreed upon, beginning dates, other repayment program, settlement amounts and dates, best time to call, phone number, and principal of authority who agreed to the payment promise or commitment of settlement, and—maybe the most important—the date of the next call. By putting the proper data in the proper area of the file, you can be sure the account is timely returned to you for follow-up.

Summary: The telephone can be one of your most powerful collection weapons—if you use it right. The essential thing is to stay in *control,* to decide for yourself whether to be easy-going or intense, firm or friendly. As long as you remain in control, there's no question that *you* are entitled to be paid, and will take whatever steps are necessary to see that you *are* paid.

6

The Fine Points Of Telephone And Follow-Up Collections

Table of Contents

6

The Fine Points Of Telephone And Follow-Up Collections

How nice it would be if we had the opportunity to hear ourselves on the phone and determine our own strengths and weaknesses! Even better, wouldn't it be wonderful if we could redo certain parts of that special conversation we knew was so important. Well, the next-best way to do that is to analyze for yourself the elements of your phone call:

What collection motivators were used? Were the arrangements reasonable, too liberal or unrealistic? Was an attempt made to negotiate a better arrangement, or did you settle for the first promise your customer gave? Did you identify yourself properly? Did you ascertain which party was authorized to make payment? Were you certain that you were dealing with the correct customer? Was your tone confident, uncertain, authoritative, harsh, routine, meek, boring or monotonous? Did you convey a sense of urgency? By what words or phrases do you believe your customer was able to detect that? Was your speech clear, mumbled, slurred, too fast, hesitant, clumsy, too verbose, decisive, or to the point? Did you take charge of the conversation, or did the customer? Did you make an explicit demand for full payment? Did you obtain a commitment from the customer, or did you make the commitment *for* your customer? Did you press for post-dated checks, promissory notes, or a letter of commitment? Did you summarize the agreement and close the call properly so that both you and the customer had a clear understanding of what was expected? How would you rate the call just completed—excellent, good, fair, or poor? In your opinion, how could the call have been handled more effectively?

SPECIAL SITUATIONS—AND HOW TO HANDLE THEM

The following situation set-ups represent examples of phone techniques in action. Included are both good and bad techniques, given for the sole purpose of illustration. The commentary on the conversation points out the strengths *and* the weaknesses of the collector's approach.

CASE EXAMPLE #1: THE BROKEN PROMISE

Background: The following case demonstrates a call to a customer who has just broken his second successive promise. (There are both good and not-so-good things in the collector's approach—as noted in the "commentary" column on the left.)

The account is for $2,000.00, and initially the entire balance had been assured immediately. Later, it was conceded that the promise had been unrealistic. The customer then agreed to forward four weekly post-dated checks of $500.00 each. Two days have passed and the collector has not yet received the checks.

Commentary

Collector:	Hello, is this Evasive Instruments, Incorporated?
Answer:	Yes, it is.
C:	May I speak with Mr. Smith, please.
Answer:	I'm afraid not. He's in conference.

*RISKY TURNOFF	C:	It's urgent I speak to him now. *I'm certain he'll want to speak with me. Please advise him that Mr. London is on the phone.
	Answer:	Hold on, please.

(Slight delay)

	Debtor:	Smith speaking.
*RISKY TURNOFF	Collector:	Mr. Smith, this is Mr. London from the Collection Division of APP Co. You know, I'm rapidly getting the impression you're *not as sincere about paying our account as you would have me believe.
	D:	You mean you didn't receive those checks? I'm certain they were mailed.
	C:	When were they mailed?
	D:	I couldn't say without consulting my bookkeeper.
	C:	Look, Mr. Smith, we're talking about a $2,000.00 account, and a creditor whose patience is rapidly becoming exhausted. Please check with your bookkeeper now and confirm the amounts, dates and numbers of the checks, when they were mailed and to where.
	D:	Hold on a minute.
	C:	I'll wait.
	D:	(after a short delay) Mr. London, my bookkeeper didn't send those checks. She says we didn't have enough money to cover the first one, and didn't want to risk it coming back. We should be able to send something next week.

*TURNOFF LANGUAGE C:	Mr. Smith, one just might get the impression you're *stalling for time. First, you said you'd remit immediately. Then, you admitted you could only pay $500 weekly. Again, you failed to come through. And now you're talking in vague terms of "something next week." *In effect, you're telling me you're incapable of paying your bills, isn't that right?
D:	No . . . no. This is just a temporary bind. We only need a little time.
C:	Mr. Smith, this bill is already three months past due.

(Language used by collector is challenging, not motivating. Unless businesslike attitude in discussion is resumed, collector may lose control of the call.)

D:	(showing irritation) Well, I'm shelling out as it comes in, a little here, a little there, trying to keep everybody happy.
*WISE-GUY ATTITUDE C:	*Obviously, we're unhappy with your philosophy. Neither a "little here," nor "a little there" has reached us. You, Mr. Smith, are going to have to make a decision. Either those checks are sent now, or we'll be forced to proceed.
D:	What do you mean, "proceed"?
*WISE-GUY ATTITUDE C:	*Let's not play coy. You've been in business long enough to know what happens when a creditor fails to get cooperation in resolving a long, past-due account.
D:	Well, what am I supposed to do about my other creditors?

C: Tell me, Mr. Smith, have they contemplated placing you for collection?

D: No.

*ON TARGET

C: *All right then, it's obvious this is the account that requires priority handling. At APP we won't wait. Failure to recognize that fact is likely to cost you more than $2,000 if you force us to proceed. And if we do proceed, you can be sure we will not tolerate installment arrangements, as we're willing to do now. Let's face it, Mr. Smith, you can't afford to delay any longer!

D: (resignedly) I suppose you're right, London. Somehow or other, I'll just have to see that the checks are covered, that's all.

C: Fine. See that those checks are mailed here today immediately.

D: I won't be able to get those checks out until tomorrow, so you should have them the following day.

C: Look, we're agreed this is a priority matter. As company treasurer, I'd suggest you use your authority to get those checks drawn and mailed today.

D: All right, I'll do my best.

SUMMARY OF
ARRANGEMENT

C: Good! I'll expect four checks of $500 each, the first current, the others dated 10/1, 10/8 and 10/15 on my desk no later than Thursday. Have you written those dates down? Do you have my mailing address?

D: Yes, I have the dates. Better give me your address again, though.

(Address is given)

D: O.K., I'll see that they get out right away.

C: Please do that, Mr. Smith, I'm counting on your cooperation. Thank you and goodbye.

Important: Be sure to record notes of the conversation in the collection file (four checks: $500 on A/C and three post-dated checks, $500 each on 10/1, 10/8, 10/15 today; per Smith, Treasurer—for example), and send a letter confirming the arrangement.

CASE EXAMPLE #2:
THE HARD-PRESSED CUSTOMER

Background: This call involves a far less successful attempt to collect by obtaining post-dated checks. While the collector has had no previous difficulty with the customer, a recent credit report shows a nominal net worth of some $2,300, slow trade payments, and poor cash position. Prospects for fast collection do not look encouraging.

Debtor: Good morning. Current Techniques. Inc.

Collector: Good morning. May I please speak with Mr. Morgan.

D: This is Morgan speaking.

C: Mr. Morgan, I understand you're the treasurer of Current Techniques, Inc. Is that correct?

D: That's right. Who's this?

C: I'm Mr. Silver of the collection division.* I'd like to discuss a serious problem with you concerning an account for $735 against you.**

*(*Poor identification. Collection division of *where?* What company?*
**Claim against you? Is it a personal obligation?)

D: I don't understand why it's so serious.
C: Mr. Morgan, the bill is three months old.

D: Is it? I don't know. I'd have to check the invoice.
C: Mr. Morgan, I'm going to have to have your check immediately. Can you make arrangements to mail it this afternoon so that I'll have it in my office tomorrow morning?*

(*On target)

D: Look, if I could have paid this bill, I'd have done so without your calling me.
C: Meaning you won't pay?*

(*What a terrible thought to put in a customer's head.)

D: That's not what I said (heatedly). I should be able to get a payment out next week.
C: A payment out next week. Mr. Morgan, evidently you misunderstand me. We want full payment now!

D: Please believe me, Mr. Silver, if I could pay this bill now, I would.
C: Well, Mr. Morgan, this bill can't be postponed any longer. Just what specific alternatives do you have in mind?*

(*Why not say, "How much are you short? We need $2,300; do you have $2,000?")

D: Will you accept $50 a month?

C: No.

D: That's all I can afford. How about if I try for $100 monthly?

C: I don't know . . . and wouldn't until I check with my superior.* However, I doubt anything less than one-half now and the balance within a week would be agreeable.**

(*If you give the customer the impression that your superior—and not you—calls the shots, the customer may use it against you and not pay until your supervisor gets involved in the discussion.
**Good recovery.)

D: One half! Look, I make electrical wire, not money.

C: You say that's unreasonable; and I say your offer is utterly ridiculous.* Be honest, Mr. Morgan, what is the maximum you could pay?**

(*Total turnoff. Collector is lucky the customer didn't just end the discussion and hang up.
**Why not continue with, "How much are you really short?")

D: Oh, I suppose I could scrape up $50 a week.

C: That's still 15 weeks—almost four months. We'll never accept that. Possibly we'd accept $200 now and $75 a week, provided a series of post-dated checks were submitted.

D: No dice. I just haven't got that much. If you'll give me a day, I think I can raise about $135; but with the way my accounts have been paying, I'd be lucky to get up $50 a week.

C: Get me a current check for $135, and 12 checks at $50 each dated a week apart starting next week by tomorrow, and I'll make every effort to get my company to go along.* I must have the checks first though, to convince them you mean business.

(*Best possible arrangement under the circumstances.)

D: I'll get you the $135, but no dated checks. They'll just have to take my word on the balance.

C: In other words, you have doubts you can meet even this nominal arrangement.* If this is the case, we're wasting our time.**

(*Negative appeal.
**Collector should encourage customer to meet commitment, not discourage confidence.)

D: I said I can pay $50 a week. But I don't want to foul up my books.

C: Mr. Morgan, what's better: a minor bookeeping inconvenience, or further action for the entire $735 plus costs?* Rest assured, if this goes any further, you will not be offered any installment terms. What's it going to be?**

(*Good alternative choice.
**Again risk; turnoff type of communication.)

D: All right, you win.

C:	I'm sure this is in the best interests of all concerned. Provided I receive the checks by tomorrow, unless advised otherwise, you can assume we'll abide by the arrangement as long as the checks clear.*
	(*Good wrap up. But summary could be improved by restating arrangement agreed to.)
D:	Don't worry. They will.
C:	Mr. Morgan, please make the checks payable to Magnetic, and send them to my attention today.
D:	Will do. And thanks for working along with me. If I can do better, I will.
C:	I'm sure you will. Goodbye, Mr. Morgan, thanks for your cooperation.

Important: Be sure to record notes on the conversation in the collection file, and send a letter confirming the arrangement.

CASE EXAMPLE #3:
THE LAST TRY

Background: The following telephone presentation represents a collector's final attempt to collect the balance due his company before seeking outside collection agency assistance. It's well done and effectively handled, as noted. The debt is 120 days old, and all prior telephone and written demands have been ignored. Balance due $2,991.18.

Commentary

Debtor/ Customer:	Hello.
Collector:	May I speak with your president, Mr. Harrington.

	D:	This is Mr. Harrington. May I help you?
*GOOD IDENTIFICATION **PROFESSIONAL PAUSE	C:	Mr. Harrington, my name is John Reed. I am with the firm of Absolute Priority.* The purpose of this call is to advise you personally that amicable arrangements must be made with our office now, to resolve your past-due balance.** Will you be mailing your check today?
	D:	Well, if I had the money, I would have paid them (you) a long time ago without your help.
BACK ON TARGET	C:	Mr. Harrington, when will the funds be available? (Pause again.) How much money are you short? How much of the total are you able to send now?
	D:	Well Mr. Reed, I'm going to need at least a few months to pay off this account.
ZEROING IN ON TIME NEEDED TO PAY	C:	Mr. Harrington, as I stated previously, I must secure this balance now. You are requesting additional time far beyond the normal terms of sale. We may agree to provide you with the necessary time, but only if you can be more specific. May I suggest that you give us negotiable instruments in the form of either post-dated checks or promissory notes payable at a bank, due on a weekly basis during the next 90 days?
	D:	Well, our company does not like having notes or checks outstanding. It is not our normal procedure.
HIGH PRIORITY	C:	Mr. Harrington, this is not a normal situation. We have a debt that is long outstanding and is now considered delinquent. We have given you fair

consideration in shipping the goods on open terms, and now we feel that we have the right to demand, in return, a little bit more consideration on your part.

D: Well, how do I know you won't slip these through beforehand? I really don't know exactly how much I'm going to have and when I'm going to have it!

OVERCOMING OBJECTION

C: Mr. Harrington, you've indicated that you need 90 days in which to resolve the account. The only question is: Exactly how confident are you that the account can be resolved over this period of time? We are requesting that you back up your statement.

In this case, it would seem advantageous to all parties concerned to have you submit a series of post-dated checks. The checks should be made payable to us, and submitted to me immediately as an indication of your

ENCOURAGING CUSTOMER CONFIDENCE

good faith. The purpose of requesting the checks is not to have them returned or disrupt your accounting procedures, but to resolve a problem situation and to obtain the additional time needed for your firm to meet its obligations. After all, if you're asking that we wait and are requesting our forbearance and understanding, you should be willing to bank on it. If you're not confident that the funds will be there on the dates that you specify, then why should we appear to be more confident in your ability than you are? Don't you agree?

D: Well, it sounds reasonable. Let me give you my bookkeeper and I will instruct her to prepare the checks on a weekly basis, payable on the Friday of each week, if this is agreeable with you.

C: Mr. Harrington, I think that is reasonable. I would appreciate it if you would have your bookkeeper come on the line right now so that there is no misunderstanding as to the amount, dates, and the urgency of the situation.

D: Hold on, I will get her.

BKR: Hello, this is Mrs. Jones.

KEEP UP MOMENTUM

C: Mrs. Jones, Mr. Harrington and I have worked out arrangements to resolve the outstanding indebtedness due Absolute Priority.

(Harrington interrupts conversation)

D: Mrs. Jones, Mr. Reed has requested that we submit a series of post-dated checks to his office in payment of the balance. I have agreed with him, and would appreciate it if you would prepare the checks for my signature to be evenly distributed over the next 12 weeks, payable on the Friday of each week.

WRAP-UP CALL SUMMARIZING AGREEMENT

C: Mrs. Jones, the outstanding balance is $2,991.18. In order to expedite the preparation, may I suggest that the first 11 checks be in the sum of $250.00 each, and the final check for the remaining balance of $241.18. These checks must be mailed today. We would like to be reassured that you are dealing with this matter as a priority item.

D: (Harrington interrupts) Wait a minute, Reed, now we've got a lot of things to do. We're running a business, and we'll get

RISKY, BUT GOOD RECOVERY

C: around to it before the week is out. Let's not start in with this "today business." Mr. Harrington, we are trying to afford you every opportunity to get this matter resolved. It is absolutely essential that this be dealt with in an other-than-routine fashion. Too much time has already passed, and you really cannot afford a delay. As President of your firm, I suggest you use your authority and see to it that they are on your desk and available for signature today, and mailed by 5 o'clock to my attention at the following address.

D: Reed, what happens if I find myself short and the checks won't clear?

C: Well, I would appreciate it if you would notify us at least one day prior to a check being presented, so that other arrangements can be made. But I must tell you now, don't count on any deviation from this agreement unless, of course, it's your intent to prepay. In the event you wish to redeem the outstanding checks prior to their maturity, naturally we will be willing to consider.

D: Okay, rest assured we will comply with your arrangements and the checks will be sent to you as you request. I suppose we'll just have to keep our commitment, because you've been fair and reasonable.

C: Mr. Harrington, I thank you and anticipate receipt within the next 48 hours. I'm counting on your cooperation. Goodbye.

Important: Record notes on the collection file: 12 post-dated checks (11—$250; 1—$241.18) as of Friday to be sent today per Mr. Harrington, President and Mrs. Jones, Bookkeeper. Confirm with letter.

CASE EXAMPLE #4:
THE CONVINCING STALLER

Background: The following account illustrates a problem we have all faced at one time or another: How to deal with a convincing staller, particularly one whom you've collected from before and who, on the surface, appears capable of satisfying the debt, but chooses to string you along instead of paying.

This case involves a customer who has made numerous promises. The collector has been trying to obtain $4,878.00, 75 days past due. Initially, recovery prospects appear good. The customer had readily admitted ability to pay and agreed to submit immediate full payment. After several defaults, however, it was agreed that the customer would proceed to the Western Union office 15 miles away and wire payment.

Funds still have not been received, and now the collector must bring the claim to a conclusion. Management is becoming restless, and it is beginning to appear as though the debtor is insincere. Here's the "last try" pair of conversations:

Commentary

Debtor:	Hello.
Collector:	Mr. Walsh, this is Mr. Reed of Absolute Priority Processing.
D:	Mr. Reed, I know why you're calling. I'm sorry to have let you down.
C:	Apologies are getting to be a chronic condition with you, Mr. Walsh.
D:	Look, I know this sounds far fetched, but on the way to the telegraph office, my car had a flat tire.

POLITE BUT
SKEPTICAL

C: Yes . . . yes, of course. And the time before that you had no one to watch the store. And the time before that the check you claimed to have mailed was mysteriously shredded in the U.S. Postal system. Mr. Walsh, you have got to be one of the unluckiest men I have ever met.

D: I know it seems I've been dealing off the bottom of the deck, Mr. Reed. but I have the money. It's true that when you first called I didn't have it, but I have succeeded in raising it.

TOUGH,
IMPATIENT
AND UNNECESSARY

C: Then you admit you were just stalling before!

D: Yes, but only because I needed a little time.

C: I will agree time is very important, but it's also important to us at APP. Your failure to pay now will force us to proceed and enforce collection.

D: If you'll just give me until tomorrow afternoon, I'll personally deliver that money to you.

C: After the lack of good faith you've displayed so far, do you really expect me to extend you more time? I've already gone way out for you.

D: Just one more day, that's all I'm asking.

C: Why not today?

D: It's late in the day, and it's a two-hour drive. And I want to deliver the money to you personally. Give me until 4:00 o'clock.

C: Sorry. The best I can do is delay placing this account for collection until noon tomorrow.

D: I appreciate your fairness, Mr. Reed. I'll see you tomorrow.

C: I certainly hope so. Goodbye.

TOMORROW

D: Hello.

*INCREASING
NO-NONSENSE
ATTITUDE
**SARCASTIC

C: Mr. Walsh, this is Mr. Reed of APP. *I called to confirm if you were on your way. It's 11:00 now. **Were you planning to charter a jet?

D: Well . . . uh . . . as a matter of fact, I won't be able to make it. You'll probably think I am lying to you again, but. . . .

SARCASTIC
AND CHALLENGING

C: (Interrupting) Your assumption is correct!

D: . . . but I had borrowed $5,000 from a relative who had just received an inheritance. When I tried to cash the check today, the bank said it was uncollected funds.

C: (Heatedly) Walsh, yesterday you specifically stated you had the money, didn't you?

D: Well, yes but. . . .

C: In other words, you stalled me again, didn't you?

D: Now wait a minute. I wouldn't exactly say that.

C: Well I would. I'm sorry, but I can't justify delaying this any longer. You've abused and taken advantage of our efforts to resolve this amicably. You have forced me to take immediate steps to protect my interests.

D: Wait, Mr. Reed, I think you should know that this morning I applied to the SBA for $5000.00. I'm to pick up the money this afternoon. I'll see that it's in your hands by 4:00. At least that should show you I'm trying.

C: You're like the boy who cried wolf once too often, Mr. Walsh. No one's listening any more. I'm sorry, but you'll have to deal with our collection agency. Good-bye.

Important: Be sure to record both conversations in the collection file, before referring it to the collection agency. Obviously, no written confirmation is needed.

HOW TO IMPROVE YOUR TELEPHONE TECHNIQUE

Checking your effectiveness against these increasingly urgent conversations can help you to improve your own telephone technique. But there are other ways, too. One way is to keep a "collector's weekly status and self-improvement" report, like the following:

COLLECTOR'S WEEKLY STATUS
AND
SELF-IMPROVEMENT REPORT

Problem Areas

I need guidance when dealing with the following types of situations:

A.   Customers who are "not in" or "in a meeting"

B.   Those who say "the check is in the mail"

C.   Those who don't return calls

D.   Those who take unauthorized discounts

Events of Interest to Management

    A.   Sales leads

    B.   Credit-line review requests

    C.   Potential problems observed

    D.   Management change reported

Call analysis is another way the collector can improve—and not only make effective calls, but make a large number of them as well. Sometimes such self-discipline is required as to warrant the presence of an egg timer right beside the telephone. This way the collector can be sure that all is said and done before the last grain of sand flows from top to bottom! It's a little intimidating at first, but it does get the job done, and it does make people cognizant of the time they spend on the phone.

The "Personal Collection Work Sheet" (see Figure 6-1) can assist the collector, as well as management, in observing the volume of activity—while at the same time enabling the collector to observe his own effectiveness.

Naturally the columns or headings can be varied depending on your particular position, and the type of activity within your department that actually take place.

Stonewalling: How To Use It, And When

The collector should never be affected by emotion, his own or a customer's; and as a safeguard should employ what is commonly known as "stonewalling." This is a defensive technique that a collector can employ when a customer is either looking for an argument, just for the sake of it, or continually bringing up subject matter the collector does not wish to discuss. By refusing to participate in such conversation, an astute collector can make the customer feel he is talking to a stone wall.

How it works: While the customer tries to start or continue an argument, the collector maintains silence, or tries to turn the conversation back to the reason for the call—the collection of the account. Should the customer continue, the collector continues too. Eventually, the customer gets the idea that talking to the collector

PERSONAL COLLECTION WORK SHEET

	Beg. Inventory	No. of Attempted Phone Calls	No. of Completed Phone Calls	No. of New Accounts Received	No. of Takeover Files	No. of Checks Received	No. of Accounts Paid	No. of Accounts Forwarded	Misc.	Ending Inventory
MONDAY										
TUESDAY										
WEDNESDAY										
THURSDAY										
FRIDAY										

Figure 6-1

this way is like talking to a stone wall, at which point the collector can pick up the conversation where he left off—and try to complete the call in a friendlier fashion.

This technique is usually successful, since the customer has vented his anger and has gotten what's been bothering him off his mind. At this point, he will usually be responsive and get down to matters at hand.

LAWS AND REGULATIONS TO KEEP IN MIND

''Third party'' collectors whose principal business purpose is the collection of consumer debts must take special care to comply with the Fair Debt Collection

Practices Act. Third-party debt collectors engaged in the collection of *commercial* accounts, on the other hand, must stay within the ethical standards set forth by the Commercial Collection Agency section of the Commercial Law League of America.

However, when using the telephone to collect your own accounts receivable, there are practices that should be avoided—to obtain best results and avoid unnecessary problems. The following guidelines, then, describe what not to do when using the telephone for collection.

GUIDELINES FOR DEBT COLLECTION CALLS

"Third party" debt collection calls, when made in a manner intended to frighten, abuse, torment or harass the debtor, are in violation of Federal law, and of many state laws as well. Specifically forbidden are:

Calls at odd hours of the day or night: These are hours, known to the calling party to be those other than the normal waking hours of the called party (before 9:00 AM and after 8:00 PM in the debtor's area), unless the customer agrees as a mutual convenience.

Repeated calls: Generally, more than two calls per week would be considered inappropriate. This would not include call backs, left word to call, follow-ups of payment promises, or instances where the principal requested an additional call (e.g., was called at place of employment and requested a call back in the evening at home).

Calls to third parties: These should generally be made for the purpose of locating the customer, or when the customer cannot be contacted directly by telephone. Requests by such third parties that no further calls be received, must be honored. Also, this includes calls during which the details of a customer's account are discussed. Failure to comply will be construed as a tariff violation.

Threatening calls: Calls threatening bodily harm or property damage as means of debt collection are prohibited and are in violation of telephone tariffs. Profanity and obscene language are also prohibited.

Calls asserting that credit ratings will be hurt, or legal action is about to be taken: Basically, the criterion should be whether the totality of circumstances indicates such statements were made solely to frighten the customer into paying, or made in good faith to apprise the customer of the possible consequences of continued failure to satisfy the obligation.

A significant indicator would be when the creditor uses such statements solely as a matter of routine to assist in the collection process. Contrariwise, knowledge that the creditor has in the past initiated legal action or reported nonpayment cases to credit bureaus would be significant.

Calls to places of employment: A request by an employer that no further calls be made to the employee at his place of business must always be honored. In addition, the General Business Law provides that it is unlawful to communicate or threaten to communicate the nature of a consumer claim to the customer's employer prior to obtaining final judgment against the customer. Failure to comply with such requests would be construed as a tariff violation by the telephone company.

A bill collector cannot discuss or communicate a consumer debt with anyone except the consumer—unless written consent is obtained from the consumer, or unless under court order. Once a consumer requests not to be contacted further, a collector can make contact one final time to advise the debtor that either no further action will take place, or to inform him of specific action planned.

If a collector knows a consumer is represented by an attorney, then he must contact the attorney and not the customer—unless the customer agrees otherwise.

Watch Out For These Further Stumbling Blocks

Even under the best of circumstances, customers who remain delinquent are apt to be difficult to deal with. At times, collectors, in their frustrated attempts to generate recovery, may be accused by customers of extortion, libel, slander, invasion of privacy, or criminal liability. You should avoid giving a customer an excuse to charge you with any of these. Even if it is denied and disproved, you will have a long delay and a problem on your hands. Mental anguish—a favorite of many super-delinquent customers—is often alleged. A delinquent customer may say a collector has threatened to expose him to his employer or credit group, or may say that he's in fear generated by the use of simulated legal forms.

The showing of "publicly exposed matter," i.e., a letter, which may reflect on the character of the person named therein may run contrary to postal regulations, and may even give rise to a cause of action for libel. Libel, in fact, is perhaps the most frequently raised issue in an effort to prove liability on the part of the collector or his company. While truth may be offered and is generally considered the best defense to libel, there's really no defense in those jurisdictions where invasions of the right of privacy based on "publication" has been violated. In such cases, it is not generally required to show special damages. All that needs to be observed is the direct injury to business, and the requirement for publication may be as simple as communicating it to a typist.

At this point, however, it should be pointed out that the interchange of credit information between legitimate people or businesses that are concerned with the credit-worthiness of a particular customer is viewed as privileged information. Such communication does not normally give rise to liability, nor would its use be considered as "publication."

Examples Of What Would Be Libelous

To charge in writing that a person is a con artist, or to accuse such a person of fraud, or publishing a statement to the effect that a company or a person is insolvent—all of these are libelous "per se."

The key topics to be cautious of concern solvency, character, and credit. Extortion should also be a concern to an over-zealous collector. In that case, however, malice is usually required. Where threats of criminal prosecution based on a bad check, or threats to distribute unfavorable credit information among members of an association that may not be otherwise interested are made, collectors may be found guilty of intending to coerce payment of the account. Of course, you can promise to do what you have a legal right to do, such as retain a lawyer, litigate, take further action, or proceed.

While libel is generally considered the intentional or careless publication of defamatory material, the collector is also cautioned about invading the rights of privacy of the individual. A person's right of privacy is his right to be void of undue and unwanted publicity. Circulating financial information on a customer's status to people with no genuine interest would violate that right. In effect, any time you communicate by telephone or by a collection letter, you run the risk of breaking the law if what you say may tend to disgrace, defame, or hold your customer up to public ridicule—and deprive him (or her) of public confidence and self-esteem.

The collector is therefore urged to use caution in his written communications, including all letters, telegrams, post cards, envelopes, and advertisements. This is not to suggest, however, that a collector should become overly cautious and shy about asking for payment. You have an absolute right to ask for payment on a just debt.

Other libelous situations are: listing the debtor's name in a published group of delinquent accounts, having words or symbols on envelopes or post cards addressed to a delinquent customer indicating that the addressee is a "deadbeat," advertising that the unpaying customer's account will be set up at public auction and the unpaid accounts will be sold to the highest bidder, or leaving a sign, note, etc. at the customer's business or residence that you were there trying to collect money.

Mailing a post card that reflects badly on the character of the addressee—in addition to being potentially libelous—may also violate the postal laws. The U.S. Post Office department has ruled that cards indicating the addressee is being dunned for an account that is past due are generally non-mailable. It has been held that postal cards threatening suit or even legal action, such as garnishment and attachment, fall within this ban. Generally, however, reminders for payment, follow-up on general collection activity, confirmation of indebtedness, do not fall within this prohibition.

Reminder: While the foregoing guidelines refer mostly to what's *in writing*, it's well to keep them in mind in considering what to say on the telephone, too. Don't risk getting a debtor's back up—and making the debt *more* difficult to collect!

Keep Your Objectives In Mind

The telephone collector should never be so busy chopping down the trees that he can't see the forest. He gets plenty of exercise by matching wits with his customers. Consider a verbal wrestling match between a collector and a customer; the collector might be climbing the walls, while the customer is beating around the bush. The collector might attempt throwing his weight around and jumping to conclusions, while the customer is dragging his heels. The collector may be swallowing his pride and bending over backwards, while the customer is running around in circles and pushing his luck. The collector might be trying to climb the ladder of success, while the customer is making mountains out of molehills.

These figures of speech—cliches, really—are nevertheless not far from the actual events that occur on a daily basis. After all, today's collector is facing a growing permissiveness on the part of customers who take advantage of competitive practices—which can break down standard credit terms and create slow payers. As a result, the collector should not accept at face value any allegations about his product, his service, or what his competition does or does not provide. Collections from today's delinquent customers require a discipline appropriate to the quality of what's at stake. And after all, the old adage, "The sale is not complete until the account is collected," is as true today as it was a hundred years ago.

With all the techniques at the disposal of an experienced collector, it still must be pointed out that techniques are just that. They are a collector's tools, a means to an end. Last year, one million drills may have been sold, but the people who bought them didn't want drills; they wanted holes.

As you probably have concluded by now, telephoning customers for payment is not just picking up a phone and saying, "Whoop-de-do, I'd like to have your check." Rather, it is a discipline that must be consistently applied. Once your customers learn that you say what you mean and mean what you say, you'll always be on top of the heap and first to be paid.

Keep in mind that despite the modern collection techniques that are available today and the automation that is anticipated in the near future, there is no machine yet conceived that can replace the telephone collector. Sure, a machine can print out lists of accounts to be collected, send dunning notices to those accounts, and perform any number of ministerial tasks, but there is no machine now—or likely to be created—that can enter into a dialogue with a customer and indulge in a give-and-take exchange necessary to generate paid-in-full results.

Bolstering Your Efforts With A Follow-Up System

With all of its advantages, though, telephone collecting still has one serious and inherent flaw: You can get all the promises, arrangements, explanations you desire, but there is no way you can be certain that the customer will actually do what he's promised. So, to be genuinely effective, a telephone collection effort must be bolstered by a prompt and determined follow-up system.

What to do: When a customer promises payment, place the account for follow up in your filing system on the date payment is due. If a promised payment date is more than five days away, prepare a reminder letter. This letter could be sent on the date of the call, or alternately, sent so as to arrive a few days *before* the date the check is to be sent. Then, if the check doesn't come in on time—call *again!*

The following outline of a typical collection call shows the sequence of events that are likely to occur as a collector engages in his daily activity. Naturally, the events may vary based on corporate policy, collection policy, or events peculiar to a specific company or its customers.

To make this chart fit your organization, you may of course disregard any steps not applicable to your operations, and add at the appropriate notch any missing procedures that are part of your collection effort. The result will be a useful outline designed specifically for your company.

OUTLINE OF
THE COLLECTION CALL

1. Review your credit file.

2. Plan your call.

3. Have all the facts ready—How much is due, what it is for, how old, account history, prior collection efforts.

4. Have all tools ready.

5. Make the call—be prepared to take control.

The Opening Of The Call

6. Be positive; the "you" attitude.

7. Identify the person with whom you are speaking as a decision maker.

8. Identify yourself and your company.

9. State the reason for your call.

Body Of The Call

10. Ask for payment in full. Create a sense of urgency.

11. Make a strategic pause.

12. Disregard the initial reason for not having paid yet.

13. Be positive. Ask how you can help the customer.

14. Control the conversation, but do not overtalk the debtor.

15. Ask questions. Does the customer need time to pay? If so, obtain a letter of commitment, promissory notes, or post-dated checks.

16. Listen closely.

17. Get full information.

18. Classify debtor and identify problem, if any.

19. Stress areas of agreement.

20. Narrow the issues and isolate areas of disagreement.

21. Sell benefits and control the direction of the discussion.

22. Don't argue. Be assertive, not aggressive.

23. Overcome possible customer objections.

24. Reassure debtor that he/she is making the right decision to pay promptly.

25. Offer debtor alternative repayment programs as possible solutions.

26. Develop the art of doing what is possible. Be sure arrangement is doable, not out of reach.

How To Close A Call

27. Make it easy for the debtor to say "yes."

28. Have the debtor write your address down and repeat it to you.

29. Review terms and summarize arrangement; dramatize importance of keeping agreement.

30. Reassure debtor that you are counting on him/her to keep the commitment.

31. Transfer important data to collection file.

32. Set disciplined follow-up date to determine if check was mailed.

How Telephone Collections Efforts Can Be More Effective Than Written Ones

Proper use of the telephone enables you to vary your approach to fit the particular personality of the customer. Naturally, the variety of circumstances will require a collector to be resilient and to be able to deal with different circumstances and people from all walks of life. Statements that may appear to be cold and without empathy in a black-and-white written communication, can lose much of their harshness if transmitted by a friendly voice over the telephone. Tension, like composure, is contagious. So proper poise is always necessary. A collector must learn to be at ease in all types of situations.

Common sense requires that an individual be steady and cool as opposed to excitable. Having a helpful, frank, sincere, honest, and ethical attitude along with good timing will enable you to at least start off correctly. Matters that could not be written without danger of libel or slander may be safely talked about over the telephone. And it is easier to make a very strong appeal for money without the possibility of offending your customer. With good talent, tact, technique and timing, you are in a position to generate the greatest recoveries for your company.

How A Customer Service Call Can Help

Some suppliers have had outstanding success from the "telephone service call" made *in advance* of a bill's due date. The collector under such conditions plays the role of a "customer service representative," inquiring if the product or service was received in good order, while at the same time making himself available for any further assistance or clarification that should be necessary. Of course, the representative should say: "By the way, our invoice was previously sent to you under separate cover, and we presume that you have found it in order and that it is being processed for payment. Is that correct?''

Where balances warrant such attention (and where time permits), this type of telephone call can go a long way toward reducing outstanding receivables—even to a point where they are paid before they fall due. Such a practice is especially effective when used in connection with special services that might be provided to major corporations, or where specific type of authorization must be obtained before bills can be approved for payment. In addition, this pre-collection customer service call may nip in the bud any dispute that may later arise to delay payment.

Going a step further: Suppose, in certain situations, even the best and most carefully prepared telephone collection techniques don't get results. Before considering turning an account over to a collection agency or attorney, there's one more approach that's worth a try: *face-to-face* collecting.

COLLECTING FACE TO FACE

Of all the techniques available to collectors involved in the collection of consumer or commercial debts, nothing can be more difficult (or more effective!) than personally visiting the account and interviewing the customer. While collectors involved in secured transactions, and banks too, frequently are required to see their collateral and service their loans, customers still view the outside call as an unusual collection procedure. That's likely to give it special meaning in the mind of a debtor. Naturally, timing also plays an important role, in that the collector should try to arrive at the customer's residence or place of business when it is likely that the customer will have funds available. When does the customer get paid, or when are the customer's accounts receivable likely to be paying him? It's important to consider this carefully.

Personal visits by collectors, while usually reserved for very large or serious collection problems because of the cost involved, often bring about the best results of all. This is because you get an opportunity to meet with customers, see their operations, and get first-hand insight into what problems they may be experiencing. It is also an excellent way to provide customer counseling, and is a good opportunity to see what potential for future business exists.

Sometimes you can even assist the customer in putting into place procedures from your first-hand experience that would be more effective if adopted by the customer—a new bank affiliation, a different loan structure, better collection procedure, personnel cost control, or the like. Most customers are also willing to show off their operations and give you an opportunity to comment on their strengths and weaknesses.

In a real sense, the personal visit can be the culmination of the entire collection effort. It enables you to say face to face what you could say on the phone, or what you would like to say by letter—but because you are there, you're guaranteed to get the customer's attention.

Pre-Visit Planning

There's a lot more to a personal visit than just holding out your hand and expecting your customer to give you payment. Pre-visit planning must be done so you're sure that you have all the necessary information that might be required during the visit. A complete understanding of the customer's payment history as well as the indebtedness is necessary.

In addition, you should determine your specific objectives and set out the guidelines for whatever compromise would not be acceptable by management, so that you appear to be in complete control and with full authority in the event that an on-the-spot decision must be made.

Working Out Reasonable Arrangements

Depending on what time during your collection cycle you make your personal visit, it will make a significant difference as to just how much counseling or how much collection effort will be necessary. Many companies only employ an outside call after everything else in their arsenal of tactics (reminders, requests, appeals, demands, phone calls, telegrams, mailgrams, etc.) has been used.

If the visit is your last resort, it's unlikely that the customer is going to hand you full payment just because you showed up. Therefore, it's important that you develop *the art of doing the possible*, and try to work out reasonable arrangements that are both doable by the customer and acceptable to you as the collector. "Offer reaching" (asking for too much) may create a default and eventually force the customer's other creditors to come down hard, and prevent the arrangement from being adhered to.

While your desire is to obtain full payment each and every time, when such is not possible, you should try to obtain a current payment for as much money as is available, and a specific commitment to retire the balance through installments, supported by post-dated check(s), promissory note(s), a letter of intent, and/or personal guarantees if warranted and possible to obtain. This is standard collection procedure, of course.

The collector must also be in a position to discuss what, if any, future business relationship would exist. Naturally, at what volume and at what terms is dependent upon the type of arrangement the collector is able to extract from the customer.

The collector has the upper hand, of course. He has the advantage of knowing that the customer's failure to satisfy the indebtedness is likely to mean further and more unpleasant enforcement of the collection effort. This could include severing any future business relationship, and perhaps repossession of collateral or merchandise, or legal action.

How To Make The Most Of Every Visit

While at the customer's home or office, the collector is in a position to observe the character of the customer. How does he keep his home or office? What type of neighborhood? The opportunity to meet with the customer provides the collector with invaluable insight into just what makes the customer tick, and how best to get a handle on what's likely to motivate him to pay.

If payment terms are to be negotiated on such a visit, try to obtain, in addition, all available financial information or a look at the cash receipt and disbursement journals, to get a good feel for what's coming in and what's going out, and where it's going. For an individual, a disbursement journal or the equivalent might be his paycheck stub and his checkbook.

The collector should be certain to *stress the urgency* and the unusual nature of the visit, so that the customer realizes that this concerted effort to bring the account current may be the last chance to resolve it amicably.

While some collectors have resorted to suggesting that customers borrow from friends or relatives, often this proves embarrassing (the customer is not likely to admit that he doesn't have a friend or relative that's willing to help). And the reaction to this could be belligerence. Remember, you are on the customer's "home turf," and once resentment builds, and lines of communication are cut, collection becomes impossible.

The collector's role in the personal interview is not much different from the role playing being done by a stage actor. The success is all in the casting. Therefore, the *quality of the people* is going to make the difference. A truly investigative collector will be a valuable asset, even if money is not collected on the account, as information regarding the best course of action to take can be attained by the visit.

Collectors occasionally encounter a problem where the customer tries to be too friendly. In order to maintain the strategic advantage, however, you must maintain your distance and avoid becoming the customer's pal, drinking partner, or buddy. (That rule should be followed even after the account is paid.)

RECAP: It is important to remember that you're competing for the customer's cash; the customer is probably paying someone, so it might as well be you. You therefore must establish yourself as the number-one priority. A personal visit is the best way to do that. However, as a technique, it is usually considered a last resort because of the cost.

WHAT ABOUT SALES PEOPLE AS COLLECTORS?

In many companies, collectors are not encouraged to visit with valued customers. This activity, in such companies, is primarily the responsibility of the sales representative. Some companies even believe that sales representatives who are already familiar with the customer may be in a better position to gather information and to get a customer's cooperation in obtaining payment than the collector, who has had no prior contact. Furthermore, the sales representative, usually already on the outside, can make the same visit at far less cost than would be incurred if the collector had to leave the office.

Whether to employ sales representatives as collection agents for seriously delinquent accounts is something that only your particular management policy can determine. There are conflicting considerations. On the one hand, sales management may claim that collection personnel are prone to regard any interview merely as an opportunity to cross-examine the customer regarding his business, and how to collect from it. On the other hand, collection personnel may claim that the sales person may feel he (she) must continue to retain the customer's good will and may tend to view the customer as his (her) personal client, not a company client, and be reluctant to say anything or do anything that might alter that relationship and dilute that personal contact.

It's true that probably no one has a more personal relationship with the account than the sales representative. It is therefore easier for him or her to approach the customer. However, the use of sales people as collectors cuts deeply into available interview time which could diminish sales performance. On the other hand, collecting the account or bringing it current may promote a more timely reorder.

Many company managers, however, want their sales people to be well-rounded business executives, and believe that the sale isn't complete until the account is collected. Those managers believe that, because of a personal relationship, the sales representative will be able to influence the customer to pay the account, making the most of friendships and personal relationships that take so long to build!

Can the sales representative effectively pre-plan the call, gather all the credit factors necessary to make an on-the-spot decision, consistent with good judgment and financial know-how? As noted, there are merits to both sides of the argument.

How To Get Effective Results Using The "Joint Approach"

Perhaps the best approach is a joint approach. Consider the advisability of asking a sales representative to make a joint call with you. Once the introductions are completed and the small talk set aside, the sales person can remove himself before the financial discussion begins. This "team effort" can produce the most effective results, by gathering the greatest strengths of each individual and placing them in their proper roles.

Reminder: In order to maintain that team spirit on an ongoing basis, it is important that communication between the two departments be on open channel—and frequent. Each should keep the other informed of major changes in a customer's status. Financial changes may either impede or assist the future growth of a customer, and both the collector and the field sales representative are in a position to obtain factual information on an ongoing basis.

In some cases, a joint meeting may prove too costly or difficult to arrange. And under such conditions, if a personal visit is to be considered as a viable alternative, the sales person should still be an important consideration, as some visit is usually better than no visit. At times, the collector may even arrange to have checks picked up by the regular sales representative (or by a different representative if there's more than one sales person in the territory).

By tapping the knowledge of the sales force, and effectively using their local proximity and customer knowledge, you are likely to make the most of a collection program that gets results without unnecessarily ruffling the feathers of your valued customers. Some people may still believe that *selling* and *collecting* are as incompatible as oil and water; but by properly channeling the effectiveness of each, a collector can obtain the best results for his company.

To Visit, Or Not To Visit

The decision on whether to visit a customer, either with or without a sales representative, can only be made after careful consideration. Keep in mind the following:

1. The nature of the company's position in the marketplace.

2. The location of its customers.

3. The quality of its sales representatives.

4. The size of its accounts receivable on an individual basis, or all of its outstanding receivables, the extent to which it experiences chronic delinquency, what its competition does, and its cost of goods sold.

That which is successful for one company may not work for another, as the procedures that worked best in a given organization usually fit that company's specific needs. However, you should be in a position to design and evaluate the best course of action to take in a given circumstance.

THE VALUE OF BRINGING UP THE "BIG GUNS"

The use of non-collection personnel in a collection effort is also sometimes helpful. Occasionally, a Treasurer, Controller, or Credit Officer will get involved in an important account. It may be specific policy of a company to do so when the indebtedness involves a certain dollar amount. While usually such activity is reserved for "jumbo" exposures, occasionally, in order to lend a degree of importance and show the customer that management is concerned with their account, such executive personnel will intercede—in either a passive or active way.

If used properly, this alternate technique can have positive effects, as long as it does not undermine the collection effort contemplated. Whether it be a Treasurer, Controller, or even company President that intercedes, each should be cautioned not to intimidate its own collector and deviate from the planned activity. The same rules and collection discipline must apply.

REPORTING TO MANAGEMENT

When it is necessary for a collector to make a report concerning his collection activity, often it is not desirable to hold the entire collection file—although that would be the best source of exactly what took place. However, when a review is required so that management understands what steps were taken to enforce payment, a "Collector's Report" (Figure 6-2) is a good idea. This means further efforts can pick up where the collector left off, and not duplicate collection tactics previously employed.

COLLECTOR'S REPORT

Account Name _____   Date _____

Street Address _____

City and State _____

Customer's Phone No. _____

How Long Have We Sold This Account? _____

Indicate below the number of times you have contacted the account relative to the past-due balance and the procedures you followed:

1. Form letters sent _____

2. Individual letters sent _____

3. Telegrams sent _____

4. No. of telephone calls _____ (type) _____

5. Reaction of customer to your telephone calls:

_____

_____

_____

6. Other collection procedures followed (i.e., personal visit):

_____

_____

_____

7. Reasons for recommending further collection action:

_____

_____

_____

Signed _____

Approved _____

FIGURE 6-2

7

Special Collection Situations, And How To Handle Them

Table of Contents

7

Special Collection Situations, And How To Handle Them

COLLECTING FROM STOCKHOLDERS
FOR CORPORATE DEBTS

Your debtor goes out of business, but is your claim against the company uncollectible? You may be able to collect *something*—if you handle things right. Many companies just fade away and go out of business leaving millions of dollars of unpaid obligations without filing any formal insolvency proceeding. While principals of partnerships and proprietorships remain personally responsible for their obligations, they limit stockholder liability by incorporating. That is its primary purpose.

The easiest cases, surprisingly, are those where the stockholders embark upon a fraudulent scheme to defeat the rights of creditors. Where such could be established, and fraud could be proven, the courts in the past have had no hesitancy in "piercing the corporate veil."

There are no fixed rules, though, from which you can predict with absolute accuracy when a court will make such a judicial determination. Whether a corporate entity should be set aside on the theory that it is being used as a shield is a triable issue. Often, there must be a combination of circumstances, such as a lack of adequate financial or business records, common officers and directors between two corporations, manipulation, insider deals and under-capitalization—or any combination of the foregoing. That would include related corporations, subsidiaries and parent corporations.

On occasion, a group of individuals will start off as partners, and subsequently incorporate without notice to their creditors. They will continue to conduct business as a partnership, and creditors will continue to rely on their personal assets as the basis for credit approval. Checks may be passed without any indication that a corporation exists. In that case as well, it must be proved that the individuals were nothing more than an alter ego of the corporation, and that the corporation was a sham designed to execute abuses upon creditors.

The following list represents the most frequent abuses to which creditors are subjected:

1. Draining off of assets

2. Paying unwarranted dividends to the principals

3. Repaying loans that were subordinated

4. Under-capitalizing or setting up a "thin" corporation

5. Embarking on a business enterprise that will expose the corporation to financial risks, many times in excess of what the paid-in capital would warrant

6. Concealment of assets

7. Payment of personal obligations with corporate checks

8. Total disregard for corporate formalities

How To Protect Yourself

Often it is necessary for creditors to obtain a copy of the corporate charter, the names and addresses of stockholders, the amount of stock held by each, and the initial contribution made by each stockholder. In addition to obtaining financial statements issued at various times during the operating period, you should seek out names and addresses of bookkeepers and accountants, copies of corporate tax returns and corporate loan accounts, and a review of the books and records. You'll want to learn the salaries paid to key personnel, along with benefits, credit cards, travel, entertainment, etc. In any matter where substantial dollars are involved, it will undoubtedly be necessary to consider employment of an accountant for the purpose of examining the corporate receipts and disbursement journals, sales ledgers, tax returns, and if possible to get a total audit.

Can You Impose Personal Liability?

There are only a limited number of instances where creditors can legitimately impose personal liability on corporate stockholders. In some states and under certain conditions, creditors have been able to hold authorized signatures on unpaid corporate checks or notes personally liable for the unpaid item, because the signer failed to sign the corporate title after his or her name. However, be sure to consult competent counsel before considering any such action.

In any instance where you try to impose personal liability and such action might be theoretically justified, it is probably not advisable to maintain an action—unless you are willing to spend a sum of money considerably in excess of that which you would spend for a normal collection case. Discovery alone could consume 15 to 20 hours, in addition to which you should expect to advance the necessary expenses for accountants as well as the cost of depositions. However, where an account is substantial and you're willing to spend the extra funds, serious thought ought to be given to whether to proceed with litigation—in an effort to "pierce the corporate veil" and impose personal liability on the stockholders of a corporation.

COLLECTING AS A SECURED CREDITOR UNDER THE UNIFORM COMMERCIAL CODE

If anything can be said about Article 9 of the UCC, it's that it would best be called a *non-uniform* commercial code. Its interpretation—and even its language—vary widely in different states. As a result, courts in various jurisdictions from time to time have reached various decisions on how Article 9 should be interpreted.

Types Of Agreements

The simplest type of security agreement is the pledge of collateral. A creditor can simply take possession of collateral and hold it until the debt which it is securing has been paid. While the pledge is used regularly in the ordinary course of business, it is not a practical method for perfecting security in property, such as cars or business assets, needed by companies to operate. Thus, the pledge is something used when a negotiable instrument is to be collateral. Items like stocks or bonds or certificates of deposit are often held by banks for just that purpose. As far as Article 9 is concerned, chattel mortgages (giving a lien on the collateral), equipment trusts, assignments of receivables, conditional sales contracts, all fall under the umbrella of "secured interest," and are treated similarly within the provisions of Article 9.

What's Excluded From The Article 9 Umbrella

Before going forward to determine what makes a security agreement valid, let's look at what is *excluded* from coverage in Article 9:

1. Landlord's real estate liens;

2. Mechanic's liens such as those given for service or materials;

3. Security agreements regulated by Federal statutes;

4. Assignments of wages;

5. Equipment liens on railway stock;

6. The transfer or assignment of contracts or accounts receivable in the normal course of business;

7. A judgment lien; a right of set-off;

8. The creation or transfer of a lien on real estate;

9. The transfer of an account maintained at a bank, savings and loan association, or similar organization;

10. A lease—if it is just a lease and nothing more.

With respect to this last point, if it looks like a sale, sounds like a sale, acts like a sale, begins like a sale and ends like a sale, even if you call it a "lease," it's still a sale. Usually such situations are dependent upon the final terms of the lease. If there's an option to purchase for a substantial amount of money, courts are likely to view the agreement as a lease. On the other hand, if the purchase price is nominal, courts are likely to believe it was a sale.

Leases for equipment should therefore contain a landlord waiver, and a clear sticker on the equipment that identifies it as the property of the leasor. In addition, a UCC-1 filing should be made in the county where the property is located, as well as the office of the Secretary of State.

HOW TO VALIDATE THE
SECURITY AGREEMENT

The first stage of determining the validity of a security agreement has to do with what is commonly referred to as "attachment." Article 9 recognizes the moment of creation of this interest lien as the point at which the secured party's interest in the collateral becomes protected. This is know as the "point of attachment." The requisites for attachment are:

1. There must be a written agreement between the parties to create a security interest;

2. The creditor must give consideration in return for the agreement;

3. The debtor must have rights in the collateral and not be in violation of the Statute of Frauds.

Once it is determined that a security agreement has attached, at what point can your position be effective against others, and how will a court prioritize who and what comes first? Basically, security agreements are valid against everyone—but a security agreement, in addition to having to attach, must be *perfected*. Perfection takes place when the secured creditor takes possession of the collateral or files financing statements as required in the specific state jurisdiction.

Security Agreement Priority

The general rule of priority is that the first interest perfected is first in line, but there are exceptions to even that. Where two unperfected security agreements are competing for first position, the first to have attached will prevail. Where one has attached and one has attached and filed, the first to have filed takes precedence.

Another way to perfect in accordance with Article 9 is called "automatic perfection," which requires neither filing nor perfection. A purchase money security interest (PMSA), a security interest relating to most consumer goods, is perfected without filing and without the creditor's taking possession of the collateral. Even so, a filing should always take place—as a buyer without knowledge of the security interest might otherwise take possession of the collateral for his own personal use. (This protection is afforded only to consumers, giving them priority over perfected but unfiled collateral liens.)

A *general purchase money security interest*, to secure all or part of the price of what has been sold (or to provide money consideration to a debtor who used that consideration to acquire rights in a collateral, in a commercial transaction) may not enjoy the same priority. There's even an exception for consumers: a motor vehicle must be registered, and if fixtures are involved, a filing is required. This is to be certain that priority can be determined.

After-acquired property provisions are frequently part of security agreements. This is especially true in the case of inventory or accounts receivable liens, or where the creditor wants the debtor to acquire future assets as a means of securing its debt. Once again, the concept does not apply to consumer goods other than goods that bear a relationship to the principal collateral, such as an improvement on the original collateral.

The Proceeds Of Secured Collateral

Another term frequently associated with security agreements concern a security interest in *"proceeds."* Proceeds are what the debtor receives upon disposing of the secured collateral. Without such an interest, if the debtor sells the collateral, a creditor may remain unprotected.

Generally under the Code, a secured party retains interest in "proceeds" for at least ten days, regardless of whether or not proceeds are claimed in the financing statement. After ten days, perfection in what is now a new collateral may be required.

Other types of security agreements that are *automatically perfected* include assignment of accounts that do not involve a significant part of the outstanding accounts, and contracts of the assignor. A security agreement in a negotiable document is automatically perfected for a 21-day period, starting from the time of attachment. It is presumed that during that time, the creditor will be able to obtain possession and formally perfect the agreement.

FILING THE AGREEMENT

Recording the agreement is, in effect, providing for public notice that you have an interest in collateral. The mailing addresses of the creditor and debtor are required, along with the signature of each. The UCC-1 form (or alternatively, the entire security agreement) may be filed. The financing statement, however, must contain a detailed description of the collateral. Most of all, since this is a record for public notice, it must show the name or names exactly.

Most commonly, the documents are filed with the county official where the property is located, as well as with the office of the Secretary of State in which the property is located. However, if uncertainty exists, it is advisable to ask competent counsel to review the agreement so that you can be sure you are properly protected.

The *statute of limitations*, generally speaking, tolls within five years, or with the maturity of the obligation if that is shorter. The exception is usually filing on fixtures, or where the debtor goes into bankruptcy. Where there is a five-year limit, a continuation agreement may be recorded so as to keep the lien in effect. The continuation agreement need only be signed by the secured party. Because of the five-year limitation, there should be a method for monitoring the due dates.

The Creditor's Right To "Peaceful Possession"

As far as the collector is concerned, all this collateral often has little meaning until the debtor is in default. But Article 9 is very specific about the secured creditor's rights to possession of collateral in such cases. It says that unless the creditor and debtor involved in the transaction otherwise agree, the secured creditor has the right to take possession of the property without judicial process—so long as it is done peaceably. Hence the term, "peaceful possession."

Assuming the collector is successful in his quest, now there's the problem of what to do with the collateral. Naturally, both the creditor and debtor would like to obtain the best possible sale price. Article 9 provides that a secured creditor can sell collateral following default, but only in a manner deemed "commercially reasonable.'' A creditor would not, for example, be permitted to sell thousands of dollars worth of assets on which it has a lien, solely to satisfy a few hundred dollars' delinquency. The creditor must also give reasonable notice of its intent to sell the collateral to all persons who have given notice that they have a claim.

In the event the collateral is not sufficient to liquidate the indebtedness, a creditor may be entitled to a deficiency judgment against the debtor. In cases involving consumer goods, a secured party in possession can propose to retain the collateral in satisfaction of the obligation, but must give written notice of the intent to do so to the debtor.

To summarize, the two problems the collector is likely to encounter most frequently in attempting recovery are: 1. in obtaining collateral as further security, and 2. in attempting to obtain payment from a debtor whose assets now are the subject to security agreements of another party. In each case, you should be certain that the filing is proper, and seek the assistance of an attorney when further advice and clarification are required.

COLLECTING FREIGHT CLAIMS

When it is your responsibility to request a proof of delivery, or to file a claim against a freight carrier for a lost or damaged shipment, the letter shown on page 711 can be very useful. Not only does it ask the carrier to supply proof of delivery, but it also serves notice of your claim for the loss.

This filing is important. There is usually a nine-month limitation (from date of shipment) on filing claims against a freight carrier.* UPS requires that claims be filed within six months.

Your customer may wait months before asking you to supply proof of delivery on a particular shipment. If more than one carrier is involved, it may take several more weeks until actual proof of delivery (if available) has been sent to you. By then, the time to file may have expired. Your letter stays the Statute of Limitations.

---

*Note: Time limitations can vary from carrier to carrier. The bill of lading will control in each situation. Some carriers may state on their bill of lading that claims or intent to file claims must be made within 90 days of delivery. The bill of lading may also have maximum stated limits on liability. Careful reading of the bill of lading is essential in each case, to protect your interest properly. As is the case with your customer, "Know your carrier!"

REQUEST FOR PROOF OF DELIVERY
AND FILING OF FREIGHT CLAIM

TO: (Carrier)
      Name
      Address
      City & State

ATT: Tracing Department

Gentlemen:

Please furnish proof of delivery for the following shipment(s):
    Shipped from _____ to _____

    Consigned to: _____ Name & Address _____

    Date Shipped _____ Invoice No. _____

    No. of cartons _____ Invoice date _____

    B/L # (or B/L date) _____ Amount $ _____

    Weight _____

Copies of the original bill of lading, invoice and paid freight bill are enclosed.

If we do not receive the requested proof of delivery within 15 business days, we will assume you are unable to prove delivery.

Accordingly, please accept this letter and the documents enclosed as formal filing of our claim in the amount of $ _____ as detailed on the invoice. Please acknowledge receipt by signing a copy of this letter and returning it in the self-addressed envelope provided.

                    Very truly yours,

When proof of delivery is not provided and your subsequent claim is denied, the bill of lading may also provide a time limit within which a legal action must be filed. Usually, you have two years and one day from the time your claim is denied to bring an action. However, time limits may vary with each carrier. Therefore, when you encounter such situations, you should look at what is stated on the bill of lading and consult with your attorney.

COLLECTING FROM THE MILITARY

The Soldiers And Sailors Civil Relief Act

The Soldiers and Sailors Civil Relief Act applies to all persons in the Armed Forces of the United States, including the Coast Guard—as well as personnel in other government services detailed on duty with the Armed Forces. The law is in effect throughout the U.S.A., and affects the collection of accounts, suits and enforcement of judgments and other civil remedies pursued against debtors. The right to enforce obligations or liability is suspended by reason of military service. While such suspension primarily applies to direct liability, the court in its discretion may also afford such protection to service people who acted as *guarantors*.

To assure protection of service personnel where an action has been filed and a default judgment is about to be entered, a plaintiff is required to file an affidavit of non-military service. Where an action has been previously filed or judgment previously entered, the court may stay any action while the person is in the service and for three months thereafter.

The scope of possible litigation is too broad to cover here, but it is important to note that many stay orders are at the discretion of the court—such as mortgage foreclosure or a lien on merchandise in storage.

In the case of an installment contract or conditional sale, in order for the contract to afford protection to the service person, a deposit on the purchase must have been made before service entry. This would prevent the collector from repossessing property or accelerating a default. Such benefits are also afforded dependents of people in the military service; and accordingly, there can be a stay against foreclosure and repossession of property (with the discretion of the court).

Various states have also enacted laws suspending the enforcement of certain litigation and granting special rights to service personnel. However, local law may provide for a waiver of these rights. Such a waiver would acknowledge the existence of the Soldiers and Sailors Civil Relief Act, make reference to an original purchase, and detail the existence of a contract. This would mean permitting the seller peaceful repossession of the property or retention of the property. (Naturally, any such agreement should be prepared by counsel and comply with local law.)

A confirmation certificate stating that an individual is in the military may be obtained from: the Adjutant General of the United States Army; the Chief of Naval Personnel; or the Marine Corps Commandant. The certificate signed by officers of each of the armed service departments represent evidence that a person is or has been in military service. It will show the time and place when such a person entered the service, the residence used at the time, the rank obtained, in addition to the information concerning discharge or death.

Special Help For The Collector

The Department of Defense has set up conditions under which it will give assistance in the collection of debts from members of the Armed Forces. The Department maintains a standard directive that servicemen/women are expected to pay their debts and conduct themselves in a moral fashion. Nevertheless, the military has no legal authority to *require* a member of the service to pay.

Military departments have assisted collectors on occasion by having a commanding officer speak with the debtor in regard to the matter. The collector who deals regularly in the collection of debts from service personnel should obtain a copy of the necessary forms to set the process in motion.

A collector can obtain a lot of information from a non-military service request, as the reply is likely to include the last known residence of the individual before induction. A collector may also take advantage of a locater service by writing to the previously mentioned Departments of the Armed Service for the address of the individual.

The following addresses of the various departments of the military are provided for the collector as a handy reference when seeking to locate military personnel.

World Wide Locater Service is available. You must provide the person's name and date of birth or social security number, and address your letter as follows:

U.S. MARINE CORP

Worldwide Locater
CMC Military Services Records Bureau (MSRB)
H.Q. U.S. Marine Corps
Washington, DC 20380
202-694-1610

U.S. NAVY

The Navy Locater Service
NO 21
Washington, DC 20370
202-694-3155

U.S. ARMY

Commander U.S. Army
Enlisted Records & Evaluation Center
Fort Benjamin Harrison, Indiana 46249

U.S. AIR FORCE

World Wide Locater
Air Force NPC/D003
Randolph Air Force Base
Texas, 78150
512-652-5774

COLLECTING FROM MINORS

A minor in most states is an individual under the age of 18, although marriage may affect this. Where a particular creditor's product is likely to be purchased by minors, a serious problem may result for the collection personnel. A minor may refuse to honor the agreement, and if so, there's not much that can be done.

The laws protecting minors may be different in each state. In some instances where the property is still in the possession of the minor, if payment is not made, the property must be returned. If that is no longer possible, however, no payment need be made. Companies doing business with this age group are likely to be proceeding at their own risk.

In general, though, the rule is that while a minor is permitted to repudiate a contract or agreement made for personal use, a minor *engaged in business* remains responsible for the debts incurred in the conduct of that business. If merchandise is ordered and received (or service is rendered in a business situation), a minor cannot change his or her mind and decide not to pay because of being under age. Such a minor is considered "emancipated."

INTERNATIONAL COLLECTIONS

There has been substantial growth in foreign trade as a result of what is commonly referred to as "multi-national corporate activity." Today, more and more companies target their products to foreign markets as a new affluence developed among third-world countries.

In spite of the creditworthiness of many businesses, exporting companies usually require that goods be paid for either in advance, or simultaneously with pick-up. As a result, the percentage of bad debts in foreign trade may actually be lower than what may be experienced domestically. Despite the variety of financing arrangements, international trade creditors are rather restrictive, and credit practices are extremely conservative. This conservatism is supported by several intermediaries that may be involved in completing the transaction—such as bankers, insurance companies, freight forwarders, and export brokers or agents.

If a company is working on a high profit margin, the rate of foreign exchange currency fluctuations is likely to prove relatively unimportant. Alternatively, fluctuations could prove extremely meaningful where the margin of profit is small. Most American export companies bill their sales in U.S. dollars and receive payments in U.S. dollars. However, the continued growth of competition for international sales will most likely result in a loosening of the credit practices, and a willingness to accept payment in the currency of the buyer's country. With that type of transaction, there is absolutely no way of making certain the future value of the currency will be equal to or greater than the current sales price.

What You Can Do To Protect Yourself

In order to protect themselves against currency value fluctuations that are frequently the result of political unrest, government intervention or an unfavorable balance of payments, a company can take a forward contract to hedge against possible losses. Such contracts may be obtained for a discount or a premium price on the "spot" market, and naturally affect the cost of doing business.

The International Monetary Fund (the IMF) was created in an effort to stabilize currency values. The Export-Import Bank, whose purpose it is to support and encourage international trade between U.S. enterprises and other foreign countries, assists by providing loans to those foreign countries, to U.S. manufacturers, and insurance against loss.

In addition to the numerous problems common to domestic collections, international collections problems are compounded by unfamiliar legal systems, language problems, currency fluctuations—and differences of time, distance, and custom. All too often, transactions may take months to complete. (Such transactions can still be very profitable, of course.)

A collector involved on the international scene, however, is likely to observe that there is no meaningful exchange of credit information among banks, mercantile agencies and insurance companies. There are professional inhibitions and legal limitations that restrict the flow of meaningful credit information.

The credit latitude of the banking fraternity in the United States is unknown in most other countries of the world. A bank or any other organization may be sued more quickly for disclosing data that may be viewed by others as unfavorable. As a result, there's a tremendous amount of discretion, which outsiders are likely to find very restrictive. It's no wonder that the greatest majority of international transactions are conducted via letters of credit.

There is a wide diversity in the laws of various countries. Even terms that effect collection judgment, such as the meaning of "corporation" or "partnership," may vary in formality and concept and differ substantially from what a collector has come to know domestically. (Consult trade definitions "Incoterms" compiled by the International Chamber of Commerce, when in doubt.) Foreign tax differences may have consequences that affect balance sheet evaluations, as would depreciation and reserve requirements. Foreign government restrictions may place demands and regulations on operating companies that cannot be easily understood within the U.S. So companies that deal abroad often have pre-arranged agreements with their export agents to pursue collection.

Specific Collection Techniques

When handled internally, initial payment demands should be made by cable, telex, or letter correspondence. A cable is more efficient though, and it cuts down the time delay that would result from routine letter correspondence. The cable or telex is most effective when supplemented by a letter, however. This technique impresses upon the delinquent customer the fact that you're right on top of the situation, and will not tolerate continued default.

Of all the appeals available, foreign customers respond most to the appeal to pride and honor. With a tactful approach, an appeal can be made to the customer's self-interest in honoring the obligation. Most customers wish to avoid the consequences of continued default that would result from having the delinquency reported to a bank, as it may adversely affect the customer's credit rating. In addition, with an unpaid note, draft or negotiable document, a formal protest attesting under oath that the account has not been paid is often enough action to generate payment. Such protests are considered to reflect very poorly on the customer's credit standing.

International collection correspondence should be more personal in nature than domestic correspondence. It should be dictated on a case-by-case basis. Furthermore, heavy use of form letters is not recommended, as there may be language barriers, requiring each letter to be translated. Letters should always be worded so as to maintain the courteous sensitive style to which foreigners have been traditionally more responsive.

Personal visits can usually be arranged through sales agents or sales personnel located in the country of the delinquent debtor. And where cable, telex, or other written correspondence has been ignored, invoking the assistance of local people can prove invaluable as a step toward achieving payment. In fact, foreign representatives are often expected to handle collections on delinquent accounts—in addition to obtaining the credit information required to approve the transaction in the first place.

"Last-Resort" Approaches

When all else fails, assistance from international collection agencies can be sought out. Many of the more prominent national commercial collection agencies have international connections with agents or attorneys in most free-world countries. But this is seldom a good idea. Litigation in the courts of a foreign land will most certainly prove to be a harrowing experience. American creditors quickly discover, much to their chagrin, that the laws of most foreign countries give them little opportunity for success. In addition to the time delays, the fees and costs necessary to generate recovery often make pursuit economically impractical. Compounding the problem even more is the fact that many countries will not honor contractual obligations—unless they are governed by the laws of the country in which the litigation is being pursued.

Arbitration is a viable alternative to the hassles of litigation. The American Arbitration Association, as well as International Trade Associations and the International Chamber of Commerce, maintain panels of arbitrators with established experts and professionals in the field of international business. The parties to a dispute may even select the arbitrators themselves, and determine the place of arbitration and the issues to be resolved.

The arbitration process has been an effective method of resolving disputes with foreign delinquents that otherwise would have resulted in costly litigation and loss of future business.

Rules for the ICC Court of Arbitration may be obtained from the ICC Publishing Corporation, 125 East 23rd Street, New York, New York. The American Arbitration Association rules can be obtained from the International Commercial Arbitration Division at 140 West 51st Street, New York, New York, 10020.

Special Problems—And What To Do About Them

A collector may sometimes encounter currency exchange regulation restrictions in a particular country. In most countries, a foreign customer need only deposit money in its bank to pay the foreign supplier, in order to have the obligation considered legally discharged. However, that country's exchange restrictions may prevent the transfer of funds to the U.S. seller. Such a situation may require the collector to contact an international money broker, in order to exchange that currency for U.S. dollars needed to complete the sale.

International collection activity otherwise involves methods similar to those used domestically. The credit policies are more restrictive; but those actually provide greater protection for the credit grantor. Documentary collections—involving sight drafts, time drafts and acceptances, bills of lading, and insurance certificates—eliminate potential collection problems before they can start.

United States overseas service offices, i.e., embassies and consulates operated by the Department of State may be consulted by a collector to obtain information on overseas markets, industries and individual companies. The International Trade Administration of the Department of Commerce also collects information for American businesses, as its primary responsibility is to promote commerce.

Aging Of International Accounts Receivable

Accounts receivable aging for foreign customers is likely to seem mind-boggling to the average collector accustomed to dealing with domestic accounts. Consider the following:

1. Standard terms may vary between 30 and 90 days with discounts of up to 3% taken for payments made even as late as 60 days.

2. Certain countries provide for payments only through a central bank.

3. In some cases, payment may not be made earlier than 14 days before the expected arrival of the product in the country.

4. Imports that involve a certain type of capital equipment or heavy machinery could involve transactions that fluctuate between making payments one year in advance to up to six months after delivery, before the matter is even considered past due.

5. The payment habits of other countries may depend on the commodities they import. Certain items may be paid for in accordance with reasonable terms, while payment for others may be delayed for one year or more.

6. There may be unreasonably lengthy installment receivables. Payments of up to 90% may be made on account within the first year, with the remaining balance of 10% carried up to an additional year.

The traditional evaluations of Days Sales Outstanding and other collection measurements have to be adjusted on a country-by-country basis, and then further adjusted for types of products sold.

You should be alert to the sensitivities of your company's foreign customers. You may even find out that the original terms of the sale offended the customer, which is the reason for the collection problem. Businessmen in certain countries may resent requests for letters of credit, for example, and unless a company's credit department is familiar with these feelings, friction may develop before the account even becomes due. Effective collection techniques can be applied internationally—but as is the case domestically, understanding must precede advice and guidance.

A GOOD WAY TO PREVENT COLLECTION PROBLEMS: LETTERS OF CREDIT

A letter of credit is a valuable financing device by which hundreds of millions of dollars and goods pass between seller and buyer, usually in an international sales transaction. It is generally a "tripartite" transaction. The buyer is the customer of the bank that issues a credit, the beneficiary is the seller of the goods (and the one who gets paid under the letter of credit), and the letter of credit itself is a substitution of the bank's credit for that of the buyer. The bank issues the letter of credit. These transactions, although related to one another, are considered to be three separate contract transactions.

How it works: The seller and the buyer enter into a contract for the sale of goods. The buyer goes to a bank and asks the bank to issue a letter of credit for the amount of money needed for his purchase. This letter of credit is issued by the bank to the seller, and provides for payment when certain conditions—as evidenced by specified documents—are met.

Definition: A letter of credit may be defined as a promise by a bank or another party of known solvency to accept and pay the draft or demand of payment by a beneficiary who has complied with terms of the credit.

Purpose: While letters of credit are also used for domestic transactions, their main purpose is to enable an exporter to draw a draft or bill of exchange on a bank or factor of known solvency instead of on the importer. The banking or factoring house promises to accept and/or pay the seller's draft or demand for payment accompanied by specific documents presented by the seller (or seller's agent, or bank).

Advantage: The advantage of a letter of credit is that the seller knows he can count on payment, once he receives a formal document issued by a bank abroad or by a confirming bank in his locale. The promise that his draft will be honored when accompanied by specific documents virtually ends the seller's credit risk. (The promise to accept and pay—or just to pay—when phrased in irrevocable terms, also provides the seller with access to bank credit or to manufacturer's or wholesale credit.) The supplier has now saved the costs of a credit investigation. And the supplier's credit with its own bankers is enhanced when a reasonable portion of sales is against letters of credit.

Types Of Letters

Letters of credit are generally broken down into revocable and irrevocable commitments. Additional types are:

1. Sight Draft Letter of Credit—where the customer pays the stipulated amount of funds on sight.

2. A Banker's Acceptance Letter of Credit—where the customer pays the available funds a specified number of days after the date.

3. Standby Letter of Credit—specifying the terms and conditions under which the supplier may activate the letter.

Under the regular letters of credit that accompany sight drafts and bankers' acceptances, the supplier bypasses the buyer entirely and looks to the issuing bank for payment. With a standby letter of credit, the supplier must first look for payment directly from the buyer. If the buyer is either unwilling or unable to pay the bill, the supplier can then present the letter of credit to the issuing bank for payment.

The promise in a letter of credit involves several degrees of certainty concerning the seller. It may be revocable, subject to the bank's unilateral cancellation without notification. In this case, the seller's certainty of enforcing the bank's promise to pay is non-existent until the bank actually accepts or pays. On the other hand, a promise in an irrevocable letter of credit becomes certain at a given moment after it is issued, usually when the letter of credit is received. An irrevocable credit may be confirmed—which means that, in addition, the irrevocable promise of another bank, usually at the seller's locale, is added.

Payment Under A Letter Of Credit

Generally, there is a specific time when payment becomes due—either at sight or at some future time. If the letter of credit states that the seller will receive payment from the issuer bank upon presentation of the instrument with the necessary documents, it is known as a "sight letter of credit."

However, drafts other than sight drafts can be drawn, usually at 30, 60, and 90 days. The bank will accept a draft submitted. It retains the beneficiary's documents, and will dispose of the draft in accordance with the wishes of the seller. Such term drafts and letters of credit are settled by the bank's acceptance of the draft—which is accompanied by writing or stamping the word "Accepted" over the date, and with the authorized signature of a bank officer on the face of the document.

Negotiability Of Letters Of Credit

There are options available in dealing with a letter of credit, i.e., to request that the draft be discounted at prevailing rates by the accepting bank at the time of presentation, or to hold the draft until it matures, and at that time pay its face amount.

Letters of credit may also be negotiable. Under such transactions, the beneficiary is not authorized to delegate his performance of the underlying transaction. Consequently he would only be entitled to negotiate his draft subject to the bank's ultimate determination of compliance with the terms of the credit. In the absence of a negotiable clause, the credit is referred to as a "straight letter of credit." Negotiable letters of credit are not necessarily by themselves transferable. But a *transferable* letter of credit also transfers the performance portion of the three-party contract.

While, generally speaking, irrevocable credits may be provided for specified periods of time, they may be repeatedly used by the seller if they are *renewable*. These are known as "revolving letters of credit." There are various types of revolving terms, the most prominent feature of which are that the amounts remain constant for a given period of time. So, whenever the stated amount is exhausted, it is automatically made available for the full amount until a specified time passes.

Documents Required By Letters Of Credit

The documents that are most frequently necessary to obtain payment on a foreign letter of credit are: the seller's invoice, a full set of on-board ocean bills of lading or airway bills, and insurance policy certificates. Additional documents may also be required such as quality inspection certificate, origin certificate, certification of weight, etc.

Caution: When documents are not available, payment may be allowed by the bank against the draft provided—such draft being accompanied by a promise to furnish shipping documents in the future. In some cases, there are provisions for allowing advances against a letter of credit *prior* to presentation of shipping documents. Sometimes even the merchandise, as part of the transaction, is stored, with title remaining with the bank until the payment is made.

Resolving Disputes

In case of a dispute and subsequent litigation involving a letter of credit, courts will generally refer to Article 5 of the Uniform Commercial Code. It contains 17 sections and deals with such matters as formal signing requirements or title transfer, presentments, rejection, etc. There are other articles that at times govern the statutory law concerning letters of credit, and that area is handled by the Uniformed Customs and Practice for Documentary Credit of the Interstate Commerce Commission. In general, the provisions of Article 5 of the UCC are not in conflict with the ICC. In some cases, they supplement each other.

Disputes about letters of credit can involve a substantial amount of litigation, much of it complex. Nonetheless, it is important for collectors to familiarize themselves with the functions and types of letters of credit, along with the general requirements involved in enforcing their collection.

In all instances where a collector has at his disposal the possible use of a letter of credit, it's a good idea to exercise it. Complicated as some disputes may be, collection on letters of credit is overwhelmingly preferred to collection from the customer directly.

"Standby" Letters Of Credit

A standby letter of credit, for domestic use, is obtained in much the same fashion as one for the export and import market. However, the domestic letter is much simpler and less costly. It doesn't deal with customs or have clearance problems; it is always in English, and it is always expressed in U.S. dollars.

The cycle starts with the buyer agreeing to purchase goods from the supplier, using a standby letter of credit. The buyer makes application for a standby letter of credit with the issuing bank. The issuing bank checks the financial viability of the buyer as regards the dollar amount of the shipment, the collateral value of the goods, and the terms under which the shipment will be paid. The issuing bank delivers the letter to the supplier, who then ships the merchandise to the buyer.

The supplier then goes to the buyer for payment. If the buyer pays, the supplier does not use the standby letter of credit. But if the buyer does not pay, the supplier presents the letter to the issuing bank for payment.

The main key to the entire transaction is the issuing bank. The costs involved may vary as well as the bank's standards for issuing a standby letter of credit.

SKIP TRACING: A GOOD WAY TO LOCATE A CUSTOMER

You cannot collect from a customer if you don't know his whereabouts. If you have security, collateral or money outstanding, finding the customer is doubly important.

A definition of a "skip" is any person whose whereabouts cannot easily be determined. Skips are those customers with whom you've lost contact, who may not have deliberately skipped, but just simply moved without telling you.

A collector in his attempt to locate an elusive customer may feel confined by ethical and moral, as well as legal, constraints—while at the same time, he may feel the customer can wander about in somewhat of a flaunting manner. Caution is advised. The collector in his skip-tracing attempt must be reminded of what's at stake: his reputation, and his company's reputation. There is no single ruse which even if successful is worth risking breaking the law.

Where To Begin

A collector in the role of skip tracer generally begins his effort right where the sale began, in the credit application and credit file. Agency reports, antecedent information, history, previous residence, businesses, employment, personal references, relatives, friends, anything and everything that might have been written on a credit application including banks, hobbies, trade association affiliations, magazine subscriptions, driver license—all represent preliminary potential leads.

Naturally, the cost of skip tracing should be commensurate with what you hope to achieve. Skips usually fall into two categories: those people that intentionally skip to evade payment of their obligations, and those people who simply move away and just lose touch with you. The planned skip is often transient enough to appear judgment-proof (unable to pay the obligation even if you were successful in locating, litigating, and reducing your claim to judgment).

If the size of the account or the circumstances involved in the skip lead you to conclude that the economics of continuing are prohibitive, then you can guide yourself accordingly and perhaps limit your efforts to mail, marked "Address Correction Requested." Some individuals and companies find it convenient to maintain a Post Office box—which can be a great help if the holder is a skip. The sample letter on the following page shows how to ask the Post Office for the business name, telephone number and address of the holder of the box.

Or you might even try a routine check with an employer or business, to see if the individual is still employed. Personnel can be extremely helpful if approached correctly. Don't discuss the reasons for your call, and be sure to have a positive attitude and avoid negative reference to your customer's character or your debt.

Sometimes the problem can be avoided simply by saving copies of checks or the envelopes that they were mailed in. By having a separate box for a new address checked on your return envelope, you will be tipped off by a cooperative customer every time there is a move. But often the box isn't checked, and you may routinely discard such information.

Sources Of Potential Lead Information

If the employer is not in position to render assistance, and the customer hasn't been transferred or isn't still employed, you should continue to review your credit

U.S. POST OFFICE

                              Regarding:

Dear Sir:

     In accordance with the U.S. Postal regulation, ASM-352-44 D, "Freedom of Information Act Regulation," Section .44d, as shown below, it is requested that you provide this office without charge the following information, if available, of the above business we are attempting to locate.

NAME _____

ADDRESS _____

_____

TELEPHONE _____

Thank you for your cooperation in this matter.

                              Very truly yours,

                                 Section .44d

     d. The business name, telephone number, and address of the holder of a post office box being used for the purpose of doing or soliciting business with the public, and any person applying for a box in behalf of a holder, will be furnished to any person without charge. The postmaster may furnish this information when he satisfied from the entries appearing on Form 1093, Application for Post Office Box or Caller Number, or from evidence furnished by the requester, such as an advertising circular, that a box is being used for such a business purpose. When the postmaster is unable to determine whether a business use is involved, he shall refer the request to Regional Counsel for advice.

file carefully, and try to locate the smallest piece of information that might help. References, friends, neighbors and landlords, relatives, former employers may provide leads. In addition, listen for gossip; some people do like to talk. And by being a careful listener, you're likely to pick something up—such as where somebody shops or what auto mechanic he uses, or what doctor he recently went to for what particular ailment.

Naturally routine telegrams, as previously discussed, can help. So can certified or registered letters with the envelope stamped "Forward to addressee—Address correction requested," and litigation checks to see if there are any pending actions (a lawyer currently in suit against your customer may have an address where service was made on your customer).

How To Put Clues Together

During your investigative stage, it is important that you take notes. Something that may not have seemed important initially, when added to something else, might prove to be an important clue. By putting together your fact sheet, you may learn that a debtor who recently was feeling ill and was suffering from allergies and asthma talked to his doctor about moving to Tucson, Arizona!

Once you get used to writing things down, you'll be in a position to develop your own technique for putting clues together. Having developed that technique, you will find yourself being still better prepared in your daily dealings with customers. Be certain, of course, to keep your credit and collection information file on each customer up to date. Sometimes changes in patterns of a customer's behavior—perhaps engendered by a marital difficulty, business reversal or medical problem—will signal a potential skip.

To be thorough, you must leave no stone unturned in your attempts, and sometimes you must even backtrack. An old girl friend, an insurance agent, fraternal group, union membership, employment agency, utility company, or even the phone company just to name a few, can be sources of potential lead information.

If the customer is involved in a profession, perhaps a license is required in his jurisdiction. That's true of a doctor, lawyer, or accountant, sometimes a service organization or even a local Department of Consumer Affairs must provide license approval. If you have a credit service that checks through Social Security numbers and the whereabouts of customers, and that information was willingly provided on your credit application, you have an invaluable source to pursue. This information is frequently provided to credit card companies.

When To Retain An Outside Skip Service

If you run out of time or run out of leads, or just don't have the time to pursue all avenues open to you, you can retain a professional skip tracer. But before you do that, be sure to check out references of the agency carefully, and verify that they are financially responsible and have the integrity to represent your company properly. After all, assuming your role, they also assume your responsibility in representing your company. So you'll want to be sure they are reputable.

Many companies require a small advance on either a per-account basis, or they may work on a contingent fee basis: no locate, no charge. Some companies have even gone so far as to send an additional order in care of a friend or relative via UPS or an overnight carrier service with instructions to "Deliver to Addressee Only" and to report where delivered. They suspect the friend or relative knows the whereabouts of their customer and are anxious to get the forwarding address.

After thoroughly checking all sources of information, the collector has actually learned more than the possible whereabouts of his customer. He has learned what type of information is important, and what must be kept current at all times in his collection or credit file. That's the best kind of on-the-job training available.

Sources Of Information From Public Records

As the collector becomes more involved in skip-tracing activities, it is probable that he's going to require assistance from a wide range of sources that are available as a matter of public record. The following are those records most frequently consulted for information:

1. Certificates of Incorporation, usually on file with the Secretary of State (and occasionally with the County Clerk in the county where the company operates).

2. Fictitious name recordings, requiring the person doing business under a fictitious or assumed name, to file with the County Clerk a certificate

showing the name under which the business is to be operated and the name of the people conducting business—usually with their addresses.

3. Partnership certificates, usually filed with the county or town where the business operates.

4. Bankruptcy petitions, on file in Federal Bankruptcy Court in the District Court where the bankruptcy has been processed.

5. Central Offices of Vital Statistics, in most states, where an official record is kept concerning births, deaths, marriages, divorces or other special events.

6. Public filings, which include notices of attachment, judgment liens, lawsuits, security interests in accordance with the Uniform Commercial Code, usually recorded in the office of the County Clerk.

7. Tax assessment records, usually maintained on all property and records and which normally include the name and address of the owner of the property. Where a corporation is concerned, those same records may also indicate whether or not the corporation has filed the required tax return and whether it remains in good standing.

8. Board of Voter Registration or party affiliation records recorded with local officials in a town, county, or school district which provide a fact sheet of information on individuals.

9. Department of Motor Vehicles. The DMV is a good source for information on people with a driver's license, as the application on record will usually include the name, address, place of business, age, date of birth and a physical description.

10. The Department of Defense Locator Service as previously discussed, enables a collector to write to the various branches of the service and with the appropriate fee, obtain the available information.

11. The Better Business Bureau.

12. Local Chamber of Commerce.

13. Local Police Department.

While Halls of Record are likely to respond to written communication, your best bet with the Better Business Bureau, Chamber of Commerce, and Police would be a phone call.

Keep in Mind: Even "problem" accounts can be profitable. But you must get the jump on them—early—and take steps, drastic ones if necessary, to protect your interests. Only then can these accounts be really worthwhile.

HOW TO RECOGNIZE SCAMS, AND WHAT TO DO ABOUT THEM

In spite of state and federal laws permitting liquidation or bankruptcy so that debtor companies can liquidate their assets and distribute proceeds to creditors in an orderly way, there are always attempts by companies or individuals to conceal assets which rightfully belong to creditors. The most undesirable of this type of business failure, in the jargon of the underworld, is called a "scam." A scam takes place when merchandise is shipped to a customer who has no intention whatsoever of paying for it. Yes . . . it is planned from the beginning.

A scam can work in several ways. The most common method is to start a company with a name similar to a company already in existence, and which enjoys a good credit rating. Orders for modest amounts are placed with suppliers. The scam operator makes certain that these bills are paid promptly in accordance with terms. Once credit has been established, larger orders are placed with these same vendors. After substantial merchandise starts flowing in, usually within a 45-day period, additional substantial credit can be obtained. This merchandise comes in the front door and generally goes out the back door. The premises are then shut, and the sting is felt by all unsuspecting suppliers caught in the scam. There are, however, other ways the scam operator is able to secure credit.

Occasionally, an investment will be made in acquiring an existing company with, yes, a good rating. The capital stock is purchased. No notice of change in management is provided to trade sources and, in effect, new principals are trading on the previous owners' good credit reputation. They will operate the company for several months, getting their investment back from existing inventory that was purchased. Then they "over-buy." Substantial orders are placed, way beyond normal means, and never paid for but are shipped out the back door for cash. The company is then collapsed.

This is the classic over-buy. The original principals have not been guilty of any wrongdoing; they sold the stock in the company for proper consideration, and no bulk sales notice was necessary. It's the new owners, of course, who are responsible. A popular time for such an operation to take place is usually just before seasonal increases are expected, and demand for merchandise is high. Fast delivery is common, and a thorough credit check is often ignored in favor of fast profit. Just as frequently, manufacturers are approached in person or at trade shows to arrange for large quantity orders. New suppliers are usually approached on a "take it or leave it" basis.

What To Do To Protect Yourself

The best protection against a scam is the old Wall Street adage, "Know your customer." But the following cautions are also suggested:

1. Verify that credit references are legitimate, read the purchase order carefully, make sure you know who you are selling to.

2. Verify the proper address and the correct composition of the company. Make sure shipments are not going to mail drops.

3. Be certain that the principals of the company are known to you, and do not have a history of planned fraud or bankruptcy.

4. Be certain to question purchase orders that seem to be different from normal orders.

5. Be certain your company is not being used as a reference by a new customer when no business relationship has developed.

6. Be on the lookout for a rash of activity on an old-line customer account that appears to be well out of the normal means of the organization.

7. Be certain to question unsolicited orders, and of course make sure shipments are not released before a credit check has been completed.

8. Scrutinize large bank deposits used as a reference out of the customer's local area, and verify them with bank officials.

9. Be certain to watch out for aliases, and make sure that type of merchandise being ordered is consistent with what is usually sold, i.e., don't ship jewelry to a garage or tire store!

In addition to the "buying blitz" in preparation for a skip, the misuse of references, or confusing requests to "ship to" here and "bill to" there, and confused title and ownership and trade style, there are also false financial statements to beware of. Was the statement submitted to you in person, even though you requested that it was to be mailed? Was it signed or unsigned? Are there unexplained shortages and liquid assets that can't be verified? Are liens or mortgages on assets omitted? Are there overstatements? Is there a history of fire, floods or other types of failures?

It is essential to recognize that the scam artist doesn't intend to pay late, he (she) doesn't intend to pay *at all*. It is a planned "bust." It's a technique that has been used successfully by organized crime in most of our major cities. Most scams are successful and go unpublished because white-collar crimes do not make the headlines; they don't seem to get the attention of an armed robbery. However, the effects of a scam can be just as debilitating. The most common scams are ones involving products that are easily saleable, such as apparel, small appliances, home entertainment equipment, computer products, electronic products, cosmetics and all types of high-technology components.

Obviously there is no easy answer, and even the most astute credit or collection executive is likely to be embarrassed by a fictitious debtor at one time or another. But it is important that your credit and collection staff be trained to spot the clues that may evolve into a fraud against your company. By being alert to the symptoms and signs of fraud, and by keeping in close contact with members of your industry to see if such suspicious activity is being experienced by others, you can do your best to minimize losses.

Avoiding Additional Costs

Credit and collection personnel, upon discovering that they've just been victimized by a scam, are likely to be even more frustrated in their attempts to determine what occurred. There are many principles at issue, and in the absence of payment, many organizations are likely to demand full investigations in an effort to obtain full financial disclosure. This could prove to be a time-consuming and expensive task that is not likely to be very successful or produce rewarding results.

Unfortunately creditor cooperation and financial support to conduct such investigations are usually nil. There is a general feeling in the marketplace that one would be throwing good money after bad. While that may be true, the real problem is that the scam operator is clever enough not to have created any substantial debts to any but a select few companies. For the most part, the debts are numerous but individually minimal. Scam operators anticipate the fact that creditors whose debts are not very substantial are not likely to invest large sums of money to pursue the fraud.

What makes things even tougher is the fact that, even if caught, the favorite explanation of the scam operator is that the company assets were dissipated as a result of gambling losses. "Gambling losses" represent the chosen favorite, in that it's customary not to ask for last names at card games or casinos, and such games are usually called at irregular hours and on an infrequent basis. The vague responses of the scam operator is likely to be even more frustrating for those who are pursuing collection, since the end result of continued investigation is likely to be *additional* cost.

In the event that creditors become more serious in their efforts to investigate and hire an accountant to review books and records, it's very common for the books and records to be missing. A favorite ploy of the scam operator is to say that the books were stolen, or destroyed in a fire or flood.

Effective collections require constant vigilance and an intimate knowledge of your customer. But it is important to recognize that no single symptom is likely to justify condemning others' possible intentions. Complete exploration must be made into a situation, so that inferences are *not drawn* from too little information. There could be legitimate explanations for items that appear suspicious. So be cautious, as it would be unfair to the customer to overreact, just as certainly as it would be unfair to your company to under-react. By looking for loopholes in personal history, and discrepancies between allegations and fact, and making certain to verify information, you can best protect yourself against this bust-out artist from the onset.

Summary: Despite all the "special" collection problems that can arise in dealing with "special" debtors, there are ways you can protect yourself—and see that your interests are properly filed and recorded. Use the techniques detailed in this chapter, and you can hold such problems to a minimum.

8

Model Collection Letters For Use In Special Situations

Table of Contents

8

Model Collection Letters
For Use In Special Situations

This chapter, like Chapters 2 and 4, contains model letters, twenty-nine of them, for use in unusual situations—where the more familiar friendly appeals and no-nonsense demands won't do.

They'll demonstrate, again in time-tested fashion, how to explain a customer's (or someone else's) oversight, how to back up claims, and how to explain adjustments—all while keeping customer good will, and encouraging future prompt payments.

BACKING UP CLAIMS

Action Approach: Enclosing Invoice Copies At Customer's Request

Date:

Vendor:

Invoice No:

Date:

Amount:

Dear Decision Maker:

Enclosed you will find duplicate(s) of invoice(s) you indicated you may have overlooked.

Will you please check your records again concerning the above, and mail us your check today.

Thank you for your prompt attention to this matter.

Very truly yours,

BACKING UP CLAIMS

Action Approach: Documentation Requested By Customer

Balance Due: _____

Dear _____ :

As you have requested, we are enclosing (proof of delivery) (the tear-sheets) (a contract copy) (bill(s) of lading), relative to the invoice(s) listed above.

With this information, we trust you will be in a position to make immediate payment.

Please mail your check in the enclosed self-addressed envelope. Why not act today!

Very truly yours,

Action Approach: Request To Pay Skipped Invoice

Balance Due: _____

Dear _____ :

SKIPPED ITEM

While auditing your account, the following item has been found to be unpaid _____. It was apparently skipped for payment.

A copy of this item is enclosed for your investigation. Should there be a question or problem, please provide us with the details. But if all is in order, your check will be appreciated.

Very truly yours,

BACKING UP CLAIMS

Action Approach: Customer Alleges Return Of Merchandise

Balance Due: _____

Dear _____ :

The merchandise covered by the above invoice(s) which you claimed to have returned, has not been received.

We therefore respectfully request that you send your check to cover the amount. If your records indicate that the return was made to us, then please submit proof of delivery.

Kindly mail payment or proof of return now.

Very truly yours,

Collection Department

BACKING UP CLAIMS

Action Approach: Request For Reimbursement For Unpaid Freight Bill

Balance Due: _____

Dear _____ :

The enclosed (statement) (bill of lading) charge represents freight prepaid by us for you.

This amount was paid out in cash as an accommodation, and there is no profit on such items. As such, they are due immediately in accordance with the original terms of sale.

You have always made payment pursuant to our terms. So we must conclude that this balance is an oversight on your part.

We would very much appreciate it if you would mail your check today, to clear the balance completely.

Very truly yours,

REQUESTING CLARIFICATION

Action Approach: Questioning Difference Between Your Statement And Customer's Payment

Balance Due: _____

Dear _____ :

The balance shown above represents the difference between our breakdown of your account . . . and your payment advice. To help clear the matter . . .

Please look over the attached explanation of your account.

If your records do not agree with ours, do write or phone, and let us work with you to resolve the difference.

But if our records now agree, then we ask that you mail a check to clear your balance today.

Thank you.

Very truly yours,

REQUESTING CLARIFICATION

Action Approach: No Record Of Payment

Balance Due: _____

Dear _____ :

While we are confident that you have long since resolved this past-due account, our records do not indicate the manner in which it has been paid.

In an effort to credit your account properly and get this matter resolved in an amicable fashion, we now ask for your cooperation with regard to the following:

1. When was the account paid?

2. To whom was the account paid?

3. Enclose a copy of cancelled check.

We are counting on your cooperation, and trust we'll have your return mail reply in the self-addressed envelope provided.

Very truly yours,

CONFIRMING SPECIAL ARRANGEMENTS

**Action Approach: Debtor Promises Payment In Full
Within 30 Days**

Balance Due: _____

Dear _____ :

    This is to confirm the arrangements you made, during our conversation today, for payment of this account in full by _____.

    We are concerned about this overdue account. Therefore, it is of the utmost importance that your check reach us as promised.

    To assure prompt handling of this urgent matter, use the enclosed self-addressed envelope and mail your check on time.

    Very truly yours,

_____

PERSONAL COLLECTOR

CONFIRMING SPECIAL ARRANGEMENTS

**Action Approach: Confirming Telephone Call With
Promise Of Payment**

Balance Due: _____

Dear _____ :

Confirming our phone conversation of Tuesday, December 20, we trust that you have already forwarded to us your payment in the amount of $ _____.

In addition to this on-account payment, we expect to receive _____ post-dated checks, each in the amount of $ _____, dated one week apart commencing _____.

If, for some reason your first checks have not been placed in the mail, then we strongly urge that you do so today—in order to avoid any additional action to enforce payment of this account.

Sincerely,

CONFIRMING SPECIAL ARRANGEMENTS

Action Approach: Debtor Promises Installment Payments

Balance Due: _____

Dear _____ :

    This is to confirm the arrangements we discussed today for the disposition of this account by partial payments, with the first payment of _____ due on _____ and the balance to be paid in periodic installments at _____ day intervals.

    We are concerned about this account; and it is of the utmost importance that each of your checks reach us as promised.

    To avoid a possible default, we again ask that you send us your current check and a series of post-dated checks covering the balance, according to the schedule we discussed.

    Cooperation on your part is essential for the amicable disposition of your account.

    We are enclosing a self-addressed envelope so that you can, without fail, promptly mail us your payment today.

Very truly yours,

_____

Collection Manager

CONFIRMING SPECIAL ARRANGEMENTS

Action Approach: Acknowledging Part Payment

Balance was   _____

Check rec'd for   _____

Balance now is   _____

Dear _____ :

Thank you for your check on account. The payment, however, only reduces your balance as indicated above.

Since the remaining balance is past due, it is necessary that you mail your check today to clear your account.

Thank you for your cooperation.

Very truly yours,

CONFIRMING SPECIAL ARRANGEMENTS

**Action Approach: Obtaining An Acknowledgement
Of Debt**

Balance Due: _____

Dear _____ :

    This will confirm our understanding that the balance you owe is in the amount of _____, and that you require additional time to pay this account in full. We are making this arrangement based upon your assurance that you agree this is the amount due.

    Please be assured that it is our intention to work with you, and will extend every effort we can to allow you to pay this indebtedness over a period of time. We are therefore confirming the schedule of payments listed below, which we have agreed to accept. All payments must be received by our office on or before the dates due.

DATE   AMOUNT

    Please sign the enclosed copy of this letter where indicated below, and return it to our office in the enclosed envelope with your initial payment and a series of post-dated checks (and/or notes) by return mail. Please do not delay. Place it in the mail today.

Very truly yours,

_____
Debtor

_____
Dated

SUGGESTING A REPAYMENT PLAN

Balance Due: _____

Dear _____ :

The purpose of this letter is to suggest a payment arrangement on your account which is seriously past due.

An additional amount of time to pay your account can be extended only if the following payments are received on time without the need of further reminders:

$500.00—12/30
$400.00— 1/15
$300.00— 1/30
$200.00— 2/15
$100.00— 2/28

We have been extremely understanding of your cash flow problem, and we trust that we will have your full cooperation in meeting the above payment schedule. If this plan is not adhered to, therefore, we will be forced to take additional measures in order to protect our interest. Please mail your check by 12/28.

Yours truly,

REQUESTING EVIDENCE OF PAYMENT

**Action Approach: No Check Received. Stop
Payment And Reissue New One**

Balance Due: _____

Dear _____ :

   Thank you for letting us know that you did send a check in full. However, we did not receive the check.

   We ask that you now stop payment on your first check, which very likely was lost in transit, and mail a replacement check to us now.

   This will clear your account and assure you that only one check can possibly be cashed. Do not delay. Please mail your new check today.

   Thank you.

                              Very truly yours,

REQUESTING EVIDENCE OF PAYMENT

Action Approach: Mail Photo Of Cancelled Check

Balance Due: _____

Dear _____ :

Thank you very much for your recent letter in which you advised us that the above balance has been paid.

Since our records do not indicate receipt of your check, we would appreciate your help in locating your remittance. Won't you please let us have a photostatic copy of the front and back of your cancelled check. Please send this to my attention today.

Your cooperation in this matter will be greatly appreciated.

Very truly yours,

SEEKING INFORMATION ON A DEBTOR

**Action Approach: Asking Help From Banks,
Landlords, Unions, Or Any Other Source Of
Information**

>   Re: Name:
>   Address:
>   Our File #:

Gentlemen:

   We wish to communicate with the above-named individual
who is listed as being (no longer) in your employ. Would you be
good enough to furnish us with the information requested below,
as this person is no longer at the address shown above?

   A stamped self-addressed envelope is enclosed for your
convenience. Thank you for your cooperation.

>   Very truly yours,

----

1. Is now employed by _____ at _____

2. Still resides at _____

3. Date of termination: _____

4. Date of birth: _____

5. Social Security #: _____

6. Have there been any inquiries from prospective new
   employers? (   ) yes (   ) no

7. If so, by whom? _____

8. Is presently residing at: _____

9. Last known address is: _____

10. Last known telephone #: _____

11. Last known bank reference: _____

12. Spouse's employer: _____

13. Is a member of _____Union

(*Note:* With variation of the first sentence, this inquiry can be used to write to all of the above inquiries.)

COLLECTING FROM AN INSOLVENT OR BANKRUPT ACCOUNT

Action Approach: Discovery Of Buyer Insolvency

(Sample Letter, Mailgram or Telegram. If you write a letter, late mail delivery could hurt your position.)

Balance Due: _____

Dear _____:

Under Section 2-702 of the Uniform Commercial Code and Section 546(c) of the Bankruptcy Code, we hereby demand payment or return of all merchandise delivered to you within the preceding ten days.

This demand covers all deliveries by the undersigned and any of its divisions to you and any of your divisions.

[In a letter only] Some of the invoices are attached; the others will be provided as soon as they are available.

Very truly yours,

_____
(Seller)

COLLECTING FROM AN INSOLVENT OR BANKRUPT ACCOUNT

Action Approach: Filing Proof Of Claim With Bankruptcy Court Or Assignee

TO: Bankruptcy Court (Send in duplicate)

     OR

     Assignee

                    Re:
                    (Customer's name)

                    Case Number:

                    Balance Due:

Gentlemen:

Enclosed is our Proof of Claim to be filed with the Court in the above proceedings.

Please acknowledge receipt on the duplicate copy attached. We are enclosing a self-addressed stamped envelope for your convenience.

Thank you for your attention and cooperation.

                  Very truly yours,

MAKING SHIPMENTS TO DELINQUENT CUSTOMERS

Action Approach: To A Delinquent Customer Who Placed A New Order

Balance Due: _____

Dear _____ :

    We are pleased to tell you that your recent order has been approved on credit. . . and shipment will go forward promptly.

    Although your account with us is past due, we did not hold this order. Instead, we chose to service your needs.

    We now believe that one good turns deserves another. We did our part by approving your order. Please do your part by mailing your check in full today.

    Thank you.

                       Very truly yours,

MAKING SHIPMENTS TO DELINQUENT CUSTOMERS

Action Approach: New Order Shipped On Past-Due Account

Balance Due: _____

Dear _____ :

When we received your recent new order, we processed it for shipment . . . even though your account was seriously past due.

In serving you, we did consider holding your shipment, but instead, we decided that you would respond by mailing your check. So we filled your order, which is en route now.

In fairness, won't you agree that your check for the above amount should be mailed at once? Please do take care of this urgent matter and mail your check today.

Very truly yours,

MAKING SHIPMENTS TO DELINQUENT CUSTOMERS

Action Approach: Pay Now, And We'll Fill New Order

Balance Due: _____

Dear _____ :

Thanks very much for your new order. We are processing it so that shipment can be made quickly.

However, before we can make that shipment, there is the matter of your past-due balance, as shown above.

Please do help us to service your needs, by mailing your check in full today. We'll respond with prompt shipment of your order.

Thank you for sending your check now.

Very truly yours,

MAKING SHIPMENTS TO DELINQUENT CUSTOMERS

Action Approach: We'll Ship New Order—When You Pay

Balance Due: _____

Dear _____ :

There are two serious problems confronting both you and us. These problems are:

1. Your past-due balance, shown above, is seriously delinquent.

2. Your new order has been received. . .processed. . .and we surely want to make shipment to you.

One type of action on your part will clear up both problems. It will balance your account and enable us to release your shipment.

That action is to mail your check in full today. The matter is now most urgent. Use the envelope enclosed and act now.

Very truly yours,

MAKING SHIPMENTS TO DELINQUENT CUSTOMERS

Action Approach: Factoring Company "Hold Order" Notice

Dear ——————— :

    As factor for your suppliers, we are continually being requested to extend credit to your company. But a review of our file indicates the following invoices are past due:

———————————

———————————

    In order that we might favorably consider approving new orders received in our office, we would appreciate your forwarding your check by return mail, to clear these past-due items.

Very truly yours,

———————————————
Credit Officer

MAKING SHIPMENTS TO DELINQUENT
CUSTOMERS

Action Approach: Factoring Company Notification
Of Past-Due Balance

(Vendor Name)

Balance Due: _____

Dear _____ :

The recent order placed with your supplier referenced above has been submitted to us as Factor, for credit approval.

However, in reviewing our records, we find that your account is past due as shown below:

_____

_____

Your prompt cooperation in mailing payment to cover this past-due amount will enable us to approve credit on your pending order.

We, as well as our client, would appreciate your attention. We look forward to receipt of your check.

Very truly yours,

_____

Credit Officer

MAKING SHIPMENTS TO DELINQUENT CUSTOMERS

Action Approach: Order Being Held

Balance Due: _____

Dear _____ :

YOUR ORDER IS BEING HELD

You were previously notified that your account is past due; now in the amount of $ _____. Your check covering this balance has not been received. Until your payment reaches our office, your (description of order) and any others submitted will be held.

To insure that there will be no additional delay in the processing of your orders, please mail your check today and bring your account up to date.

Very truly yours,

CUSTOMER'S CHECK RETURNED

Action Approach: For The First Time

Balance Due: _____

Dear _____ :

Your check has been returned to us dishonored for payment by your bank, for the reason indicated below.

We are redepositing your check today, and request your cooperation in arranging with your bank to have this item honored for payment upon re-presentation.

If there is any reason this check will not clear your bank, please send us a Cashier's Check, Certified Check or Money Order by return mail now.

A self-addressed envelope is enclosed for your convenience.

Very truly yours,

Check #

Dated:

Amount:

Indicated reason for dishonor:

CUSTOMER'S CHECK RETURNED

**Action Approach: Second Request For
Replacement Check**

Balance Due: ————————————

Dear ————————— :

It was a surprise to learn today that there was no response to our recent letter requesting a replacement check.

When you advised us that you had sent a check to clear your balance, we promptly responded, "No check received," and asked that you stop payment on your first check and mail a new check to us to cover your balance.

Your account is now seriously past-due, and we urge you to mail a replacement check today.

Very truly yours,

CUSTOMER'S CHECK RETURNED

Action Approach: For Insufficient Funds

Balance Due: _____

Dear _____ :

Your check in the amount of $ _____ dated December 1, _____, check # _____, has been returned by your bank due to insufficient funds.

It is imperative that you make arrangements to replace this check with a Money Order or Certified check immediately.

We trust that you realize the seriousness of this matter, and that there can be no reason for a further delay in payment.

Please utilize the enclosed envelope and mail your payment in guaranteed funds today.

Very truly yours,

CUSTOMER'S CHECK RETURNED

**Action Approach: Letter To Bank Requesting
Certification Or Collection**

TO BANK

> Re: Creditor
>
> Vs: Customer, City and State
>
> Balance: $

Gentlemen:

Please handle the enclosed check for certification or collection. We understand that there are sufficient funds on deposit to enable you to certify this check. If that is not correct, please handle it as a collection item.

If the check is certified, return it to us less your fee. If collection is made, deduct your fee and remit the proceeds to us.

In either case, please return this letter with your reply, or give your depositor's full name, address and telephone number.

Your assistance will be appreciated. A self-addressed envelope is enclosed.

> Very truly yours,

9

How To Get Money From Insolvent Or Bankrupt Debtors

Table of Contents

9

How To Get Money From Insolvent Or Bankrupt Debtors

When a company becomes insolvent, there are many ways of handling its financial distress. It doesn't always have to go into court to straighten its affairs. The company can call a meeting of its creditors and attempt to solve its financial difficulties out of court. The *advantage* of such voluntary settlements is that they are straightforward and proceed traditionally under common-law rules. The agreements made are strictly between the creditors and the debtor, and only those creditors who choose to accept are bound by the conditions.

Whether a debtor in financial difficulty is to be *restored to solvency* (thereby enabling the company to maintain a business relationship with its customers), or *put out of business* (and the assets distributed pro-rata among his creditors) are often the only choices. You must therefore be familiar with all types of insolvency proceedings and the advantages and disadvantages of each, so as to be able to protect and preserve the assets of your company.

905

VOLUNTARY VS. INVOLUNTARY SETTLEMENTS

The Benefits Of Extension Agreements

Voluntary settlements can be initiated either by the debtor or his creditors. Usually a debtor who is in financial difficulty will consult with an attorney, who in turn will confer with a number of major creditor representatives. Occasionally, the major creditors themselves will insist that the debtor convene a meeting for the purpose of solving his financial problems.

If the creditors' meeting is successful, the adjustment that results may take the form of an extension agreement, if the debtor proposes to pay his creditors in full over a period of time. There will be no need to involve the courts.

Extension agreements are a favorite of creditors because they usually provide for substantial payment; but they ought not be considered unless the debtor's financial responsibility has not been seriously impaired. They're desirable where the debtor's inability to pay its debts as they mature is a temporary situation, and where an extension is likely to improve its position for the future. Allowing for the honesty of the debtor, another major consideration is whether or not the extension agreement will accomplish its purpose of rehabilitating a troubled customer. Does the debtor have sufficient strength to carry on, and sufficient ability to turn the situation around? The answers to these questions depend on the seriousness of the debtor's predicament.

In considering whether an extension agreement is worth approving, remember that a debtor facing an extension agreement is likely to find it very difficult to attract new suppliers and customers. It's therefore likely that additional inventory support will have to come from the present creditors, including yourself.

While it's tempting to accept in the interest of good customer relations, an extension agreement could be followed by liquidation, and you could be caught with more indebtedness than previously. So caution is in order.

Other Possible Out-Of-Court Arrangements

(1) A composition settlement where the creditors agree to accept payment of a lesser sum in full satisfaction of their claims. The amount is usually the

most creditors can extract, and often it's the most the debtor is able to pay. This is also called a "pro rata" cash settlement.

(2) A combination of (1) and an extension agreement, calling for a pro-rata cash payment on account, with additional payments expected to come at regular intervals until the total obligation is paid. (Usually the remaining portion of the settlement will be secured by company assets, or guaranteed by principals of the company or third-party individuals with substance.)

(3) A moratorium on payments for a specific period of time, at the end of which a cash settlement, a combination settlement, or an extension agreement will be proposed.

Agreements of this type usually permit creditors to exercise partial control over the company's affairs, so as to prevent further dissipation of assets and deterioration of operations. As an example, merchandise purchases may be limited to specific amounts, and checks may have to be countersigned by representatives of the creditor body. If a corporation is involved, the capital stock may have to be deposited in an escrow account until specific terms of the agreement have been carried out. On occasion, new agreements require the subordination of existent claims to new ones. This can enable the debtor to obtain credit from new sources to function, and ultimately to pay out the agreement that's been negotiated.

Before any agreement or settlement can be worked out, however, a creditor must distinguish between a business which can be rehabilitated financially, and one which would best serve the community by its liquidation. Experienced credit and collection personnel, of course, have learned to recognize the honest as well as the dishonest. And one of the most important questions to be considered is not *how much* the settlement is going to be, but whether the debtor making the offer *deserves rehabilitation*.

The dishonest debtor should, of course, be prevented from re-establishing his business at the expense of its creditors. Creditors faced with a dishonest debtor should remain steadfast in their refusal to cooperate and, in each instance, insist on full payment or liquidation, and even prosecution for wrongdoing. By taking a good hard-line approach to the dishonest operator, creditors are afforded the best protection from the offender.

What Precedents Are There?

Settlements are usually unique unto themselves. Each plan itself has to be hammered out, individually, through extensive negotiation.

Creditors frequently disagree as to the best course of action to take, some being optimistic and others pessimistic. Many actually believe that a business, because of its insolvent state, actually belongs to the creditors, and that they are the ones who should decide the fate of the company. Their reasoning is that stockholders (meaning the debtor's principals) are usually the last to be paid under the liquidation rule of absolute priorities. The creditors therefore believe they're entitled to make the decisions as to what's in *their* best interest. This often accounts for the difficulty in persuading the debtor to accept creditors' proposals.

HOW ARE CREDITORS PROTECTED?

Additional controls: Creditors may also suggest that debtors execute an assignment for their benefit, to be held in escrow by a selected committee. The assignment will only become effective, however, if there's a default in performance or payment amounts. The assignee may then liquidate the assets of the company for the benefit of creditors. These types of controls afford the creditors the best protection—and provide the debtor with an incentive to pay or face liquidation.

In the case of a corporation, the committee may also ask for *resignations* of officers and directors or for specific individuals to be held in escrow, and exercised only in the event of non-compliance or performance. On occasion, accountants or attorneys may be requested to supervise operations, and designated creditor representatives may be asked to authorize all expenses and, in some cases, countersign checks on a new number-two bank account. Additionally, creditors may request new liens on inventory or fixtures, an assignment of accounts receivable, or combinations.

Getting Written Consent From Creditors

Often before a settlement of any kind can take effect, the written consent of a substantial majority of creditors, usually between 85% and 90%, must be obtained. If a creditor does not consent, it is not bound by the agreement and is still in a position to take unilateral action, i.e., it can sue the company and try to obtain a judgment for its entire claim amount.

A creditor can also join with other non-consenting creditors in an attempt to petition the debtor company into more formal bankruptcy proceedings. Involuntary petitions may be filed seeking liquidation or reorganization. However, the petition must be filed by three or more creditors holding "uncontingent" and "unsecured" claims totalling at least $5,000. For an involuntary petition, it is sufficient for the creditors to allege that the debtor is generally not paying its debts as they become due.

Of course, should such action take place, this means that no settlement or extension will go forward. So, as a practical matter, creditors who dissent may have an opportunity to make other arrangements and, if small enough, could even be paid in full. In fact, it is not at all uncommon for creditors whose claims are small to be paid in full anyway, so as to reduce substantially the number of creditors with which the debtor has to deal. In some cases, creditors are even permitted to reduce their claims to $100, $200 or $500 figures, and to accept that amount in full payment of their obligation.

Getting The Debtor's Consent

In actually executing the settlement, the creditors' committee has negotiated and approved the plan with the aid of its counsel and accountant. The secretary of the committee will usually prepare a letter explaining the developments, and its recommendations that creditors accept the plan as outlined. An acceptance form is enclosed as well.

On occasion, the acceptance will also contain language suggesting that acceptance of the arrangement may be used by the debtor as a vote in favor of this plan in the event the company is to file for reorganization under Chapter 11 of the Bankruptcy Code. Since it is always the debtor's right to file voluntarily for reorganization, such a statement is frequently done for the purpose of intimidating creditors into acceptance. If the requisite number do not accept, the debtor may be able to get the exact same plan confirmed in a Chapter 11 proceeding, where such great percentage of acceptance is not needed as would be required out of court.

Another method of forcing compliance upon creditors in an out-of-court situation is the use of a bulk sale. The debtor in effect sells all the assets of the business to another corporation, sometimes even a new corporation formed *for the sole purpose of acquiring the business*. By selling off the assets and providing for pro rata distribution to creditors, the debtor leaves dissenting creditors to pursue an empty shell.

From time to time, litigation results suggesting that such activity is in violation of the "bulk sale" intent, and that the new corporation is nothing more than an alter ego of the old one—and that the sale was created as a sham to avoid payment. However, such allegations are very difficult to prove and are extremely costly to pursue. Hence, the bulk sale is used (or just as often, abused) as a tool to implement out-of-court settlements.

Advantages Of A Voluntary Settlement

The main advantage to the voluntary settlement is its simplicity. Because of this, a voluntary settlement's cost is substantially less than other more formal assignment or bankruptcy proceedings. And since the administrative costs are lower, the dividends creditors would receive are likely to be *higher*. That is the main attraction for creditors, and certainly an incentive to make the concept of voluntary settlement work.

Furthermore, such settlements are frequently accomplished more quickly than those involving court proceedings. The result could be a healthier potential customer with whom creditors are able to continue a profitable business relationship, thereby offsetting the losses that are likely to be encountered during the rehabilitation stages.

Future business potential also plays a major role in determining what amount of pro-rata payment to be made would be acceptable. On occasion, an independent appraiser is brought in to determine the value of the business as a going concern, based on expected earnings, or on the value of the business in liquidation. Sometimes the value of the business in liquidation may exceed the value of the business from expected earnings. At that point, the future of this debtor as a potential customer has to be seriously weighed against the loss liquidation would yield, compared to the debtor's offered settlement.

Disadvantages Of A Voluntary Settlement

There are some disadvantages to an out-of-court arrangement. For example, during the period of negotiation, the debtor remains in control of his business and assets. In addition, and perhaps more serious, is the fact that during this same time, other creditors are free to institute lawsuits which could lead to attachment of the debtor's assets. Likewise, landlords and taxing authorities are likely to remain restless, and could tilt the situation and force the debtor into the filing of a Chapter 11 proceeding, which would then permit an automatic stay against pending actions.

In order to realize the benefits of an out-of-court settlement and bring the case to fruition, the full cooperation of all types of creditors as well as the debtor is essential. As pointed out earlier, if the debtor fails to keep records or falsifies records, issues false financial statements, or makes substantial preference payments or conceals assets, creditors should demand full payment or a full investigation.

Potential problems: The out-of-court settlement is very difficult to arrange when there are secured creditors such as banks controlling accounts receivable, inventory, or other noted property which the debtor must use in the normal conduct of its business. In addition, where priority claims exist, consisting of wages, taxes, rent (up to specific amounts), or other types of creditors who are entitled to priority of payment over unsecured creditors, those priority creditors must be prevented from taking precipitous action. Assurance that claims have been properly dealt with must be obtained before any hope of out-of-court settlement can be realized.

There are situations where an honest debtor intends to discontinue his business, and may propose a compromise settlement based on the liquidated value of the assets, or an amount that would exceed the liquidated value of the assets. Where it is decided to liquidate a debtor's business without court supervision, competent appraisers should be consulted.

Out-of-court settlement and extension agreements do not seem as popular today as they had been in the past. Today we live in a more litigious society, and there seems to be a race to the courthouse to collect one's debts from the creditor's vantage point, and a rush to obtain protection in the form of an automatic stay by the debtor. Perhaps greater awareness as to the benefits afforded all parties in an out-of-court agreement will eventually lead to their increasing use. All too often the question asked is "How much will the debtor pay?" instead of "How much *can* the debtor actually pay?"

WHAT A CREDITORS' COMMITTEE DOES

A creditors' committee is usually chosen at a meeting of the larger creditors. Such a committee is essential because decisions concerning financially distressed companies can only be made through a small, representative creditor body. A seven-member creditors' committee is chosen from the seven largest creditors who are eligible to serve—and wish to serve. (In case of an out-of-court settlement, however, the creditors' committee need not be composed of the seven largest; and in fact it is often worthwhile to have the smaller creditors on the committee.)

While the matter remains out of court, the committee is designated as unofficial. If a Chapter 11 proceeding is subsequently filed, that unofficial committee can be designated as the official committee if it was fairly chosen and is representative of the different kinds of claims recorded. Being a member of the creditors' committee is the best way to keep in touch with the debtor's financial position. A creditor who's not a member of the committee may find other creditors moving in directions that are detrimental to his interest.

How The Committee Works

Once convened, the creditors' committee immediately chooses a chairman, a position traditionally reserved for the largest creditor. Once the chairman is chosen, the secretary is then designated to record the minutes of the meeting. The secretary also communicates with other members of the committee, the creditor body, and counsel to the committee. The creditors' committee usually authorizes the retaining of an accountant and an attorney.

The creditors' committee does not run the debtor's business, but it does take appropriate steps to see that the debtor's financial situation is properly monitored on a regular basis, including review of salaries, purchases, inventory levels and monthly profit-and-loss statistics. The committee often works with the debtor in liquidating parts of a business by selling off assets, and generally assists in all future major decision-making areas. The ability of the committee to act as a representative group helps to minimize the risk that any individual creditor will take independent action as a result of lack of information.

Liability of the creditors' committee membership is relatively limited. Under most circumstances, members (or the companies they represent) are liable only for fraud or malfeasance. Poor business judgment or imprudent recommendations made to a debtor or to a general creditor body would not render the members liable for damages.

The creditor controls which exist in out-of-court proceedings are far more strict than those that would be available if the debtor were to file under Chapter 11. However, in exchange for those controls, the creditor's committee provides the debtor with a vehicle to reorganize out of court, and to avoid the stigma usually attached to the more formal and costly bankruptcy proceeding.

What To Expect At A Creditors' Meeting

Word of a meeting of creditors could come from a lawyer, an accountant, a major supplier, or the debtor itself. Whenever it happens, there is likely to be a certain amount of anguish. But it is important, as always, for the collectors to remain calm and courteous and to get the facts—such as the place, the date and hour of the meeting, and the name and address of the person (frequently the debtor's attorney) who signed the notice of the meeting. In addition, if possible, try to confirm the information directly with the debtor's principals—and only with them, because the debtor might not want its staff to know about the meeting just yet.

This first meeting can be a well-planned and well-organized effort that proceeds in an expedient fashion, or as a chaotic and confusing shouting match. Much depends on the preparedness of the debtor. If the debtor company comes well prepared with both counsel and accountant, the meeting will probably progress nicely. The debtor's counsel will outline the debtor's situation generally, and then point out the reasons for the financial difficulty. (Questions fired at the debtor are often sharp and acrimonious—requiring careful responses.)

In addition, the debtor's financial statements—both balance sheet and operating statements—are sometimes provided to the members of the creditor audience. Those papers, along with a verbal explanation, should provide the entire financial history of the business, as well as the reasons for its present condition. Even when this is not done, however, a debtor may still make a favorable impression upon the general creditor body by showing that he's come to grips with the seriousness of his financial condition, and is prepared to work towards a solution.

Developing Essential Information

The debtor's attorney, either at the end of the presentation or after the questions, might give some idea of what kind of offer or settlement his client is prepared to make. Most frequently, though, the question of an offer is left until later—and the attorney merely expresses the desire for his client to continue in business. Only in rare cases will a satisfactory plan of arrangement evolve at a first meeting—though it is essential for the debtor to come to peace with his creditors. Frequently, however, obtaining new financing is essential to a solution.

After the question-and-answer part of the proceedings is over, the work of organizing a creditors' committee gets under way. Nominations are made, and usually representatives of the large suppliers of various merchandise or service organizations, or banks or insurance companies will be included on the committee. Each class of creditor is entitled to form its own committee. (Secured creditors would not serve on the unsecured creditors' committee, and vice versa.) Members of the committee also are requested to come forward and advise the others if they possess any additional collateral or guarantees, or if they plan to take any action that may not be consistent with the interests of the entire unsecured creditor group.

After the committee is selected, it will go into session and choose an attorney or law firm to represent it as well as an accountant, if necessary; and, nearly always a secretary—who may be an employee of the adjustment organization where the meeting is being held.

Arriving At A Meaningful Settlement

When the committee's organizational work is complete, it may start negotiating with the attorney for the debtor—but frequently such negotiations do not come until later. Creditors will usually then request that the accountant make an independent audit of the debtor's books and records—at the debtor's expense. The creditors try to hone in on the realistic values of debtor's assets at forced liquidation, rather than full market value. It is important, of course, for members of the committee to get an indication of what might be realized if the debtor were liquidated or placed in bankrupty. Creditors naturally should try to obtain at least that amount.

Depending on the size of the case, it will require from one to three weeks to complete the audit; but some of the procedures could go on for months. The same holds true for arriving at a meaningful settlement.

At the conclusion of the meeting, the committee should have a fairly clear picture of the debtor's status, and whether or not the debtor has been honest and deserves rehabilitation—or whether it has concealed assets or has been guilty of other fraud. The committee should be convinced that the debtor can be rehabilitated and should already be in a position to suggest economies in the debtor's operation.

Shortly thereafter, the secretary will send out a notice to all creditors advising them of the proceedings, providing a synopsis of the meeting, and asking that the creditors file statements of account with the committee to assure participation.

How Decisions Are Made

Each creditor who attends the meeting is entitled to one vote. The committee hammering out the plan of arrangement with the debtor, however, should usually *not* be empowered to make final decisions without creditor approval. Any agreement negotiated should be submitted to the entire creditor body for their individual approval.

Suppose irregularities are uncovered? There is a definite relationship between the number of irregularities uncovered in the conduct of debtor's business affairs—such as preferences to other creditors or company officers, or concealing assets—and the ability to conclude a settlement with creditors. The more irregularities uncovered, the more likely that the committee may decide that bankruptcy proceedings are preferable to continued negotiations. Bankruptcy proceedings would provide opportunities for fully investigating and perhaps denying a discharge to the debtor from his obligations, or even imposing criminal sanctions.

As noted, the debtor remains in possession and is always in control, under such a committee. Nonetheless, the committee can and often does greatly influence the operation during the negotiating stages.

Important: It is never safe to assume that because something happened in the past under similar circumstances, it is likely to happen again. Each case is different.

Costs And Compensation

Service on a committee of creditors is purely voluntary and does not provide compensation. It is nonetheless very worthwhile. Cases with active committee participants tend to work out much more successfully than those with less-interested or weaker committee representatives. Active participation is likely to benefit you, your company, other creditors—and perhaps even the debtor—in the end.

In all cases of voluntary settlement, the costs of administration are reviewed by the committee. Bills are submitted by the accountant, attorney, and secretary. The committee will review the fees incurred, and the expenses approved will be deducted usually as a percentage from each creditor's claim—or in some cases, paid directly by the debtor.

The following list of steps will assist you in understanding the continuity of activity from the beginning of an out-of-court settlement to the ultimate outcome.

AN ANATOMY OF AN OUT-OF-COURT SETTLEMENT

   I. Debtor convenes meeting of his creditors
  II. Creditors select a committee
 III. Committee selects—
    A. Chairman who coordinates activities
    B. Secretary who reports to the entire creditor body outlining—
      1. status of company,
      2. the amount and method of payment,
      3. who is to be paid and when, and
      4. any special conditions or circumstances needed to conclude an agreement.
    C. An attorney who—
      1. investigates the legal affairs of the debtor, i.e., liens
      2. checks possible irregularities, i.e., preferences or fraud, and
      3. reports to committee with a recommendation to accept or reject debtor's proposals for continuing in business.
    D. An accountant who does an independent audit and provides financial reports to the committee, including:

1. liquidation analysis,
2. a company's ability to pay, and
3. the actual cash value of the ongoing business.
  E. An appraiser who evaluates the assets as an ongoing concern, or assists in the preparation of a liquidation analysis.
IV. Meeting to decide fate if payment is not made. Options are:
  A. Assignment,
  B. Bankruptcy filed, Chapter 11 or 13,
  C. Company to be liquidated out of court or Chapter 7 bankruptcy.

AN ASSIGNMENT FOR THE BENEFIT OF CREDITORS

This is a voluntary transfer of assets by the debtor to another person in trust, for the purpose of liquidating the assets and distributing the proceeds to creditors. The debtor in this instance is the "assignor," and the person receiving the assets is the "assignee." Such action is purely at the discretion of the debtor, and cannot be an *involuntary* assignment. Generally, a document setting forth a list of assigned assets must be executed by the debtor and delivered to an assignee.

Every state has statutes relating to assignment proceedings, and while the outcome of the proceedings may be the same, the procedures may vary from state to state. A collector interested in answers to specific legal questions concerning assignment should therefore consult with competent counsel.

An Assignment Vs. Bankruptcy

A debtor may file an assignment proceeding without prior consultation with his creditors, or it may be executed as a result of a creditors' committee request, when it becomes clear that voluntary settlement or compromise is not likely. Assignments are frequently used as a method of liquidation in lieu of bankruptcy. However, as noted above, bankruptcy may be the more appropriate vehicle to maximize recovery and protect the interests of all creditors wherever there are suspected irregularities, preference payments or fraudulent transfers of assets.

An assignment is usually a good choice, mostly because the expenses of an assignment are considerably less than those of a bankruptcy. The legal fees, accounting fees, and administrative fees may be substantially less than would be the case in bankruptcy. Usually, then the assignee will proceed to liquidate the assets by public sale, with appropriate advertising to assure competitive bidding. Occasionally, a private sale is held, but only where the assignee feels that the price is likely to exceed a public bid.

On rare occasions, a collector may learn that a company having made an assignment and having liquidated its assets is back in business, under a similar name and with the same principals. In fact, the collector may even learn that the new company is in possession of many of the same assets. This may be the result of selling the assets to a person who sold them back to the original debtor, or who was bidding on the original debtor's behalf. Of course, it could be that the new company legitimately purchased the assets and intended to hire the previous owner/debtor to manage the business. But a collector who learns of such a situation should immediately investigate, and consult counsel to be sure of protecting his interests.

Where the assignor has listed Accounts Receivable as an asset, the assignee will attempt collection or sale of those receivables. And once all the assets have been liquidated and the costs of administration accounted for (including compensation to the assignee and occasionally to an attorney), proceeds are distributed among unsecured creditors on a pro-rata basis.

How A Common-Law Assignment Works

In a *common-law assignment*, the proceedings are not under the supervision of any court, and dividends to creditors may be higher than with a proceeding under court control. A *statutory* assignment accomplishes much the same as the common law assignment; but in that instance, the assignee must file a final accounting and request the court to settle the records and approve of the distribution. Which is better?

In some cases, administrative costs in common-law assignments are lower; and therefore, given the same effort, the collector is likely to conclude that the yield to creditors on a pro-rata basis would be higher. On the other hand, without court control and somebody to oversee the activities of the assignee, the flow of information and the outcome are often suspect.

In either type of assignment, the debtor does not receive a discharge from his obligations. Assets may have been sold and the proceeds distributed among creditors, but the balance can still be pursued. However, usually the assignor is incorporated. Since all corporate assets have been liquidated, pursuit of any balance by corporations would be wasted motion.

Assignment And Settlement: Another Alternative Recovery Method

A more recent method is a *statutory assignment and settlement*. At the end of this proceeding, the pro-rata distribution is accompanied by a statement to the effect that endorsement of the check constitutes acceptance of the payment with "full accord and satisfaction." Creditors do not have to accept payment with the qualified endorsement, but they're usually better off doing so. The alternative is pursuit of a worthless debtor.

There are many states that afford the debtor the opportunity to ask creditors to consent to the assignment before their claim in the proceedings will be accepted. Creditors almost have to accept this. If they do not approve, they will not receive distribution and may be forced to pursue, independently, a worthless shell of a company.

Despite the opportunity to obtain greater recovery because of the smaller administrative expense, there are disadvantages to the assignment. Assignment proceedings in general provide creditors with little or no opportunity for examination of the affairs of the debtor. There is often no way to determine whether possible improprieties took place. In addition, an assignee acquires only the title previously afforded to the debtor. The assets assigned are still subject to liens, claims and encumberances which would have been valid against the debtor. Once the assignee is involved, he in effect has the status of a *lien creditor*. There's an exception, though. A landlord may have a recorded prior lien that will be superior to that of the assignee. The same would be true of a lien creditor or secured creditor with a properly perfected security agreement that's been filed.

The assignee's duties and responsibilities are similar to those of any trustee, but may vary in different state jurisdictions. Even the powers of an assignee functioning as a trustee in a given state are likely to differ, depending on the type of assignment statute in force. Some states require recording of the assignment, filing of schedules, listing assets and liabilities, giving notice to creditors and even bonding of the assignee, and additional reports as required by the court. Other states may permit the assignee to set aside prior fraudulent conveyances to avoid pre-assignment preferences previously remitted by the debtor.

Despite its flexibility and informality, creditors are further cautioned concerning the assignment proceeding, in that while a complete assignment of assets is not under bulk sale regulation, a partial assignment of less than all of debtor's property might be viewed as a fraudulent conveyance of assets.

What About Friendly Assignments?

You'll have to remain alert to the differences that appear in each situation, and try to make informed judgments as to what is likely to generate the highest recovery and represent the company's best interest. This is especially true when encountering what is commonly referred to as "a friendly assignment."

A friendly assignment happens when the assignee is a friend of the debtor, or of the debtor's attorney, or any person likely to favor the debtor's interests rather than the interests of creditors.

Watch this: In assignment liquidations, always be certain that the creditors are in control. When friendly assignments occur, the assignee and the attorney for the assignee frequently try to set things up so each will participate—and earn a fee.

When creditors believe they have encountered a friendly assignment, they should consult with counsel, and consider filing an involuntary petition in bankruptcy. This would enable the matter to be brought under the jurisdiction of a federal court, and a complete impartial investigation to be made into the disposition of the assets. This also makes impartial liquidation of that which remains far more likely. Act quickly in attempting to remedy the friendly assignment, in order to get the greatest return on the assets before they're liquidated!

RECEIVERSHIPS

A receivership is another method of collecting from the assets of a financially distressed debtor—usually because of dissipation of assets or deterioration of property. Receivership proceedings can be instituted by one or more creditors, who file a Bill of Equity in a state court, seeking to collect on their claims. While this dramatic action may have some rehabilitative possibilities, the proceedings most often will result in liquidation.

Receivership action is often used where, after having obtained a judgment, a creditor is unable to enforce payment on the judgment. The creditor hopes, in making application to the court for the appointment of a receiver, that the pressure resulting from the action (which may result in the debtor's losing control of its business) would be sufficient to obtain payment of the claim.

Receivership, like garnishment, may be both a pre-judgment and post-judgment collection action. The appointment of a receiver is discretionary, however, and courts are very reluctant to appoint pre-judgment receivers—as they have been very reluctant to provide for pre-judgment garnishment.

Once appointed, the receiver is required to take possession of the property as soon as possible. However, his role may be one of holding the property for the purpose of preserving it, or the receiver may even be requested to find the means to continue the debtor's business activities.

Again, the motivating factor behind the creditor's application for the appointment of a receiver against the debtor company is to produce payment. There's no special advantage to the petitioning creditor, as all creditors share in the proceeds of any liquidation. The receiver, like the assignee, takes the property subject to existing liens; and creditors can even create new liens. But they are unable to enforce payment and disturb the receiver's possession of the assets without asking for relief from the court.

Receivership proceedings have the same effect on all creditors, and provide the same discharge limitations as general assignments. Occasionally, for example, creditors meetings are held for the purpose of examining the debtor, much the same as in an assignment or out-of-court settlement proceeding.

Who's Subject To Receivership?

Such proceedings may be undertaken against partnerships or corporations, but receiverships cannot be applied for against *individuals*. Interestingly enough, though, in some jurisdictions, individual principals of corporations can apply for the appointment of a receiver to take over their own corporations.

The primary function of the receiver is to conserve the assets of the debtor company, and distribute them according to certain priorities. To do this, the receiver may have to continue the business, and seek out the cooperation of the creditors or a creditors' committee, and eventually either return the business back to the debtor or completely liquidate it. However, before the receiver is discharged, he must file a final accounting with the court that appointed him. At that time, creditors can have an opportunity to review and question items in the final report.

Impact Of The Bankruptcy Code

Before the new Bankruptcy Code, creditors filing an involuntary petition in bankruptcy would frequently ask the court to appoint a receiver to take custody of a debtor's assets. The new Bankruptcy Code, which permits debtors to remain in possession (DIP) has made this a far less common procedure. It is, however, one with which you should be familiar.

WHAT TO DO ABOUT INSOLVENT CUSTOMERS

The Meaning Of Insolvency

Within the meaning of insolvency, there are a wide variety of possible definitions. But the usual one is this: "A person or company is 'insolvent' who has ceased to pay debts in the ordinary course of business, or cannot pay those debts as they become due."

A person or company is also considered insolvent whenever the aggregate of assets at fair market value is less than liabilities. Occasionally, good companies become temporarily insolvent. So long as a debtor is able to meet his (its) obligations, no action is likely to be taken against him. In the majority of instances, however, both debtor and creditors wait too long before recognizing the trouble. Where the situation is recognized and remedied immediately, further deterioration can probably be prevented.

Getting Merchandise Back From An Insolvent Customer

One of the most exasperating situations a collector has to face is to learn that his customer is insolvent or has filed bankruptcy—and that recent shipments have been made to the customer's account. While there is a natural feeling of outrage, it must be quickly quashed in favor of judicious and timely action, to assure that the necessary steps are taken to protect your position.

Whether the merchandise is in transit or already in the hands of your customer, the following chart (Figure 9-1) will provide you with the necessary understanding as to what should be done, when it should be done, and why it should be done. Compilation of this information is in no way designed to provide legal advice or guidance to you as a collector. It is given here to show you some ways of handling recent shipments to an insolvent account and protecting your interests. A sample of the necessary demand is also included.

WHAT YOU MUST KNOW ABOUT BANKRUPTCY LAW

The safeguarding of company assets is as much the responsibility of the collection executive as the credit executive—whose decision it is to take sales risk in the first place. That responsibility is the main reason a collector should take an interest in both insolvency procedure and bankruptcy law.

Bankruptcy law is complex and very technical. Note, however, that the following information is not intended as a complete explanation of a very specialized subject. It's designed primarily to serve as a guide to assist the collector in working with bankruptcy practitioners who are experts in the field.

The bankruptcy courts provide the forum where interests of debtors and creditors can be thrashed out. By safeguarding the interests of creditors, and relieving honest debtors of obligations they're unable to cope with, it can help society to be the ultimate benefactor. However, this scenario is not always how it works out; and depending on your vantage point, it may appear that creditors exert too much control, while others may believe that debtors get a head start and not a fresh start.

How The Bankruptcy Court System Works

Under the new law signed by the President in July 1984, bankruptcy cases will be initiated in the U.S. District Court and then automatically referred to the U.S. Bankruptcy Courts, which now function as adjuncts to the Federal District Courts. The Bankruptcy Courts currently have jurisdiction over all cases under Title II, and any and all ''core proceedings.'' A core proceeding is one which is routinely part of

Rights Of A Seller Upon Discovery Of Buyer Insolvency

Situation Where	UCC	Bankruptcy Code	Remedy
Merchandise in possession of seller	2-702 Sec (1)	546 (c)	May refuse to deliver merchandise unless paid cash for new and old invoices, even if prior terms were on credit and bill not due.
Merchandise in transit	2.705	546 (c)	Stop delivery of merchandise in possession of carrier may be effective as long as buyer has not taken possession.
Merchandise delivered to buyer	2.702 (2)	546 (c); if buyer is in bankruptcy, Code will govern. Written demand a must.	(A) May reclaim merchandise if demand for merchandise is made within 10 days after merchandise received; but buyer must be insolvent and sale must be on credit only as part of 2-702; cash sale is okay only under 546 (c), i.e., NSF check. (B) After demand is served: (1) file complaint for reclamation; (2) obtain order restraining disposition of merchandise. (C) Result: (1) court may deny claim; (2) grant seller priority as administrative expense; (3) secure claim by lien on property; (4) return merchandise; (5) pay.
If misrepresentation of solvency was made in writing to seller and relied upon	2.702 (2) Balance sheet and financial statement either signed or unsigned is okay, or letter signed is evidence. Three mos. from date presented to seller.	Not valid under code.	Seller can make demand any time to reclaim, but the longer you wait, the less merchandise will be available.

Figure 9-1

Definition of insolvency	Has ceased to pay debts in the ordinary course of business; can not pay bills as they fall due or as per Bankruptcy Code.	Insolvency when debts are greater than assets at fair valuations. This Balance Sheet Test is more difficult to prove than insolvency under UCC.

Footnotes:

1. Notify carrier with reasonable diligence to prevent delivery.
2. Does not violate automatic stay of code 362(c), or does not constitute voidable lien of 545 of the code.
3. Demand is effective to reclaim only the merchandise on hand at the time of receipt of demand. It is therefore important to get confirmation and verification immediately, to avoid later dispute.
4. Secured creditior usually has rights superior to reclaiming seller.
5. UCC does not state whether demand must be written or oral.
6. UCC is silent on how to compute 10-day time. Must be 10 days after receipt, not after title passes; UCC SS 2-103. Demand must be received by buyer in 10 days; date of receipt, not date of sending notice controls.
7. Type of demand best is a telegram with time and date; confirmation should include all credit and cash sales (assume any checks received will be NSF), and refer to 2.702 and 546(c), sample attached.
8. BUYER'S RIGHTS WITH SOLVENT SELLERS: Under 2-502 of the UCC, a buyer has the right to recover goods from an insolvent seller when the following conditions are met:
   . . . The buyer has paid in part or in full the purchase price of the undelivered goods;
   . . . The seller becomes insolvent within 10 days after the receipt of the first installment payment for the undelivered goods;
   . . . The undelivered goods can be identified to the contract of sale; and
   . . . The seller still has control over the undelivered goods. When *partial payment* has been made, goods can be recovered only when the buyer pays the balance of the purchase price. When *no payment* has been made, there are no recovery rights.

Figure 9-1 (Cont'd)

Rights Of A Seller Upon Discovery Of Buyer Insolvency:
Sample Mailgram Or Telegram

(If you write a letter, late mail delivery could hurt your position dramatically.)

BUYER

                     Balance Due: _____

Dear Decision Maker:

      Under Section 2-702 of the Uniform Commercial Code and Section 546(c) of the Bankruptcy Code, we hereby demand payment—or the return of all merchandise delivered to you within the preceding ten days.

      This demand covers all deliveries by the undersigned, and any of its divisions to you and any of your divisions.

      All invoices will be provided as soon as they are available. Please advise your intent to return the merchandise, or mail your check today.

                   Very truly yours,

              _____

                      (Seller)

the administration of a bankruptcy case. In non-core matters, i.e., "a wrongful death suit," the bankruptcy judge will hear the matter first and then make recommendations to the U.S. District Court for final action.

Bankruptcy judges serve as judicial officers of the district court. They are appointed by the U.S. Court of Appeals for each circuit, for fourteen year terms. Current judges serve four years from the date of their last appointment or until October 1st, 1986 whichever is later.

In addition, Congress has authorized the continuation of ten pilot programs (involving eighteen judicial districts), where the Attorney General appoints a U.S. Trustee to assume administrative responsibilities in bankruptcy cases, and to maintain and supervise a panel of private trustees.

Any appeal must be filed within ten days to the U.S. District Court which then may elect to hear a matter all over again, as if no prior decision had been made. If a further appeal is requested by either party, an appeal is then made to the U.S. Circuit Court of Appeals.

Your lawyer will handle any possible dealings with the Bankruptcy Courts, of course.

CHAPTERS IN THE BANKRUPTCY LAW—AND HOW THEY AFFECT YOU

The Bankruptcy law is a Federal law. The chapters commonly referred to in the marketplace concerning insolvency are contained in Title II of the United States Code, which is divided into eight chapters: 1, 3, 5, 7, 9, 11, 13 and 15. Chapter 1 contains the general provisions, definitions and rules of construction. Chapter 3 contains the commencement and case administration; Chapter 5, the debtor and its estate and the trustees' avoiding powers; Chapter 7, liquidation proceeding; Chapter 9, debt adjustment for municipalities; Chapter 11, reorganization; Chapter 13, adjusting the debts of an individual with regular income; Chapter 15, dealing with the United States Trustees Pilot Program.

Let's take a closer look at some of these chapters:

Liquidation: (Chapter 7)

Liquidation under Chapter 7 is commonly known as "straight bankruptcy." Individuals or companies involved in it will have their non-exempt property liquidated and distributed within each class of creditors in accordance with the rules of absolute priority.

After the filing of a Chapter 7 proceeding, an Order of Relief is entered and then the court immediately will appoint a Trustee from a panel of private trustees. However, creditors may elect a trustee at the first meeting of creditors, if creditors holding 20% in amount of allowable claims request it. (If creditors do not elect a trustee, the interim trustee serving will then be designated as trustee.) The creditors' committee in this situation, consisting of between three and seven creditors, consults with the trustee in connection with the administration of the estate, and makes recommendations to the trustee. The committee represents the entire creditor body, and may submit to the court any questions affecting the administration of the estate. At the first meeting of creditors, the debtor is required to attend, and may be examined under oath.

Most of the administrative tasks performed by the creditors' committee are similar to those performed outside of a bankruptcy proceeding. However, the rules regarding creditor controls and debtor negotiations are not applicable to a Chapter 7 liquidation.

Because of the fact that Chapter 7 involves liquidation, there is a tendency for creditors to pay less attention to this type of proceeding than to a reorganization. But caution is advised in this area. In a Chapter 7 liquidation, proofs of claim must usually be filed with the court within 90 days after the first meeting of creditors. The rules change from time to time, however, and the collector must remain alert to the changes.

In addition, the court may convert a case under Chapter 7 to a Chapter 11, and permit *reorganization* in lieu of liquidation. Furthermore, the court may dismiss a case under Chapter 7 for cause, such as unreasonable delay by the debtor, or nonpayment of fees by the debtor. If the case is dismissed, creditors will once again be free to pursue recovery.

The Discharge

Of equal concern to the collector in Chapter 7 liquidation is whether or not the debtor will be given a *discharge* of the obligation. The court may not grant a discharge to a debtor who hindered, delayed, defrauded, concealed, transferred, removed, destroyed, mutilated, or permitted or aided in doing any of these. This will hold true for any assets within one year prior to the filing of the petition, or property in his possession after the filing date. Discharge may also be denied where the debtor failed to keep proper books and records from which its financial condition can be ascertained. (However, there may be extenuating circumstances—as debtors often lose their books or report their destruction as a result of fire, flood, or even robbery.)

Discharge may also be denied if it can be proven that the debtor made a false statement under oath, that the debtor has refused to obey lawful orders of the court, or that the debtor has been granted a discharge in a previous bankruptcy case within the past six years.

Either the trustee or individual creditor may object to a discharge, and where it can be proven that a discharge was granted but obtained with false information, it may be revoked. If the debtor desires, the bankruptcy court may also permit the debtor to execute a written waiver of discharge, provided it was executed after the filing of the petition.

Denial of a discharge will permit every creditor to pursue its original debt. On the other hand, discharge relieves the debtor of almost all pre-petition liabilities.

Under the 1984 law, certain debts—up to $500.00 in luxury goods and $1,000.00 in credit card cash advances incurred 40 days and 20 days before the order of relief in bankruptcy—are considered *non-dischargeable*.

Reaffirmation

In past years, it has been quite common for bankrupt debtors, especially consumers, to undertake particular obligations again *despite the fact that they were dischargeable*. Whether agreed to as the result of friendships or scare tactics, such reaffirmation was an effective legal basis for pressing a claim.

However, the Federal Bankruptcy Code as amended, now limits this technique, and provides specific requirements for reaffirmation agreements to be enforceable. A reaffirmation agreement must, for example, have been made before the granting of a discharge. And the debtor has the right to rescind the reaffirmation agreement within 60 days after making it. The agreement must contain a clear statement of this.

Furthermore, individual debtors are no longer required to appear before the court to reaffirm a debt. That means any reaffirmation agreements should be secured and filed as early in the proceedings as possible, so they will be final and not subject to repudiation by the debtor.

Non-dischargeable debts: While it may appear that there's a "rush to the courthouse" because of the benefits afforded a bankrupt, keep in mind that the following debts are not dischargeable . . . certain taxes, debts incurred by fraud, embezzelement, larceny, unscheduled debts or alimony, maintenance and child support. In addition, student loans or debts from a previous bankruptcy in which discharge was denied—as well as judgments resulting from driving while intoxicated—are not dischargeable.

Adjustment Of Debts For An Individual With Regular Income: Chapter 13

Chapter 13 is available to an individual who is stable and has a regular income that enables him to make payments under a plan. There are, however, debt limitations. The individual must have unsecured debt of less than $100,000 and secured debt of less than $350,000—with the income of husband and wife totaled together. (Note that Chapter 13 is not available to corporations or partnerships.)

There's no such thing as an involuntary Chapter 13, as only the debtor may file a Chapter 13 plan. There will be a trustee appointed in every case; and in some districts, the bankruptcy judge will appoint a standing trustee to serve in all Chapter 13 cases.

The plan in a Chapter 13 case may impair the rights of secured creditors (except those secured by a mortgage on the residence of the debtor), and also unsecured creditors. However, unsecured creditors do not have the right to vote on an arrangement under Chapter 13; it requires only court approval. Unsecured creditors are protected by the court under the "logic of best interest." This means the amount the debtor proposes to pay must be at least equal to the amount that creditors would have received in a Chapter 7 liquidation. That kind of plan is likely to be approved by the court, and if confirmed, is binding upon the debtor and all of his creditors.

However, a creditor does have the right to oppose the plan in an attempt to block its confirmation by the court, unless the plan provides for full payment for that creditor or provides for the debtor to commit all of his (her) disposable income to thc plan over a three-year period, with the first payment to begin 30 days after the plan is filed.

A business debtor in Chapter 13 is likely to operate as a debtor-in-possession (DIP); and is likely to be paid from the profits of the business—not from an individual's salary. But in either case, the money is paid to the trustee, who will act as disbursing agent of the court.

Changing To Chapter 7

Under certain conditions, the court may dismiss a Chapter 13 proceeding or convert it to Chapter 7. A collector must therefore stay on top of the proceedings and be on the lookout for irregularities, so as to protect his interests.

However, the Code gives the court power to reject certain Chapter 7 petition filings—if it believes a consumer has sufficient disposable income. The court may require a payment of a percentage of pre-petition debt, in exchange for a discharge.

After completion of the payment provided for in a Chapter 13, the debtor receives a discharge. However, the court may grant a discharge in a Chapter 13 case *even though the debtor has not completed payments* as mandated by the plan. Where it can be demonstrated that the debtor's failure to complete payment was due to hardship and circumstances beyond his control, the court may discharge the obligation. However, for this to be done, the value that creditors received already must have equalled or exceeded what they would have received in liquidation; and it must be further demonstrated that modification of the plan would not be practical.

Important: If a discharge is given, a second discharge will not be granted in any Chapter 7 case filed within six years of the date of the original Chapter 13 filing, *unless* payments to creditors under the Chapter 13 plan were substantial (approximately 70%). Where a case was dismissed by the court for willful failure of the debtor to abide by orders of the court where the debtor obtained a voluntary dismissal of a proceeding, a debtor would have to wait six months before refiling. Thus, a diligent collector may be able to reach assets during the first three months after dismissal without being subject to the possibility of a later preference claim by the debtor, trustee or other creditors.

A debtor who files a Chapter 13 can also file a Chapter 11 petition. Under Chapter 13, a business debtor is less likely to have a trustee appointed, as might be the case in Chapter 11. Most courts permit the debtor to operate as a Debtor-In-Possession. In Chapter 13, as creditor acceptance of debtor's proposed plan is not necessary, there is no need for creditors' committees.

Co-Obligors

An automatic stay remains in effect not only against creditors of the debtor, but also against many co-debtors or guarantors of a consumer debtor's obligation. There is an automatic stay against such co-debtors, and creditors cannot proceed to collect or commence any action to collect, unless such guarantor became liable for the debt "in the ordinary course" of each individual's business. In fact, if the guarantor received direct consideration for the guarantee, there may be an opportunity for a collector to proceed by asking the court to lift the automatic stay. If the plan proposes not to pay such a claim, or if a creditor can show that its position is likely to be irreparably damaged, a creditor may ask the court to lift the automatic stay.

In a Chapter 13 consumer filing, creditors with claims against co-debtors are permitted to proceed against the co-debtors 20 days after the creditor files a request for relief, unless the debtor files written objections to the creditor's request. In Chapter 7 and Chapter 11 cases—unless local rules apply—there must be a preliminary hearing on a request for relief from the automatic stay within 30 days and a final hearing within 60 days.

A debtor may even elect to treat co-signed obligations differently than other unsecured claims, and create a separate class for such creditors in his plan of arrangement with the Bankruptcy Court.

Exemptions Under Chapters 13 And 7

Generally, federal law recognizes two types of exemptions: specific property, and a dollar amount designed to give the debtor a means to start over. (Note: Some states have enacted their own set of exemptions which may be less liberal than the federal list and prohibits debtors from use of federal exemption.)

Under both Chapter 7 and Chapter 13, the bankrupt debtor is allowed to keep many assets: the Federal exemption for personal property exclusive of one motor vehicle valued up to $1,200.00 and jewelry valued up to $500.00 is limited to $200.00 per item to an aggregate of $4,000.00. Debtors can also obtain a super benefit by getting $3,750.00 additional exemption of any unused amount of a

$7,500.00 residential real estate exemption if debtor actually uses the property as residence. Debtor is also entitled to a floating wild-card exemption of $400.00, and is permitted to retain up to $750.00 in books or tools of trade.

Protecting Your interests

Your main objective upon receiving notice in a Chapter 13 case is to be certain that a proof of claim is filed for the proper amount due. A proof may be deemed filed for any claim that appears on the list of schedules filed by the debtor, provided it's not listed as "disputed," "contingent" or "unliquidated." However, creditors rarely get the opportunity to know the amount for which they're listed; and accordingly, the best protection is a timely filing of a proof of claim with the court.

The Involuntary Petition In Bankruptcy

An involuntary petition in bankruptcy may be filed against the debtor by any three or more creditors holding non-contingent and unsecured claims totalling $5,000.00 or more. (Where the debtor has less than twelve creditors, the petition may be filed by one or more.) They may allege that the debtor is "generally not paying debts as such debts become due" (excluding debts which are in bonafide dispute), or has had a custodian of all of his assets appointed. A "custodian" includes an assignee for the benefit of creditors.

Creditors could seek liquidation of such a debtor's assets. However, creditors can also file an involuntary bankruptcy petition, as provided by the new Bankruptcy Code, and apply for reorganization under Chapter 11. A Chapter 11 plan can be a plan or arrangement that calls for the orderly liquidation of a business under court supervision.

What Determines "Failure To Pay Debts"?

Such a determination will be dependent upon a comparison of the total debt with the amount of debt that remains unpaid. In addition, to prevent a possible rash of filings, debtors are protected from improper petitions by certain provisions of the Code. These allow the court to charge the petitioning creditor for attorney fees, and even damages for loss of profit, if it concludes that the involuntary petition was filed in bad faith—and should be dismissed.

The court may also dismiss any petition if it finds the interests of creditors and the debtor would be better served by such suspension. This provision is primarily designed to protect the debtor who is only in a temporary cash bind from being adjudicated as "bankrupt."

After the filing of the Chapter 7 involuntary petition, the debtor may convert the matter to a case under Chapter 11. This is frequently done if the debtor has a change of heart, and wants to remain in business. Alternatively, the debtor may convert the case to Chapter 11 so that he can remain as debtor-in-possession and, at the same time, propose a plan which calls for reorganization or for liquidation of the business. The Bankruptcy Code now permits the debtor to convert its assets into cash and to liquidate substantially all of its property—and distribute the proceeds to its creditors.

A Chapter 11 Bankruptcy Petition

A Chapter 11 case is commenced by the filing of a petition in bankruptcy court, and is usually filed voluntarily by the business debtor. Sometimes a debtor will voluntarily convert a creditors' involuntary Chapter 7 petition to his voluntary Chapter 11.

In Chapter 11, the debtor will usually be allowed to remain in possession of its business and to operate during the reorganization process. It's quite usual for creditors to be dealing with such a debtor on an ongoing basis after the filing of this type bankruptcy petition.

What Chapter 11 Does

In its petition for relief, the Chapter 11 debtor will state its intention to file a plan that will deal with existing debts. The plan may seek to accept or reject leases or other types of contractual obligations. It may seek to pay out debts over long periods of time, or compromise debt, sell off portions of the debtor's assets, issue new stock, liquidate divisions, merge, seek new capital to assure the future of the business, or liquidate the entire operation in an orderly manner.

For the first 120 days of the proceeding, the debtor has the exclusive right to file a plan. After that time, any trustee, creditors' committee, creditor, or any "third party" may offer a plan or arrangement, if the debtor's plan is not accepted by creditors.

If a debtor's plan is not acceptable, it doesn't immediately follow that there will be an adjudication and liquidation. Because others beside the debtor may propose a plan, the true value of the debtor's business will depend on the "marketplace"—it depends on what will give creditors the greatest possible return.

The creditors' committee, in a change from common law, will be appointed by the court, generally from among the seven largest unsecured creditors willing to serve. The court may also appoint a representative group for other classes of creditors, each of whom may employ counsel, an accountant and a secretary—as would be the case under common law. But all outside employment is subject to court approval.

In the event that the case began as an out-of-court meeting, a creditors' committee that was organized before the petition was filed may be maintained. The court may even appoint that committee as the official creditors' committee, provided there's adequate representation and the committee was fairly chosen.

If there are limited assets in a given case, the committee may not wish to retain the service of professionals. The size of the committee and the administrative expenses which reduce the funds available for distribution to creditors must be held down, and must be commensurate with the size of the debtor and the recovery likely to bc achieved.

What The Committee Does

The primary functions of a creditors' committee in Chapter 11 will be similar to those functions conducted by a committee in an out-of-court situation: investigation into the operations of the debtor's business, to determine the desirability of continuing the business. Where there are signs of irregularities, the committee may request the appointment of a trustee or examiner to conduct further investigation. The committee may participate in the formulation of a plan, report its recommendations to the entire creditor body, and then tabulate the votes and file the results with the court.

The committee will consult continually with the debtor in possession regarding problems that are discovered, and offer suggestions for change. Such areas might include reduction of salaries and other fixed costs, and elimination of all but the most necessary personnel. Such committee activity may actually be welcomed by the debtor, as the discussions often involve acquisition of additional operating capital or new ways to control production and inventory. By doing this, the committee can significantly reduce the cost of operations and improve the debtor's profitability.

Under Chapter 11, the committee does not get the opportunity to put in the controls that would be possible in an out-of-court settlement. However, it can make good use of the monthly financial statements the debtor is required to file with the court. The debtor's plan of reorganization, in fact, is basically a schedule of payments for discharging any remaining pre-petition debt.

It's important to remember that the creditors' committee is appointed only in Chapter 11 bankruptcy cases. In Chapter 11, because the debtor may seek to rehabilitate, reorganize, or liquidate, while at the same time remaining in possession and control of his business—the creditors' committee serves as a vehicle through which creditors can have a direct voice.

How A Plan Is Adopted

Once the required number of acceptances (⅔ in dollar amount and more than ½ in number) have been obtained and the plan is approved, creditors who don't agree are barred from taking any action. If a class of creditor does not accept, the plan may even be confirmed over their objections if (1) that class is not affected by the plan, and (2) the plan meets all other tests for confirmation, and that creditor class would receive more than it would otherwise receive if the debtor were liquidated.

Additional Benefits

A Chapter 11 proceeding offers many opportunities for debtors to improve the position of their companies, beyond just the restructuring of their debt. As a review of the public records of the major companies involved in Chapter 11 filings will show, reorganization can provide the opportunity for (1) cutting dead wood out of a company's operations; (2) renegotiating (or even terminating) leases, contractual agreements and even employment contracts; and (3) giving a company an opportunity to reorganize its method of doing business. As an added benefit, it can take write-offs that would otherwise be necessary to protect its credit standing while under the protection of the court umbrella.

From all of the foregoing, a collector should quickly observe that Chapter 11 can be very helpful.

If a stronger company can emerge and not leave a group of angry exasperated creditors in its wake, it's likely to prove to be a better customer for the future. Any company given the opportunity to renegotiate its loans and its debt, so that it can once again operate more profitably, is likely to take advantage of the opportunity—which will in turn benefit its creditors. But you should of course see to it that your company stays clear of companies who could abuse Chapter 11. When confronted with organizations that do not deserve rehabilitation, you should do everything in your power to see to it that the facts come out.

Rights Of The Secured Creditor

The Bankruptcy Act classifies debts by types of claims, not names of creditors. A creditor is said to have a *secured* claim if it holds a lien or security interest on property. However, secured creditors are allowed a secured position only to the extent of the value of the collateral on which they have perfected liens. To the extent that the value of the collateral is less than the amount of their debt, they have an *unsecured* claim.

If you have a secured claim, your lien on that property survives the bankruptcy of the debtor. You may not, however, try to collect the debt while the bankruptcy case is in process, and are subject to the same automatic-stay provisions as would be the case if you were an unsecured creditor. You do have a right to petition the court to stop the debtor from using the property; but in general, the court determines how the property is to be used.

A distinction is made, in such cases, between cash collateral and other collateral. The debtor may use cash collateral only after notice and hearing is provided to the secured creditor. But the debtor may use non-cash collateral in the ordinary course of business. In all instances, however, the secured creditor may require the debtor to provide adequate protection of the creditor's interests. The secured creditor will have to apply to the court for such protection and may even be allowed to recover attorney fees and interest, if the collateral is insufficient to pay the fees as well as the amount owed.

As a secured creditor, you're not required to file a proof of claim in a liquidation case if you intend to rely on the collateral, and no challenge to your security is made. However, as with all creditors, it's a good practice to file a claim, to be certain that your interest is protected. Secured creditors, of course, are treated differently from unsecured creditors. They do not serve on the same committees, and rank differently in order of satisfaction of their claims. When you have a secured claim and your security interest survives a bankruptcy, you're protected; you can even wait until the entire proceeding is over, and then attempt to seize your collateral or collect your debt. Be sure, however, to file a proof of claim (see below).

Periodic payments may be required of the debtor-in-possession. If the collateral is an important part of the operation of a debtor's business, the debtor may be required to provide periodic payments—on the grounds that the use, sale or lease of the property decreases the value of the property.

If there isn't adequate protection, the court may provide for a "replacement lien," and grant the secured creditor the equivalent of its original collateral. The court may also provide for the protection of the secured creditor by entitling it to a "super priority" administrative expense (they're number one)—where the collateral is necessary for the continuation of the debtor's business.

The Proof Of Claim

The filing of a proof of claim is a collector's single most important duty in a bankruptcy case. Unless the claim is filed, his company may not be able to share in the dividends paid, or vote for a Plan of Arrangement, or participate in the election of the trustee. Unfortunately, though, many collectors overlook this important task. A collector should keep ample supply of the necessary forms for assignment, receivership, and bankruptcy proceedings. These may be obtained at any legal stationery store.

The filing of a claim itself is a rather straightforward procedure. A collector can simply fill out the form and attach to it an itemized statement or any other instrument on which the debt is based. A receipt of filing should be maintained, and correspondence should be sent certified mail or regular mail in duplicate, with the request that a receipted copy be returned. It is best under those circumstances to provide a prepaid self-addressed envelope.

As it has been previously stated, in a Chapter 11 proceeding, a proof of claim need not be filed—but a creditor may participate in the proceedings *only* for the amount that it's listed for on debtor's schedules. Since the information on debtor's schedules may not be easily accessible, it is always best to file a proof of claim immediately in all proceedings. Occasionally, a creditor is asked to provide Power of Attorney to a creditors' committee, a recognized adjustment bureau, or an attorney. Creditors should not, of course, provide Power of Attorney to someone they don't know.

It is not uncommon for attorneys wishing to participate in the bankruptcy proceeding to offer to file a creditor's claim without charge. "Without charge" may, however, refer only to the filing of the claim. Should any recovery take place, the attorney is likely to take a fee on the dividend, leaving the creditor with less than others in the same circumstance. There's actually no reason for the services of an attorney, in the majority of cases, simply to file a proof of claim.

Reminder: Carefully scrutinize any request to provide Power of Attorney, but at the same time keep in mind that—by acting in concert with other creditors or a creditors' committee when requested to do so—you'll be likely to insure greater creditor control of the situation and hopefully greater recovery.

10

How To Get The Best Recovery From Accounts Placed With A Collection Agency

Table of Contents

10

How To Get The Best Recovery From Accounts Placed With A Collection Agency

In many respects, the decision to place an account for collection is the most difficult, and important, of all. If you act too soon you:

1. deprive the company of the right to earn potential profit;

2. cost the company more money;

3. open yourself to possible criticism for not working the account hard enough;

4. involve your office in the indirect costs of increased file handling and correspondence;

5. may perform a disservice to the debtor (customer).

On the other side of the coin, the dangers of not acting soon enough are often far greater. Delay may bring about:

— uncollectibility. Assets may be conveyed, concealed, disposed of—or an insolvent condition may develop—while you procrastinate;

— the necessity for suit. This means more time and collection expense. If given an account while the element of timing is still a factor, amicable collection by others is often possible. However, accepting too many promises and stalls often creates a callous debtor who may try to do the same thing again.

WHAT TO DO BEFORE YOU PLACE AN ACCOUNT FOR COLLECTION

It is not always easy to decide when the best time is to move the account along, even for experienced collectors. But experts agree that timing and information are the most important factors in determining when to place an account for collection, and what is needed to obtain the best results.

Before placement, be sure your efforts have been thorough and vigorous. Where no contact has been made and communication is non-existent, make sure you have:

— checked phone directories and information operators for phone numbers;

— checked city cross directories, where warranted by size. Often, neighbors can tactfully be "sounded" for similar information;

— scoured available credit reports. Frequently, a name or fact buried in the body of the report will give you the lead needed to generate results.

In cases where contact has been made, but where you are experiencing difficulty reaching the principals, or where you are having trouble extracting a commitment or holding the debtor to one, have you:

1. tried a personal visit? If warranted by size of claim and is geographically practical, this often works wonders.

2. sufficiently impressed the message-taker with the vital importance of getting an immediate response?

3. tried the third-party approach? The debtor may be impressed, if you're getting nowhere, and you let the manager or another collector try. No one

man is all things to all people. This is certainly true as applied to debtors. It's the mark of a seasoned, mature collector who realizes this, and utilizes other personnel to the fullest. Maybe a new voice or personality will motivate the debtor/customer to respond. This is called a "T.O." (take-over tactic), and can be extremely effective as a final demand.

4. been firm enough? Does the debtor know you mean business?

5. reminded the debtor it's either pay you or the agency? Which does he prefer?

6. been overly aggressive? If you are too pushy, the debtor may feel "boxed in." And if he's genuinely unable to pay in full, he may feel there is no other way out. With proper guidance, he might be led to volunteer a partial payment.

7. considered alternative arrangements? Perhaps the initial arrangements may be unrealistic.

8. given the debtor a firm deadline? A *firm ultimatum* sometimes provides the catalytic spur needed to produce results.

When, despite your most diligent efforts, the debtor has refused to respond, a decision to proceed further must be reached. The discipline, of course, must be maintained.

Warning Signs

There are certain "red flag" situations which will facilitate the decision to place the account for collection. Some of these are obvious, others are not. For example:

1. no phone

2. phone disconnected

3. new unlisted phone

4. an absolute refusal by debtor to cooperate

5. refusal to acknowledge responsibility for debt

6. refusal to issue dated checks or notes, or to bind a payment schedule with a letter of commitment

7. record of NSF checks or notes

8. default, followed by request for lower payment schedule

9. erratic payments

10. partial payments of steadily diminishing amounts

11. poor record of principals in other related businesses

12. admission by debtor that other bills must first be paid

13. more than 2 or 3 defaults at the most

14. increasing evasiveness of principals

15. unbalanced financial condition

16. talk of refinancing

17. talk of paying less than 100%

18. threat to go bankrupt if pushed. (If bills cannot be met, the debtor is admitting his insolvency anyway—and you may as well formalize it.)

19. has a record of partnership, marital or business difficulties

20. over-buying

21. admission of inability to pay

22. debtor defers to an attorney

How To Develop A "Collection Sense"

There are numerous other "tip-offs," but the preceding list is fairly representative. Knowing these clues to assess collection prospects and the means for using them, constitutes what is commonly referred to as "collection sense."

The astute collector is constantly aware of his obligation to serve his company's best interests. Therefore, he guards against allowing his pride to blind his judgment, and against becoming emotionally involved. In addition, he recognizes the importance of getting prompt assistance when he cannot achieve reasonably fast and fairly substantial arrangements. And he understands that this is the only way he can get maximum recovery of his company's dollars. After all, recovery is the name of the game!

BENEFITS OF USING COLLECTION AGENCIES

There was a time when the collection position was not truly recognized in financial circles; but today, collectors responsible for converting asset receivables into cash have truly come of age.

During these times of increased economic awareness, business professionals are forced to focus greater attention on the collection function. Collection agencies are being put to the ultimate test. In an effort to capitalize on collection facilities available, so that recoveries can be maximized, a thorough understanding of the true purpose of a collection agency is essential.

The collection agency owes its existence to necessity. As a safeguard to our national credit system, utilization of a knowledgeable collection agency offers the prudent person the most effective implement for converting overdue receivables into paid-in-full collections.

Collection accounts, whether the result of errors in judgment, inefficiency, overoptimism, lack of ability, or acts of God, will always be with us. Collection control, bad debt identification and recovery are of concern to all in the credit fraternity. But they are of special concern to the collection agencies. It is apparent that collection activity is really an extension of credit activity, rather than a legal problem.

The agency should be employed as a tool, and not as a crutch. A disputed claim will not be improved by its having been placed for collection. It will remain disputed, if the dispute is genuine and not merely a sham to avoid payment.

WHEN TO PLACE AN ACCOUNT FOR COLLECTION

Historically, 90 days past due has been the point at which maximum effort has been employed not only to collect, but to prevent total loss. It is after this point—after every reasonable means available has been exhausted—that *timely placement* with a collection agency is made.

There is no magical answer to the question of: When is the best time to place an account for collection? As already pointed out, acting too soon may result in the loss of a potentially good customer by destroying the rapport and good will; waiting too long may result in a credit loss if the company owing you the money should go out of business.

When a claim is submitted to an agency, the entire file should be forwarded to it. All the preceding correspondence will be important, as well as the invoices, contracts, and credit information. After all, the agency would not want to cover old ground. It should be able to pick up where a creditor leaves off, and then move forward. This maintains the continuity of the entire collection effort.

A Key Preliminary Service

An account can be called in by telephone, or mailed to the agency. Either of the two will usually involve initial pre-collection service called "free demand." It consists of a written demand on agency letterhead advising an account that, unless a check is received by a certain date, collection activity will begin. If the account pays, there is no charge made by the agency. Hence the term "free demand." (See Figure 10-1 for a sample agency free demand letter.)

The free demand concept, when used in its proper context, can be almost 100% effective. This is not to suggest that each time a notice is sent to a debtor, informing him that if payment is not made by a certain date his account will be placed for collection, a check will be forthcoming.

Experience shows that checks will be received 16% to 23% of the time, depending on the industry, age of the account at placement, and the nature of the product or service involved. But the accounts that remain unpaid have all said something; by remaining silent, they have thus confirmed that they are the collection problems they were thought to be all along. These types of accounts are the ones most in need of vigorous agency action.

How An Agency Determines The Best Approach To Take

When an agency becomes involved, as outlined earlier, collection cycles previously employed by creditors are not duplicated. An account is analyzed, based on the specific collection activity that took place in the creditor's own department,

"Sample Agency Free Demand Letter"

STa (logo)

STANLEY
TULCHIN
ASSOCIATES

A PERSONAL SERVICE

THROUGHOUT THE NATION

CREDIT AND COLLECTION CONSULTANTS • 591 STEWART AVENUE • GARDEN CITY, N.Y. 11530 • (516) 222-2750

DATE

TO

ATTENTION

AMOUNT
PAST DUE **$**

You have left us with no alternative but to place your past due account with

STANLEY TULCHIN ASSOCIATES, for immediate collection unless your check is in this

office by

Your prompt attention to this notice will avoid the necessity of further proceedings.

CREDITOR _____

ADDRESS _____

CITY & STATE _____

By _____

COPY TO   **STANLEY TULCHIN ASSOCIATES**

©MCMLXXXII STA Rev. 6/82

NEW YORK   •   CHICAGO   •   LOS ANGELES   •   ATLANTA   •   DALLAS

Figure 10-1

the age of the invoice, amount involved, and previous agency experience with the account. Then an action technique is decided on. This, coupled with knowledge of the remedies available to the creditor in a particular geographical area, all help to determine the best possible approach to a given collection account.

It is important for the agency to know the law, in doing this—but not for the purpose of interpretation or giving legal advice. This knowledge plays a role in the collection effort, and protects the creditor as well as the agency itself. The laws governing creditors' rights in a given area are a matter of public record, and it is vital that they be considered.

For example, when a lengthy payout program is put forth in an attempt to resolve a debt, such as $25.00 a week to pay a $500.00 account, knowing the alternatives (if and how that payment program can be improved upon, or should legal action be instituted, how much time it may take) means that invariably a more intelligent decision can be reached regarding acceptance.

A debtor usually does not want a collection agency—and possibly other creditors—to know he pays his accounts slowly. If at all able, he usually prefers to avoid such a reputation by paying the creditor in full or by discussing a mutually agreeable way of settlement. Only when all efforts fail, when creditor and agency alike agree that there is no alternative, are accounts forwarded to local attorneys for further action.

It is usually advisable for a creditor to request preliminary investigation rather than issue instructions for the agency to retain counsel for the purpose of instituting immediate suit. In most cases, no such action is necessary. Litigation can often be protracted as a result of dilatory answers being filed by the debtor's attorney. Creditors are much better off with on-account payments that reduce their exposure, than with docket numbers.

The creditors' attorney who specializes in collection practice will, after a thorough investigation, provide a recommendation with regard to the advisability of instituting legal action.

Special Considerations In The Use Of A Collection Agency

Once having made that final decision to place the account for collection with an agency, creditors find such action has several advantages:

1. *The agency can provide third-party influence.* Often the introduction of a third party into the collection effort will produce in itself a collection result. The delinquent customer knows you mean business when you turn the account over to a collection agency, and it is likely that your customer/debtor does not wish to obtain a reputation of having to pay an agency. The customer may be worried that his bank will find out he's been placed for collection, because if he sends a check to the agency they will endorse it. This accounts for the greatest number of payments going directly to creditors immediately after an account has been placed for collection. (This quick result often amazes many collection managers.)

2. *The agency provides collection experts.* The personnel in a collection agency are trained in the collection of all kinds of delinquent accounts. Many of them are experts with special knowledge, sophistication and experience in collecting your money.

3. *The agency can save you time and expense, and generally promote good use of your own people.* The time it takes your in-house staff to maintain long-term intensified collection efforts against the toughest delinquent accounts can be better spent. A good agency has the time and personnel to give you the service you require, thus turning over your receivables a lot faster.

4. *The agency has knowledge of local conditions.* In many cases, the agency will have an intimate knowledge of your account's operations through prior experience with it. Collection tactics can then be tailored to fit the individual debtor's circumstance. By targeting the effort, the agency can generally obtain better and quicker results.

5. *The agency is in a position to provide a total collection service, and has access to local attorneys* in the event such action becomes necessary. If legal action is required, an agency knows which attorney is best to deal with the account concerned. Developing relationships with only the best legal professionals concerned with creditors' rights, a good agency is in a position to advise you when it feels such action may be required.

WHAT TO LOOK FOR IN CHOOSING A COLLECTION AGENCY

There are extensive criteria to consider in deciding which collection agency is best for you. While you need an agency with a proven track record for effecting recovery, you also need an agency whose ethical conduct is beyond reproach. First and foremost in the selection criteria is the *financial responsibility of the agency*. You should find out the following:

1. *Whether the agency, owner, partner, or corporation is financially responsible*. Are its employees bonded? Is the agency itself bonded and willing to provide you with a copy of a meaningful bond? In addition, the collection agency should be in a position to furnish a financial statement with the names and addresses of all owners. It should also supply bank and trade references, and a copy of the bond along with significant coverage limitations, if any.

After all, by trusting your accounts receivables to your collection agency, you're in effect extending a potential credit to that agency. You want to be sure it has the financial strength, along with the capital capacity and collateral, to collect and remit the proceeds of what's collected.

2. *Reputation of the agency*. You should obtain references and check into the agency's ethics and tactics. You should interview at least three of its clients, so that you can determine firsthand if its performance is satisfactory. The key question is whether it makes effective and timely collection with dispatch, and without excessive antagonism, which could damage your company's hard-earned reputation. Remember that the agency represents you. If it uses abusive tactics, it's as if you had used them. Be sure not to deal with any organization that fails to comply with the Fair Debt Collection Practices Act, or whose efforts and reputation may be subject to question.

3. *Experience of the agency*. Verify the length of time the agency has been in business, especially checking the experience of its collection staff. Remember, favorable collection results are gained through well qualified and experienced personnel.

4. *Size of the agency*. How many collectors does it employ? It should be small enough to give you personal attention; yet large enough to handle all your accounts satisfactorily. In addition, it should have branch offices and good contacts in your geographical area. This will help to speed communication, and to provide you with face-to-face collections where the situation warrants it.

5. *Results the agency produces*. Performance ratios are important. Check out not only the dollars collected, but how long it took to collect them. Keep a record by agency, of placements and collections on a monthly basis.

A sample chart, like that shown in Figure 10-2, can act as your guide towards evaluating results. Compare agency against agency, and do it often. Don't be afraid to reward the better performer with increased activity.

6. *If a license is required* in your state, be sure that the agency maintains one, and that it remains in good standing. In addition, it is often better to deal with an agency that is an active member of its industry association. In that way, the agency's executives are likely to attend continuing educational meetings, and become acquainted with the latest rules and regulations pertaining to the collection industry. They're also likely to know the newest collection techniques.

When seeking out a *commercial* agency, you should be sure to choose among the professionals holding a Certificate of Compliance from the Commercial Law League of America. The group has established a Commercial Agency Section, headquartered in Washington, D.C. Before being admitted to this Section, a commercial agency must meet rigid standards, and applicants must be thoroughly screened as to staff reliability, financial responsibility, experience and professionalism.

When choosing a *consumer* agency, be sure the agency is a member of the American Collection Association (ACA), or the American Commercial Collector's Association (ACCA).

7. *The fees the agency charges.* Although there are established recommended rates for each type of claim, there can be a wide range in the services provided and in the rates charged by different agencies. It is up to you to make a judgment as to what service provides the best value. But it's important to remember that you get what you pay for; and often the lowest rate generates the lowest recovery and the least effort. In addition, avoid the "no frills agency"—low rate, lower recover, little effort, and perhaps no remittance.

8. *The service the agency provides.* Make sure that the agency furnishes at least the following services:

A. An effective Free Demand Service, under your direction and control, so that you are in a position to know if, when and how it's mailed—and when the "clock starts ticking" on your Free Demand Service.

B. Be sure the agency is willing to assign to you an experienced account representative who knows your industry, and is dedicated to your needs. When the

Company name _____

ANNUAL EVALUATION OF COLLECTION AGENCY OR ATTORNEY

Agency's _____ Name _____

Attorney's _____ Address _____

19___

L I N E	1	2		PRIOR YEARS	LAST YEAR	AMOUNTS PLACED THROUGH PERIOD ENDED												
						JAN.	FEB.	MAR.	APR.	MAY	JUN.	JUL.	AUG.	SEP.	OCT.	NOV.	DEC.	TOTAL
				3	4	5	6	7	8	9	10	11	12	13	14	15	16	17
1	PLACED																	
2	January																	
3	February																	
4	March																	
5	April																	
6	May																	
7	June																	
8	July																	
9	August																	
10	September																	
11	October																	
12	November																	
13	December																	
14	TOTAL																	
15	BALANCE OUTSTANDING																	

Collected By Month During Current Year

FIGURE 10-2

agency provides personal and individual attention, you will avoid having to educate collectors regarding the peculiarities unique to your industry. Nothing is more frustrating than having to call an agency and being transferred to seven different representatives, each handling a different phase or geographical location of your collection effort.

C. Be sure the agency agrees to maintain a separate trust account into which all monies rightfully belonging to creditors are placed. It is important that proceeds on your collection not be used for operating overhead, and in that regard remittance should be made promptly upon clearance, or within 30 days of each collection.

D. Be sure the agency keeps you informed of its progress without being prodded, relieving you of needless correspondence and the burdensome details required in the follow-up.

E. Be sure the agency respects the privileged nature of your communication. It should only report the status to you, and should not disseminate information to the trade or publish debtor lists, or violate your confidence in any way. That may create a drain on the debtor by producing a rash of activity all at the same time—so that collection becomes problematic or for that matter impossible.

F. It is also important to consider the source of revenue for your agency. Since its fees are contingent, you should be sure that the agency specializes exclusively in the collection of delinquent accounts, and that collection represents its major source of income.

G. Be sure your agency will provide monthly or quarterly, manual or computerized listings of the accounts placed for collection and their present status, along with a summary analysis of results accomplished to date. This should not be its only method of reporting, but simply a double check and overview of your activities with them.

H. It is important to consider the agency as an extension of your collection department, so that you are comfortable calling your representative to discuss your collection problems whenever the need arises. Let's face it, when you turn your delinquent account over to your representative, you do so with a great deal of concern. It is therefore equally important that your representatives react with empathy and understanding, and be able to transfer that sense of urgency into action.

I. It is important to ascertain that you are getting a full collection service. Many companies operating at a substantially lower commission rate provide nothing more than a letter service. This, in effect, duplicates your own collection effort, and could do more harm than good, as a result of a delay in further proceedings. Credit Managers and collectors should make sure that the agency they retain is not so automated as to handle all accounts in a predetermined fashion, regardless of balance due or the circumstances surrounding the particular collection.

HOW BEST TO WORK WITH YOUR COLLECTION AGENCY

After an account has been placed for collection, it is important to cooperate as fully as possible with your agency. The quickest and most effective results can be achieved when there is a smooth transition, and the efforts of the agency pick up right where the efforts of the prior collector left off. In fact, that it is similar to what you would expect to occur in a relay race, the moment the baton is passed. You certainly wouldn't get very far if the baton, instead of being passed, was dropped, thrown to the rear, or for that matter thrown in the woods and completely lost. It must be a team effort.

A smooth transition is facilitated by full disclosure and the placement of complete documentation to support the balance of the account, along with any written communications between you and the customer that bring out salient points. Any acknowledgement of debt in the form of NSF checks, letters of admission, or written statements of account should be sent in as well.

Despite the need for supporting documentation, accounts are often telephoned to the agency, so that action can be started immediately—with full detailed explanation given by phone and later supported by the documentation that follows. This is sometimes enough. While documentation is helpful and important, if the only available information is a statement of account or a copy of an invoice, that is sufficient for an agency to begin its collection effort. The creditor can, in the meantime, attempt to obtain additional information in support of the balance.

What To Do When A Debtor Contacts You Instead Of The Agency

Once the agency efforts have begun, it is quite common for customer/debtors to contact their creditor directly. This is a mistake. Creditors should refer all further communications to the agency, so that continuity in the collection effort can be maintained. Otherwise, customers may try to play the agency against the creditor, (1) trying to create confusion, (2) trying to buy additional time by stalling, or (3) just to avoid being thought of as a collection problem requiring agency action.

Creditors should promptly advise the agency regarding any direct contact, and immediately refer any payments to the agency for clearance. If the matter being handled by the agency has already been referred to counsel, and if the attorney retained has proceeded with suit, creditors who accept checks may be jeopardizing the chance to recover the court costs advanced. For that reason alone, creditors should not accept direct payments once an account has been placed for collection.

In order to be certain that customer/debtors do not benefit from communication delays between you and your agent, you should promptly respond to requests for documentation, offers of settlement, or any other written communication. Debtor's allegations must be dealt with promptly. A dispute—that may be nothing more than a sham to avoid payment—must be dealt with right away.

On occasion, it may be necessary to respond to the requirements for suit as submitted by the creditor's local attorney; and just as often it's necessary to obtain acceptance and creditor approval for a negotiated pay-out. Best results are achieved by open and timely communication with the agency. Nothing helps an agency's effort more than personal contact with the client.

What To Do About "Dead Wood" Accounts

From time to time, accounts referred to an agency may be out of business at the time of placement. However, based on either the size of the account, or the creditor's desire to obtain further information, these accounts cannot simply be written off, but must be investigated further. The agency will usually undertake this investigation, and may even provide sufficient additional information to confirm the hopelessness of any recovery.

When working on a contingent fee basis as collection agencies do, such non-productive accounts are not considered revenue producers. But by providing information and servicing even the "deadest" of accounts, the agency hopes to win the confidence of its clients improve the quality of placements, and make its relationship a long-term one. However, a creditor that consistently places accounts for collection against companies whose phones have been disconnected or whose mail has been returned, or organizations that have been closed and are out of business, is really wasting an agency's time.

LEGAL PHASES OF COLLECTION

While you probably won't become involved in the legal side of collection very often, this is still something you should be familiar with. You should know the legal steps an agency sometimes recommends *if they become absolutely necessary.*

Here's what can happen:

When a customer/debtor has been totally unresponsive to payment demands, the agency can recommend an attorney(s) to the creditor, and transmit accounts to an attorney on terms and conditions authorized by the creditor. There is a separate rate schedule that permits no division of attorney's collection commission or suit fee. However, that fee is usually combined with the agency's total contingent collection rate previously provided to its client/creditors.

Creditors usually authorize an agency to act as their agent, to conduct correspondence of a routine nature on their behalf with the attorney to whom the creditor's account has been transmitted for collection, and in general to carry on activities similar to those ordinarily carried on by the collection department of a creditor organization. However, the attorney will institute no proceedings, incur no expenses, make no compromise and grant no extensions unless authorized by the creditor. It is usually decided in advance as to whether copies of correspondence between the attorney and the agency are shared with creditors. In some instances, all communications are transmitted; in other such situations written correspondence is minimized.

How Much Will It Cost?

The service charges of the agency usually remain fixed whether there is a lawsuit or not. The agency service to the creditor is intended to relieve the credit or collection manager from the details concerning the handling of claims and correspondence. The agency gives to the servicing of the collection account its special skills and experience, and usually provides the creditor with the up-to-date reports and file record data necessary for efficient collection management.

After conducting a preliminary investigation, the attorney is usually in a position to report on the possibilities of collection and provide suit recommendations—in the event suit is believed to be advisable. At that time, the attorney will state exactly what papers and costs will be required.

What Documentation Is Needed By The Attorney To Bring Suit

In many cases, the documentation needed by the attorney to start a lawsuit is similar to the documentation desired by the agency. The most important consideration in each instance is "Know your customer," that is, the one against whom the action is to be brought.

You should provide the legal identity (composition), the names and addresses of the principals or proprietors, or partners. Naturally, a good address where service can be made is extremely helpful. Copies of customer's purchase order, contract(s), invoices—including terms of sale, delivery dates, and types of merchandise, bills of lading, or any original unpaid negotiable instruments submitted, such as a bad check, promissory note, or trade acceptance, will help. Of course, at this time, it's important to provide all information concerning any possible banking connections, and if it's a commercial matter, to review if there are any possible security agreements or any encumbrances on assets or property.

In addition, depending on the particular county, state, and court jurisdiction where the action is to brought, a specific affidavit is likely to be required, which must be signed and notarized. The state of incorporation and the proper identity of the plaintiff are necessary, along with copies of any written agreements or signed contracts. If there are finance, service, or interest charges included in the principal, they must be isolated at this time, and a proper explanation of each should be provided.

Miscellaneous information that would prove to be unusual or that could materially effect the outcome should also be submitted. This includes letters to and from the customer which may be of help to clarify a dispute or acknowledge a debt. Usually the attorney will require original documentation of these. In most states, however, copies of the originals are considered acceptable and admissible as documentary evidence.

As is the case with preliminary collection efforts, delay should be avoided at all costs. When not all documentation is available, it's important to consult with the attorney and to determine whether action can begin on an "account stated" basis—which is usually when an account has been promising payment and where no dispute exists. If additional documentation is later required, at least the original action need not be delayed.

When an account of yours is placed in the hands of an attorney with instructions to commence suit, it takes on a different complexion. Before, your relationship with your customer was one of creditor/debtor. Once the suit action begins, however, it becomes one of plaintiff and defendant. Using the definition of debtor in its simplest form "one obligated to pay" and comparing it to defendant "one who is innocent until proven guilty," it's easy to see how even the most simple lawsuit can prove troublesome. By starting legal action, many creditors feel that confirming the obvious is all that's needed—that the outcome can only be what they knew when they started, and that their customer owed them the money. But they of course have to prove it, in a procedure which might prove to be time-consuming, costly, and with no guarantees that collection will result.

WHAT HAPPENS IN A COLLECTION LAWSUIT

Upon receipt of the necessary documentation, the attorney will commence the action by serving a summons upon the debtor. This can be done either personally, or in some other way, as required or permitted in the state. Once served, the debtor/defendant is allowed a certain amount of time to answer the allegations as set forth in the complaint. In his answer, the debtor may set up whatever defenses he believes he has to the action, including a denial of the allegations, any special defenses and, in some cases, even new matters—introduced by filing cross-complaints or counterclaims.

Ways That Collection Actions Can Be Resolved

Sometimes, through pleadings (such as exchange of questionnaires known as "interrogatories" or "discovery proceedings") solutions can be found for resolving all difficulties. However, each jurisdiction may deal with the intricacies of a particular lawsuit in a different manner. If, despite every effort, a settlement is not possible, then the matter will be either sent to arbitrators, or placed on the trial calendar of the court. Under the laws of most states, the parties are entitled to a trial by jury as a matter or right; but a trial by jury is usually waived, and the case proceeds to trial before a judge.

In cases where no answer is filed by the defendant, or there's an overwhelming amount of evidence including acknowledgment of indebtedness on the part of the defendant, a creditor is in a position to take a default judgment or summary judgment. If, either as a result of arbitration or judicial decision, a judgment is entered, that judgment becomes part of the permanent records of the court. It also becomes a lien upon property which the debtor may own.

Most collection actions are resolved through default or summary proceedings, arbitration, or settlement before trial. In a rare instance where a trial is necessary, a witness may be required. There are many who do not understand why they must appear in court, and regard it as an inconvenience or imposition. The usual comment is, "Why can't the attorney show the judge the relevant documents, and prove the case without them?" But our system of justice requires that the *plaintiff* prove his case, not the plaintiff's lawyers.

In order to prove a case in court, it is necessary to have an appropriate witness (preferably one who is genuinely familiar with the books and records of a company) swear under oath that the facts being presented by your attorney are accurate and truthful. The judge will not permit the attorney to swear that his client's information is accurate, nor can the documents speak for themselves. Judges will rely only upon the testimony of live witnesses who are present in the courtroom, and who are sworn in to tell the truth.

How Collection Is Effected

Once the judgment confirming the amount due from a defendant to a plaintiff is entered, the next step is to request an order of the court directing the sheriff or other officer to seize the judgment debtor's property to satisfy the judgment. In some cases, the judgment debtor doesn't really have the funds or property which can be used to satisfy the execution. And sometimes there are numerous exemptions allowed the judgment debtor, so that collection cannot be effected through normal means. A debtor may, for example, claim that he is unable to pay.

In certain instances, garnishment proceedings are used to effect recovery. This enables you to compel an employer to pay you directly, instead of paying the defendant/debtor. Wage executions, salary garnishments and the like vary in each state (and in some states are not permitted at all). But the only real problem is the fact that in commercial cases, companies could go out of business, and in consumer cases, the sheriff or court official cannot find any property on which to make a levy. The problem now is how to find the money or property which can be used to liquidate the judgment.

How To Find A Debtor's Assets

The search for a debtor's assets usually begins with a supplementary proceedings examination, more commonly referred to as a "sup-pro." Such action differs in accordance with the statutory provisions of each state. Basically, it provides that a judgment creditor may by subpoena direct the judgment debtor to appear before the court or other appointed official for examination by the judgment creditor. The examination is used by attorneys to establish under oath what property is owned by a judgment debtor (if any), and what the real possibilities are concerning the recovery on the judgment.

The subpoenas contain a comprehensive list of questions concerning the source and use of funds of companies, the checkbooks of individuals, and each and every item that a company or individual may have been known to possess. Frequently, the judgment debtor is asked to provide copies of prior tax returns for review.

While the main purpose of this type of subpoena is usually to obtain information that will lead towards collection, occasionally the activity itself produces results where both husband and wife are involved. Sometimes it's easier to pay an obligation than to resolve a marital argument that may result.

The sample financial statement (Figure 10-3) is used for a personal or business situation, and contains the information that is likely to be the subject of a comprehensive questionnaire in the supplementary proceedings process.

The following list entitled the "Key steps in a collection lawsuit" will be helpful to collection managers. In fact, it will help to guide any executive to understand better what's likely to happen when a collection account is pursued through suit. The step-by-step process can take a few months to a few years to complete. Payment, while it can occur at any time, is most frequently the end result of a successful action.

A collection manager, now being more familiar with what lies ahead if legal action is pursued, should seriously consider such action only as a last resort. Suit action should only be taken when customer/debtors are unresponsive to agency demands for payment. In that way, the collection process is likely to maximize recovery and minimize expense in the shortest period of time.

Form CR 107 (Revised May 1977)
Statement Form Suggested By
FEDERAL RESERVE BANK OF NEW YORK

FINANCIAL STATEMENT

As of .... 19 ......

PERSONAL

NAME..RESIDENCE..
OCCUPATION   BUSINESS
  OR PROFESSION .... ADDRESS ....

I make the following statement of all my assets and liabilities at the close of business on the date indicated above to

....
(Name and Location of Financial Institution)

and give other material information for the purpose of obtaining advances on notes and bills bearing my signature, endorsement, or
guaranty, and for obtaining credit generally upon present and future applications.

ASSETS		LIABILITIES and NET WORTH	
Cash on Hand	$	Notes Payable to Banks — Unsecured	$
		Direct borrowings only (Sch. No. 1)	
Cash in Banks		Notes Payable to Banks — Secured	
(Sch. No. 1)		Direct borrowings only (Sch. No. 1)	
Notes Receivable		Notes Payable to Others — Unsecured	
(Sch. No. 2)			
Accounts Receivable		Notes Payable to Others — Secured	
(Sch. No. 2)			
Loans Receivable		Accounts Payable	
(Sch. No. 2)			
Life Insurance — Cash Surrender Value		Loans against Life Insurance	
(Do not deduct loans) (Sch. No. 3)		(Sch. No. 3)	
Securities — Readily Marketable		Real Estate Mortgages Payable	
U. S. Govt. & listed on Stock Exchanges (Sch. No. 4)		(Sch. No. 7)	
Securities — Not Readily Marketable		Real Estate Taxes & Assessments Payable	
Unlisted stocks & bonds (Sch. No. 4)		(Sch. No. 7)	
Mortgages Owned		Federal & State Income Taxes	
(Sch. No. 5)			
Real Estate		Other Taxes	
(Sch. No. 6)			
Automobile(s)		Interest Payable	
Registered in own name		On loans, mortgages, etc.	
Other Assets		Brokers Margin Accounts	
(Itemize)		(Sch. No. 8)	
		Other Liabilities	
		(Itemize)	
		Net Worth	
TOTAL ASSETS	$	TOTAL LIABILITIES & NET WORTH	$

SUPPLEMENTARY SCHEDULES

NOTE: The following data should be furnished as of the same date as this Financial Statement. Fill in all spaces; insert "NONE" where appropriate.

No. 1 — Banking Relations — List all bank accounts, including savings accounts:

Name and Location of Bank	Cash Balance	Amount of Loan	Indicate How Loan is Endorsed, Guaranteed or Secured
	$	$	

No. 2 — Notes, Accounts and Loans Receivable — List the largest amounts owed to you:

Name and Address of Debtor	Amount of Debt	Age of Debt	Nature of Debt	If Secured, Describe Security	Date Payment Expected
	$				

No. 3 — Life Insurance — List all policies in which you are named as the insured:

Beneficiary	Insurance Company	Type of Policy	Face Amount of Policy	Total Cash Surrender Value	Total Loans Against Policy	If Assigned, Indicate To Whom
			$	$	$	

No. 4 — Securities — List all stocks, bonds, etc.:

Face Value (Bonds) No. of Shares (Stocks)	Description of Security	Registered Owner(s)	Cost	Market Value	Book Value	If Pledged, Indicate To Whom
			$	$	$	

(Continued on Reverse Side)

Figure 10-3

SUPPLEMENTARY SCHEDULES — (Continued)

No. 5 — Mortgages Owned —

Location and Description of Mortgaged Properties	Assessed Value	Market Value	Amount of Owned Mortgage	Mortgage Interest Due & Unpaid	Indicate if First or Second Mortgage	Amount of Prior Mortgage
	$	$	$	$		$

Mortgage Income — During the 12 month period ended..19......., I received interest payments of $.................... and principal payments of $......................... on the above described mortgages.

No. 6 — Real Estate —

Location and Description of Owned Properties	Cost with Improvements	Assessed Value	Market Value	Book Value	Annual Gross Rental Income	Annual Net Rental Income (Before Depreciation)
	$	$	$	$	$	$

Title to Real Estate — The title to all of the above described properties is in my name solely, except as follows (give details): ....

No. 7 — Real Estate Mortgages Payable — List all mortgages on the above properties; follow the same sequence:

First Mortgages		Second Mortgages		Mortgage Payments Due Within One Year	Mortgage Interest Due & Unpaid	Taxes and Assessments Due & Unpaid
Amount	Maturity	Amount	Maturity			
$		$		$	$	$

No. 8 — Brokers Margin Accounts — List the names and addresses of the brokers and indicate the net amount due to each:

SUPPLEMENTARY INFORMATION

Personal Data — No. of Dependents............

Income and Expense — Alimony, child support, or separate maintenance income need not be revealed if you do not wish to have it considered as a basis for repaying this obligation.–My gross income from all sources during the 12 month period ended................................19........, amounted to $.................... My personal living expenses and those of my dependents during that period amounted to $...................., and I had other expenses for income taxes, insurance premiums, interest on debts, etc., of $...................... I expect no important changes in my income or expenses during the current year or next year, except as follows (give details):......................

Contingent Liabilities — As of the date of this financial statement, I had no contingent liabilities, except as follows: Notes Receivable Discounted or Sold $....................; Accounts Receivable Assigned or Sold $....................; Co-maker $....................; Accommodation Endorser, Guarantor or Surety $....................; Mortgage Bonds $....................; Leases $....................; Claims for Taxes $....................; Other (describe)....................

Pledged, Assigned or Hypothecated Assets — Describe all assets not noted elsewhere in this statement as having been pledged, assigned or hypothecated and indicate the liabilities which they secure: ....

As of the date of this financial statement, I had not pledged, assigned, hypothecated or transferred the title to any of my assets, except as noted on this form or on a supporting schedule, nor has any such action been taken since that date, except as follows (give details): ....

Legal Actions — No lawsuits, claims, judgments, or other legal actions are outstanding or pending against me and, to the best of my knowledge, no legal actions are to be started against me, except as follows (give details): ....

Insurance Coverage — Fire Insurance: Buildings $...................., Automobile(s), Household Effects, etc. $....................; Indicate if policies have extended coverage endorsement: ....; Liability Insurance: Automotive $...................., Personal $...................., General Public $....................; Other Insurance (describe): ....
Date of latest independent analysis of insurance: ....; Indicate adequacy of coverage: ....

Certification — This is to certify that all the statements contained herein and in any supporting schedules are true and give a correct showing of my financial condition as of the date indicated. I further certify that I had no liabilities, direct or contingent, business or accommodation, except as set forth in this statement, and that the title to all assets therein set forth is in my name solely, except as may be otherwise noted. IN THE EVENT OF ANY MATERIAL ADVERSE CHANGE IN MY FINANCIAL CONDITION, I AGREE TO NOTIFY THE FINANCIAL INSTITUTION NAMED HEREIN IMMEDIATELY IN WRITING.
Signed this....................day of...................., 19......   ....
                                              (Signature)

NOTE: If space is insufficient, separate schedules, which should be clearly identified as being part of this statement, may be attached hereto. Such schedules should be dated and signed in the same manner as this statement.

Figure 10-3 (Cont'd)

KEY STEPS IN A COLLECTION LAWSUIT

1. Preparation of summons and complaint

2. Defendant/debtor is served with notice

    A. personal service, or
    B. substituted service

3. Time to answer expires

4.1 Answer filed

    A. request for details; Bill of Particulars
    B. exchange of interrogatories or discovery questionnaire, to narrow the issues of dispute
    C. pretrial examination; efforts to settle
    D. arbitration
    E. appeal (Trial de Novo)
    F. settlement
    G. trial
    H. judgment

4.2 Summary judgment
4.3 No answer filed

5. Default judgment

6. Execution, levy, garnishment attachment

7. Supplementary proceedings, examination in aid of execution in an attempt to discover assets

8. Payment

(Some jurisdictions require creditor completion of non-military service affidavits before the entry of judgment, swearing that their debtor/defendant is not in the military service.)

COMPULSORY ARBITRATION

Various jurisdictions throughout this country have now put in place a policy of compulsory arbitration. In many states and counties, the size of the balance of a collection account may mandate that the matter be referred to *arbitration* rather than trial. In general, the arbitrators are more lenient with the rules of evidence and allow considerable amount of leeway in proving a case—a leeway which might not be allowed in a courtroom. Nonetheless, many attorneys view this as a process of collection equity—not collection justice.

Arbitration procedure has the advantage of getting quick attention in lieu of waiting for a trial docket number. Knowing that a matter is going into arbitration also is likely to engender a settlement. However, when arbitration actually does occur, and a decision is rendered, the losing side can file an appeal of the case and request an actual trial. The procedure is called "Trial de Novo." There does not have to be any reason for this. It simply has the effect of eliminating all the prior informal proceedings. At that point, the matter will simply remain on the court docket until the trial actually takes place.

The arbitration system works well in resolving many matters in an expeditious fashion that might otherwise be sitting on a court docket, and in providing the creditor with a chance for quick recovery. But it does allow the defendant the opportunity to wait 30 days after the decision to consider an appeal. Collection-type cases seem to lend themselves well to arbitration, and it is likely that as time goes on, arbitration will be expanded to more and more jurisdictions.

COLLECTING THROUGH SMALL-CLAIMS COURT

While each state handles its small-claims court in its own way, for the most part, small-claims court is not a "court of record." That means that there is no transcript of what took place, and hence no opportunity to appeal any decision. Generally, the proceedings are not actually handled by a judge, but rather by a referee, arbitrator or business person.

In larger-city jurisdictions, small-claims court may be conducted at odd hours. The rules of evidence in formal courtroom procedures are usually not followed, and a lawyer is generally not necessary. The court will usually set a maximum balance limit. If the creditor has a larger balance, it will not be able to use small-claims court.

Adjournments are rare, and no summary judgment proceedings are granted. When counterclaims are filed, there is no appeal, and therefore if a case were to be lost in small-claims court, any counterclaim filed by a defendant would be final. In effect, by using a court of record, plaintiffs are protected against adverse decisions.

In small-claims court, plaintiffs are permitted to tell their own stories in their own words; but they must bring proof to support their positions. Corporations must represent themselves, and since the action is usually brought in the area where the defendant lives or works, it's likely that the court is more conveniently located to the defendant than the plaintiff. Whenever the defendant appears, the plaintiff must appear (and it is for that reason that lawyers recommend against getting involved with small-claims court actions).

After hearing both sides, the judge will usually award a judgment—which will automatically be entered by the clerk of the court. Occasionally a decision is reserved, which means you will be notified at some future time as to the outcome.

Remember: If you win the case and obtain a judgment, this does not mean that the person you sued will pay. The judgment means that the person owes you a specified amount of money, but it's up to you to enforce payment. If the defendant fails to pay the judgment, you must contact the sheriff of the county where the defendant lives or works, or has a place of business. The sheriff will attempt to collect the judgment, after you pay a fee in advance. Of course, you would have to assist the court official—whether it be sheriff, marshal, or constable—and provide as much information about the defendant's property, bank accounts, and assets as possible.

Because it's highly impractical for business people—whether they deal in consumer or commercial transactions—to represent themselves in person, just to get judgment and then have to worry about how to collect on the account, small-claims court is not usually the method chosen to enforce payment of debts. It is more frequently reserved for isolated disputes, and for people who don't normally have access to an attorney to handle such matters.

11

How To Gear Your Collection Efforts To Today's Business Conditions

Table of Contents

11

How To Gear Your Collection Efforts To Today's Business Conditions

Customers these days seem to be more ingenious than ever at delaying payment—and having the use of *your* money—for as long as they can. This, in turn, can make it more difficult for your company to keep its own Accounts Receivable current. The whole effect can snowball.

The Impact Of Slow Collections

Slow-paying accounts—in addition to hurting your company's "image"—lead to lack of cash flow or lost sales, which forces a company to borrow at high interest rates in order to operate. This, in turn, increases the debt burden that drains available cash, and is likely to cause a slowdown in the way a company pays its own bills. In addition, an uncollected dollar fast becomes less and less valuable. The chart in Figure 11-1, taking typical collection costs into account, shows how quickly this can happen.

The actual value of accounts receivable should be determined by their age.

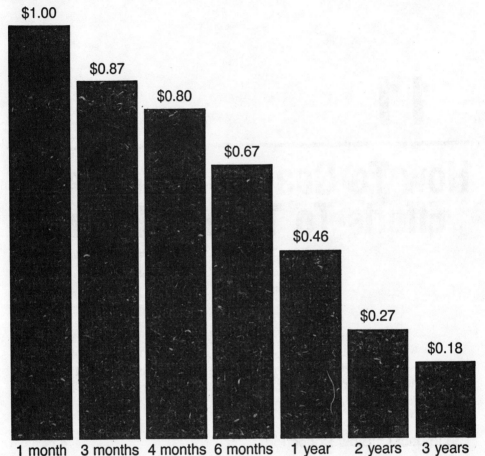

The longer an account remains unpaid, the less it is worth, and the greater the chance it will never be paid.

Figure 11-1

That's why it's increasingly important to establish collection policies and procedures that will build respect for your company in the minds of today's customers. Your reputation for firm, even-handed collections will reassure good customers—and act as a silent "motivator" for those who might be tempted to over-extend or pay slow.

"CONSUMER" VS. "COMMERCIAL" INDEBTEDNESS

"Consumer debt" traditionally means any obligation of a consumer to pay money where the property, insurance, or services rendered are primarily for *personal, family,* or *household* use. Generally, this is the form of credit extended to an individual who uses the goods and services produced by industry. In the consumer area, obligations frequently result from installment credit used in the purchase of large household appliances, automobiles, and home furnishings. Consumer loans—usually supported by promissory notes, or secured by the item to be purchased or by other personal belongings—are another popular consumer indebtedness. Charge account credit is typically short-term credit (30-day), extended by department stores or retail outlets as a convenience to the customer to pay at a later date. Usually interest is fixed to balances remaining after the billing, and minimum payments are required.

Typically, any service professional or service industry—accountant, doctor, lawyer, dentist, oil company, hospital, phone company, etc.—where cash is not demanded upon performance of the service, and a bill is requested, involves creating a service credit consumer-type obligation. Of course, mortgage credit, extended to consumers for the financing or refinancing or making improvement upon homes, represents the more permanent type of long-term consumer credit obligation. For the most part, however, such obligations—as always—are collateralized, and represent *secured* indebtedness.

It is important to recognize that collection of today's commercial accounts may involve some different techniques from those employed in collecting consumer accounts. This is because—

1. Commercial debtors traditionally are corporations, partnerships, or proprietorships conducting business; and in general, such business people have become relatively sophisticated in business practices.

2. Commercial indebtedness is usually for services, merchandise or equipment used in the manufacturing or processing, or for merchandise sold and delivered to distributors or retailers. Such merchandise or services rendered is not for personal, family or household use or consumption.

3. Commercial debts usually are of a larger average amount, although balances in individual situations can vary substantially.

4. Communications with commercial debtors are usually at their place of business during normal working hours, and are not likely to take place at a customer's residence.

5. In commercial collections, you may be dealing with layers upon layers of various people, each of whom refers responsibility to another. But when you deal with a consumer, the party involved is usually the entire "team"—that is, the person who created the indebtedness, as well as the party responsible for payment. It is not likely that a consumer will tell you that the bookkeeper or controller is not in, or the party responsible for payment is unavailable.

6. Commercial indebtedness, while substantial, is likely to be voluntary. Consumer indebtedness may not be. Merchandise purchased but not paid for is one thing; but with a large hospital bill, the consumer surely did not wish to run the bill up so high! Many such involuntary indebtednesses are forced upon the person by misfortune. In such situations, "third party" recoveries from state or federal agencies or insurance companies may be available—a situation not likely to occur in a commercial setting.

MATCHING COLLECTION TECHNIQUES TO YOUR SPECIAL NEEDS

The techniques that work best are likely to be unique to a particular case or organization, and not necessarily the best approach to all collections. In today's world of business it's not what you think or in fact know that's important, but rather what you are able to do with what you know. Recognition can be gained only by demonstrating consistent excellence. The knowledge, style, sophistication and tact demonstrated by real pros come from hard work and application.

Accounts Receivable must be approached as if like a portfolio of investments. Accounts Receivable management is *asset* management.

A collector must have a good grasp of what's expected, in the same way that a mathematician must understand the formulas before calculations can even begin. The qualities of a good collector parallel those one would expect to find in any valuable employee.

The following list of adjectives, often used to describe collection personality traits, no doubt could also describe qualities of company presidents:

Sales-oriented	Courteous	Dependable
Decisive	Common Sense	Tactful
Poised	Organized	Understanding
Businesslike	Enthusiastic	Patient
Accurate	Mature	Firm
Expedient	Mathematical	Disciplined
Imaginative	Motivated	Analytical
Empathetic	Resourceful	Quick thinking
Tenacious	Drive	Confident

Who's In Charge?

In a small company, the collection function today may be performed by an officer, or even the owner. Under such conditions, his authority is total. In a larger company, the range of authority could vary from a person who has to ask permission to make any decision, all the way to a collector who has independent authority to stop shipment on future orders—and even determine when to authorize a settlement or lawsuit.

Again, depending on the size of the company and the approach to collection, an entire collection department may be in operation, with the greatest authority resting with the collection manager.

How Customer Attitudes Affect Collection Policy

Today's customers will pay because of any one of the following reasons:

1. a puritan payment ethic involving pride in meeting obligations.

2. good will and a general liking for the people with whom business is being conducted.

3. the feeling that bad treatment begets bad treatment.

4. an absolute need for the product or service provided.

5. the moral obligation inherent in an indebtedness.

6. the wish to avoid the consequences that may result if the payment is not made.

7. the desire to enjoy the respect that results from a good credit reputation.

8. outright habit, supplemented by the desire to increase available credit lines which may result in the ability to make additional profit.

Undoubtedly there are unique exceptions or variations, but this list should provide you with a better understanding of what motivates your customers to pay. Consequently, the appeals selected by you should be those that will appeal to people's real motives.

In spite of the benefits that will accrue to a company as a result of improved collection style, effort, or procedure, there is always a reluctance among corporate financial planners and those within a company who make decisions to institute change—unless it's going to turn a profit. Many present-day executives believe that while credit is a tool of profitability, it is competition that really determines trade terms and how collection policy is enforced. Those who remain flexible and willing to learn and test new ideas are undoubtedly going to achieve the best success, and make the most profit out of their credit and collection tools.

SETTING A POLICY THAT PROMOTES SALES

The change from "customer" to "debtor," of course, occurs when new credit will not be available to the account until the old invoices are paid. If you are unwilling to extend credit to a customer because of delinquency, and if you are not able to resolve your differences with the account or motivate the customer towards payment, then he or she is no longer a customer. He now becomes a debtor.

It's also interesting to note that, in many cases, your customer won't ask to buy from you because he is either embarrassed or realizes that credit might be denied. So there is a good chance he will look elsewhere. Such a customer may use whatever funds may be available to establish a business relationship with one of your competitors. A prompt follow-up, though, can often reactivate such an account and thus rejuvenate a customer.

If you can bring the account to a more current level, it's possible additional order arrangements can be made. Psychologically, your customer, having just paid you, will certainly want to continue the relationship with your organization.

Much of the right policy for today, of course, depends on sound credit limits. Naturally, accounts with $5,000 credit limits could be past due by only $500. Pressing for payment too harshly may create a debtor out of a customer you wanted to keep. So do not over-react to such situations, but do *react*. Interrupt your normal collection routine and have the customer's credit limit re-evaluated. If the customer is still worthy of $5,000, try a sales-oriented call to a decision maker with a view towards cleaning up the old balance. Determine why credit was under-utilized, and how you can be of service to the customer in the future. Remember, the relationship has to be good for both companies.

What Aging Of Receivables Can Show

With an aging schedule, you will know at a glance how much money is tied up in accounts receivable, and what portion is current—or 30, 60 or 90 days overdue. Comparison of industry figures—by products lines, by profit margin, by geographical area or region, domestic or foreign country, by sales person, by customer, etc.—enable you to learn of any strengths and weaknesses. In addition, the use of graphic aids to demonstrate and illustrate results proves to be invaluable. (Pie charts, bar graphs, line graphs can point up hidden facts or relationships quickly and dramatically.)

You can also get a quick and dramatic view of the cost of receivables, if you consider what you have to earn to make up for a bad-debt loss. For example:

ADDITIONAL SALES REQUIRED
TO OFFSET RECEIVABLE LOSS

If You Have An Actual Loss Of:	And Your Net Profit Margin Is:		
	4%	6%	10%
	You Need Additional Sales Of:		
$100	$ 2,500	$ 1,666	$ 1,000
$500	$ 12,500	$ 8,333	$ 5,000
$1,000	$ 25,000	$ 16,666	$ 10,000
$10,000	$250,000	$166,660	$100,000

YOUR LONG-TERM INVESTMENT IN TRADE RECEIVABLES

Days Sales Outstanding (DSO) measures how long money is tied up, but makes no distinction between accounts that are within agreed terms, and those that are delinquent. As such, it is not a good measure of today's collection department performance.

However, DSO does offer important benefits. It enables you to compare yourself to industry performance, and to your own performance in prior periods. You can also compare the *actual* DSO to the *best possible* DSO. Here's how:

Actual DSO formula =

$$\frac{\text{Average Receivables for 3 Month-Ends} \times 90}{\text{3-Month Sales}} = \text{DSO}$$

Best possible DSO is:

$$\frac{\text{Average CURRENT Receivables for 3 Month-Ends} \times 90}{\text{3-Month Sales}} = \text{BP DSO}$$

If all customers paid exactly on the due date, all receivables would be in the current aging column. Hence, if you use the current receivables figure in the formula for DSO, you will get best possible DSO or Average Terms.

To carry the reasoning one step further, if you subtract Average Terms from DSO, you have "Average Cost of Delinquency" in days, or ACD.

What you have accomplished is to break up DSO into its two components, Average Terms and ACD. Now you can spell out the impact of terms that have been established. Since Average Terms, by definition, take into account only the current receivables, the measure isolates the actual selling terms on which the calculation is based. Further, it permits an examination of those terms, to see if they are reasonable within the industry and justifiable in terms of your production time, ability to carry receivables, and alternative corporate uses. You'll see how those funds may be used to increase income, increase return on investment, or used to lessen external borrowings.

Let's see how these calculations work out:

DAYS SALES OUTSTANDING

$$\left(\frac{\text{Average of 3 Month-End Receivables} \times 90}{\text{3-Month Billings}} = \text{DSO} \right)$$

	Days
This Month	
Last Month	
Last Year Industry Average	

AVERAGE TERMS

$$\left(\frac{\text{Average of 3 Month-End \underline{Current} Receivables} \times 90}{\text{3-Month Billings}} = \text{Average Terms} \right)$$

	Days
This Month	
Last Month	
Last Year Industry Average	

AVERAGE COST OF DELINQUENCY

(DSO—Average Terms = ACD)

	Days
This Month	
Last Month	
Last Year Industry Average	

The answer to excessive costs of delinquency, of course, is *policy*.

HOLDING COLLECTION PROBLEMS TO
A MINIMUM

While you can't avoid collection problems entirely—you'd be missing some real profit opportunities if you could—it is possible to keep these problems within bounds. The way to do this, of course, is by proper *credit checking*. You'll need to do some thorough checking in advance, to weed out the obvious bad risks; and you'll need to keep your credit information current, as well. Besides the familiar four C's—Character, Capacity, Capital, and Conditions, you'll need to consider the following:

1. size of the order

2. potential for future business

3. risk in relation to profit margin

4. competition

5. quality of customer

6. timetable for delivery

7. total credit exposure

8. special orders not readily marketable to other customers

Additionally, references (both trade and personal) should be verified. Mercantile agency reports containing ratings also help you to zero in on a decision. Sources of information include: industry credit groups, Dun & Bradstreet reports and ratings, retail credit company reports provided by local credit bureaus, TRW reports, banks, accountants and other trade suppliers. Most legitimate customers will be glad to supply you with helpful information.

Controlling Your Credit Risk

Some companies insist that every account should be re-checked each time it's granted credit. When the risk appears too great on an unsecured basis, special arrangements can often be made to help insure payment—and to avoid the loss of a sale. By changing the character of the credit from "unsecured" to "secured," or by obtaining a personal guarantee or lien for example, the complexion of risk is dramatically altered, and a comfort zone can be put in place.

However, the extension of secured credit requires constant vigilance; and collateral, while providing additional protection, should not be thought of as more than a collection tool that can be used to enforce payment. Therefore, it's a good idea to consult with counsel who's expert in the workings of the Uniform Commercial Code, to assure that you're legally protected. (See Chapter 7.)

SETTING THE BEST COLLECTION POLICY FOR TODAY

Most dictionaries have a secondary definition of ''policy'' as follows: a form of gambling in which bets are made on unpredictable numbers; the word ''policy'' also seems interchangeable with parimutuel betting, and the numbers game and policy racket in a gambling context. Well, this is not what collection policy should be! Rather, collection policy is a course of action based on guiding principles and procedures that are advantageous, prudent and expedient.

Striking The Right Balance

If policy in either department were set so as to assure zero bad debt losses, more than likely it would be an indication that there's a weak credit and collection policy, designed not to take risks. But sound credit and collection policy requires an understanding of *how* and *when* to take a risk.

When such policy is too restrictive it's quite obvious that marketing and sales deficiencies will be apparent; while there are no losses, there are also diminished profits. Accordingly, there has to be a willingness to take risk, which is usually reflected in sales to marginal accounts. The right collection policy should therefore contain a discipline for dealing with such customers.

From time to time, some customers may consider your company's collection policy too restrictive, while others may find it too lenient. This customer perception could arise despite optimum ratio numbers measuring performance. In fact, if the measurement criteria indicate outstanding performance, it could be the result of a too-restrictive credit policy.

Therefore, substantially curtailing potential delinquency is not collection efficiency. Where credit policy is too restrictive, outstanding accounts could be the result of too drastic an approach to a collection effort which at some future date might have a negative impact on sales. Actually, favorable statistical measurement could be the result of any combination of collection policy variations.

To be effective, the policies designed by the collection department should not be cast in concrete, but rather be *flexible* and in *harmony* with the general goals set forth by management. As new products or new markets are sought out, or as the business objectives change, so should there be changes in collection policy to reflect the new objectives.

A well-defined collection policy, in addition to synchronizing with the credit department and being in harmony with sales and marketing, should complement the on-the-job objective of the collector. A successful policy will necessitate—

1. defining the objective, and setting a balance between firmness and flexibility. It will require balancing the collection of 100% of unpaid accounts receivable, and keeping good customer relations and a sales awareness.

2. the establishment of a method and procedure guide, which must involve planning in order to determine *what* type of action is to be taken, *when* that type of action is to be taken, and *who* is to take the action.

3. the delegation or assignment of responsibilities for implementing needed action.

4. accountability and follow-up, to evaluate results and determine whether procedures are being followed and timely actions taken. This will necessitate evaluation on collection procedures and results.

5. constant re-enforcement. Re-enforcement must be made internally with collection personnel and externally with customers, so that the policy is known by all, and commands the respect of everyone involved.

6. periodic review with modifications made, to correct any procedure deficiencies. Sometimes easing a restrictive collection policy and permitting a more understanding approach may prove to be a more successful collection technique than would be accomplished by absolute firmness.

An effective collection policy, in addition to being ethical and businesslike, should involve principles of good collection procedure. Collecting the money through effective communication within the framework of a disciplined follow-up gets results—and preserves good will.

A systematic follow-up, which helps to mold collection discipline, should be the single-most important part of the policy. It should set forth the method of contact (by statement, letter, telephone, telegram, or personal visit). The hierarchy establishes a *persistent consistency* as to when each of the variety of payment demands is to be used, and the frequency of contact.

Depending on the type of business a collector is collecting for, he or she may be regulated by the Fair Debt Collection Practices Act. To the extent that there are industry or local legal restraints, such restraints (including the times of the day when collection calls may be permitted, and items such as calls to neighbors or employers) should be included in your policy guidelines.

A firm's collection policy should be created with the idea that it will build respect for the company in the mind of the customer. A company's reputation for a firm, efficient and attentive collection staff will, in and of itself, act as a silent motivator to customers who otherwise might be tempted to over-extend or pay slowly.

COLLECTION POLICY: WRITTEN OR UNWRITTEN?

In spite of the complexities of business today, numerous organizations carry on collection activity based on ideas that have been taken for granted for a long time. Each time someone new is hired, procedures that perpetuate the system are passed along. It is very common for top management as well as collection personnel to operate under unwritten informal arrangements that have become too comfortable and routine. Well, complacency breeds mediocrity. There is no such thing as the single-most effective collection policy. If nothing else, this fact alone suggests that policy should be re-evaluated periodically, to maintain its effectiveness.

The Collection Department acts in the role of *Sergeant-At-Arms* in an overall organization that has many departments—each with its own systems, procedures and policies.

Significant *items* that may be *predetermined* by credit policy play an important role in establishing collection policy. Items such as terms of sale, cost-of-goods sold, profit margin, trade custom and competition, must be considered. The financial condition of the company as well as the accounting procedures followed also may result in a tightening or loosening of collection procedure, which impacts cash flow or the lack of it. A company may desire more write-offs in one period than another, and adjust policy and procedure accordingly.

Conservative Policies

Conservative policies will probably be effective when a company operates under the following conditions:

1. limited competition

2. slim profit margin

3. uncertain political environment or economic situations

4. custom-designed products

5. insufficient cash flow

6. demand usually exceeds supply, and production is at full capacity

7. large average-size order (the larger the order, the greater the risk, the greater the risk, the less likely the company is willing to take the risk)

8. stability of the market to which they sell

9. availability of credit information

10. size of the staff available to perform immediate functions

Conservative policies are more time-consuming, and thus more costly. Operational costs directly effect profit margins, and it's clear that conservative policies take more time to implement than their less-expensive liberal counterparts.

A strict conservative credit policy usually requires more *credit* effort, but less *collection* effort.

Advantages Of A Written Collection Policy

There are distinct advantages to having a written policy:

1. it provides a mechanism by which the policy makers are required to think through their objectives and procedures before they are put in final form.

2. it provides for hard-copy facts, and leaves little room for misunderstanding.

3. it eliminates the need to rely on memory alone, especially in a small company where procedures may be known by a limited few, or a larger company where turnover of personnel is frequent. In such an environment, unwritten policy will require constant and excessive retaining.

4. with properly written review provisions and flexibility requirements, it will enable revisions and improvements to be timely implemented.

5. it assures consistent application and interpretation by all employees and customers. Unwritten policy tends to be subject to interpretation and, where customers are concerned, subjective.

6. it can be distributed throughout a company, to sales personnel, department heads, financial management, accounting, accounts receivable department, or any other interested party. Unwritten policy through such distribution channels, could not possibly remain consistent.

7. it may later on act as a guide to help *computerize* the collection function.

A SAMPLE COLLECTION POLICY

(*Objective:* Collect the account as close to terms as possible and preserve good will.)

1. Collection effort is to begin no later than five days after the bill is due.

2. Where a series of forms or computer letters are used, no more than four are to be sent to any one customer without a reply. All are to be sent to

the attention of a decison maker. Letters may vary with the customer type. Management agrees that the collection department gets "priority-one" status for EDP scheduling.

3. All collection efforts must be documented on customer's file.

4. (A) All accounts over $2,500 should be telephoned in accordance with established techniques after being 31 to 45 days past due. A call should be made to a decision maker.

    (B) Promises of payment are to be followed up promptly, so as to be certain that the check has been mailed before the file is advanced.

5. Payment programs and extension requests are acceptable only when and where it can be demonstrated that the request or payout is reasonable and likely to be in the company's best interest. However, where a delinquent balance exceeds $5,000, management approval is necessary.

6. Customer claims deduction (returns, shortages, damages, discounts, freight adjustments, price adjustments, etc.), must not linger; process within 20 days of receipt, with a confirming acknowledgement sent to the customer.

7. Settlements may be negotiated where it can be demonstrated that such action is in the company's best interest. (See format for settlement work-up as outlined in Chapter 7.) However, two signatures are required where amount to be written off is greater than $2,500.

8. As part of a final collection effort, all accounts should be considered for a personal visit where economically practical.

9. The seven most troublesome, the seven oldest, and the seven largest accounts must be reported to management, along with all customers on "credit hold alert."

10. All accounts receivable are to be pursued diligently and placed for collection no later than 120 days past due, before write-off will be considered.

PUTTING YOUR COLLECTION POLICY INTO ACTION

At first glance, examination of an accounts receivable aging schedule reflects a listing of various accounts, ranging from those that are nearly current to other customers that may have . . .

- skipped invoices

- requested additional information before payment

- been chronic slow-payers

- responded that "the check is in the mail"

- overlooked an invoice

- disputed the account

Actually the categories are limited only by the imagination of the delinquent customer. Yet each situation requires a different type collection technique, to stimulate payment without alienating that particular type of customer. No matter what the cause of the delay, however, these steps are essential:

1. *identification* of various types of customers;

2. deciding *what constitutes being past-due*. Once an invoice falls due and remains unpaid, technically it's past due. Delinquency, therefore, is a question of degree.

3. *making decisions* about where and in what manner the collection effort will begin. Follow-up should begin one to five days after the bill is due—but most companies stretch it from six to ten days.

It is at this point that written policy is really an improvement on any verbal approach.

Concepts such as "quick action," "moving fast" and even the word "immediate" mean different things to different people. You must be more specific, whether your approach is friendly or firm—or a combination of both. Give people deadlines, and you'll get results.

THE IMPORTANCE OF TIMING

Time has always been the enemy of a successful collection effort. Accounts receivables decline in value as they get older. But keeping a close follow-up on collection activity will help to minimize these time delays. As comedians have said, "Timing is everything"; this is true both in intervals of follow-up, as well as the chosen collection technique!

A favorite procedure at the preliminary collection stage is the use of a statement of account, listing the invoices outstanding. An equally effective and comparable alternative would be a past-due statement, which lists only those invoices actually past due. If the majority of sales are made with EOM (end of month) terms, sending complete statements of account can be very desirable. Such a procedure may encourage customers to pay the entire statement at once. However, mailing such statements to all customers regardless of terms of sale, size of the customer, or type of customer could prove to be a waste of postage. It could impede rather than accelerate cash flow.

How A Customer Service Call Can Help

Where the accounts receivable are particularly large, or where the transaction is complicated—as we have seen—some companies have had outstanding success from the "telephone service call" made in advance of the due date. The collector under such conditions would play the role of a customer service representative, inquiring of the customer if the product or service was received in good order—while at the same time offering any further assistance or clarification that may be necessary now or in the future. Of course the call includes a "By the way, our invoice was previously sent to you under separate cover. We presume that you have found it in order, and that it is being processed for payment . . . is that correct?"

Where balances warrant such attention, and where time permits, incorporating such a telephone call into collection procedure can go a long way toward reducing outstanding receivables—even to a point where they are paid before they fall due. Such a practice is especially effective when used in coordination with special services that might be provided to major corporations, or where specific authorization must be obtained before bills can be approved for payment. This pre-collection customer service call, in addition to expediting payment, may nip in the bud any dispute that might later arise to delay payment.

The degree to which practical applications of policy are implemented as procedure is very difficult to control. Decisions concerning the severity of follow-up, including the tempo and tone of both written and verbal communication, should be spelled out. The limits of authority already in place will enable the collector to handle the routine situations, such as what type of initial demand should be made, and at what intervals to send specific demands. Situations such as when to accept and acknowledge on-account payments, requests for extensions, settlement proposals, when to place an account for collection, and when to prepare an account for write-off may be included in policy guidelines, but will most certainly be considered "red flag" situations that require special attention.

PAYMENT DEMAND SCHEDULE: INTERVALS FOR FOLLOW-UP

Once determination has been made of when an account is past due, intervals for follow-up must be decided. Common practice is to permit 5 to 10 days past the due date before action begins. Aside from the external influences such as economic considerations, shorter sale terms by necessity suggest closer follow-up.

How Long Should Your Collection Cycle Be?

The collection cycle, measured by the time between the first payment demand and the final demand (prior to seeking outside assistance) typically falls within a 45, 60 or 90 day time frame. With the new Bankruptcy Code and the redefined "preference rule" (payment must be made in the ordinary course of business and according to business terms), numerous companies have been shortening or telescoping their collection cycle and tightening up their terms.

Determination must be then made as to what type of initial reminder is to be sent (pressure, sensitized label past-due statement, form letter, invoice copy, etc.), with the reminder being followed by the request, then the appeal, then the demand for payment—all sent within prescribed intervals. However, this initial stage of the collection cycle should not be exclusively reserved for correspondence. A telegram or mailgram, a telephone call to a decision maker, and a personal visit—discussed earlier—are all viable options and may be interspersed within the collection cycle at any time. In fact, such variations often result in prompt payment.

Customers often develop payment patterns as a result of what a company will permit them to get away with. Collectors frequently hear customers comment, "Why are you calling me now? You know I don't pay until that fourth letter of yours that says, 'This is your Final Notice' "! The fact is, customers not only know that they're past due, but they know your routine—probably better than you do.

Keeping Tabs On Your Collection Policy

To keep your system fresh and your customers from becoming complacent, a monitoring system should be maintained so as to check on how much pulling power your collection notices really have. When you observe an unexplained drop-off, perhaps it's time to switch gears and try updating your system or creating a new demand letter.

A collection policy must deal with all types of customers even-handedly, including:

1. customers who pay promptly or discount (such customers are particularly sensitive to their credit reputation).

2. good accounts that pay slowly (more thick-skinned to appeals than would be the case in #1).

3. delinquents who may lack the desire or the ability to pay.

But once your normal collection cycle is evaded, it is you who must choose the best type of demand, the one likely to be most effective in obtaining payment.

The subtle appeals and variations in approach which a collector may choose from are comparable to the notes on a piano keyboard . . . but getting the customer to dance to your tune means you have to make precise and efficient use of all the "notes" at your disposal, and strike a responsive chord in the mind of the customer.

Here is the collection procedure likely to be followed in most industries:

KEEPING COLLECTION POLICY AND PROCEDURE SHARP AND EFFECTIVE

The following suggestions are offered for keeping your collection policy and procedure in "racing trim":

1. Tighten up your collection procedures by starting earlier on over-due accounts; keep on schedule and be persistent; maintain collection discipline.

2. Review and shorten the interval between your collection letter series; select the style and cycle which best fit your terms of sale, product line and customer type. Remember, timing is everything.

3. Revise and shorten your collection letters, if possible. Make them more specific, stronger, and consequently more effective.

4. Be versatile in your collection procedure, so that a customer will not feel he can just wait out your old routine. Don't wait for end-of-month printouts before partial payments are pursued. Acknowledge such payments immediately, with a request that the balance be promptly paid.

5. Screen out your largest and oldest accounts from your aging, and give them preferential collection treatment early on. Remember, from time to time a call or visit will do a lot more than the usual collection letters.

6. Narrow the gap between the due date and the time when credit privileges on such past-due accounts are suspended and new orders are held.

7. Use all the available and effective tools in the various stages of the follow-up period. This improves your versatility, and keeps the customer guessing as to what's your next step.

8. As business conditions change, maintain or re-establish a firm collection policy. Be sure that the policy is known by your customers, and never be embarrassed to ask for money justly due. Stay in touch with your market; the business affairs of customers do not remain static. Keep credit files current and refer to them regularly. Know as much as possible about your customers.

9. Screen requests for extended payment terms carefully, and enlist your sales department to discourage these requests.

10. Accelerate the point in your collection cycle at which past-due accounts are turned over to a collection agency. Your good judgment will let you know when you've exhausted all of the means at your disposal to negotiate payment. At this point, you can take positive action by referring the account to a professional collector. Once your final demand has been made, you can't just sit and wait forever for something to happen. A discipline must be maintained. Fix a date to begin further action.

11. Say what you mean and mean what you say; stand by your statements. When a decision is made, carry it out.

12. Be sure that you're dealing with a decision maker, and always keep the lines of communication open. Remember, sometimes it's the company that may owe you the money, but it's the *people* who pay the bills.

No checking is foolproof, of course. And when collection problems do arise—as they're bound to, sometimes—you need the surest, most up-to-date techniques for dealing with them. In any case, you need to be prepared for such problems, and to move swiftly and firmly when circumstances warrant it.

Summary: Match your collection techniques to today's realities, and you'll not only help to keep operations profitable, you'll also earn your customers' respect for your firm-but-fair approach.

POLICY IN ACTION:
A MODEL COLLECTION PROCEDURE

Days Past Due	Balance Less Than $2,500	From $2,500 to $10,000	Over $10,000
5 to 30	Send form letter, sticker, statement or invoice copy or #1 reminder letter, or any variation thereof	any reminder variation	courtesy phone call and reminder variation

31 to 45	#2 request letter variation	#2 request, inquiry phone call	telephone call to decision maker; request letter follow-up
46 to 60 classify delinquent accts. as good/fair; slow payers seasonal credit hold alert problem account report to management	#3 appeal letter variation	#3 appeal letter; follow-up telephone call	telephone call; #3 dictated follow up if necessary
61 to 75 76 to 90	#4 demand letter; telephone call	telephone call; follow-up demand letter	telephone call; follow-up demand letter, dictated if necessary
91 to 120	telegram, mailgram, personal visit from collector, credit or sales reps. Account referred to manager for final T.O. (take over). Final demand, special letter, phone call, pick-up check, wire money.		

120 and over—Place for collection with agency.

(*Note:* This is only a sample of collection procedures that can be used to follow up accounts. There is no single "right" procedure. Collection policy details the interval of follow-up and the cut-off amounts to be pursued in each category. Naturally when customers respond to payment demands, and request documentation or promise payment, correspondence and follow through are handled appropriately outside of this dunning cycle.)

Index